S0-BAK-218

Lou Gehrig

An American Classic

LOU GEHRIG

An American Classic

RICHARD BAK

TAYLOR PUBLISHING COMPANY

DALLAS, TEXAS

Also by Richard Bak

Cobb Would Have Caught It

Ty Cobb (Taylor)

Turkey Stearnes and the Detroit Stars

Published by
Taylor Publishing Company
1550 West Mockingbird Lane
Dallas, Texas 75235

Designed by Timmons Willgren Design

Photo credits follow index.

Library of Congress Cataloging-in-Publication Data

Bak, Richard, 1954–
Lou Gehrig : an American classic / Richard Bak.
p. cm.
Includes bibliographical references and index.
ISBN 0-87833-883-7
1. Gehrig, Lou, 1903-1941. 2. Baseball players—United States—Biography. I. Title.

GV865.G4b35 1995
796.357'092—dc20 94-46151
[B] CIP

Printed in the United States of America

10 9 8 7 6 5 4 3 2 1

CONTENTS

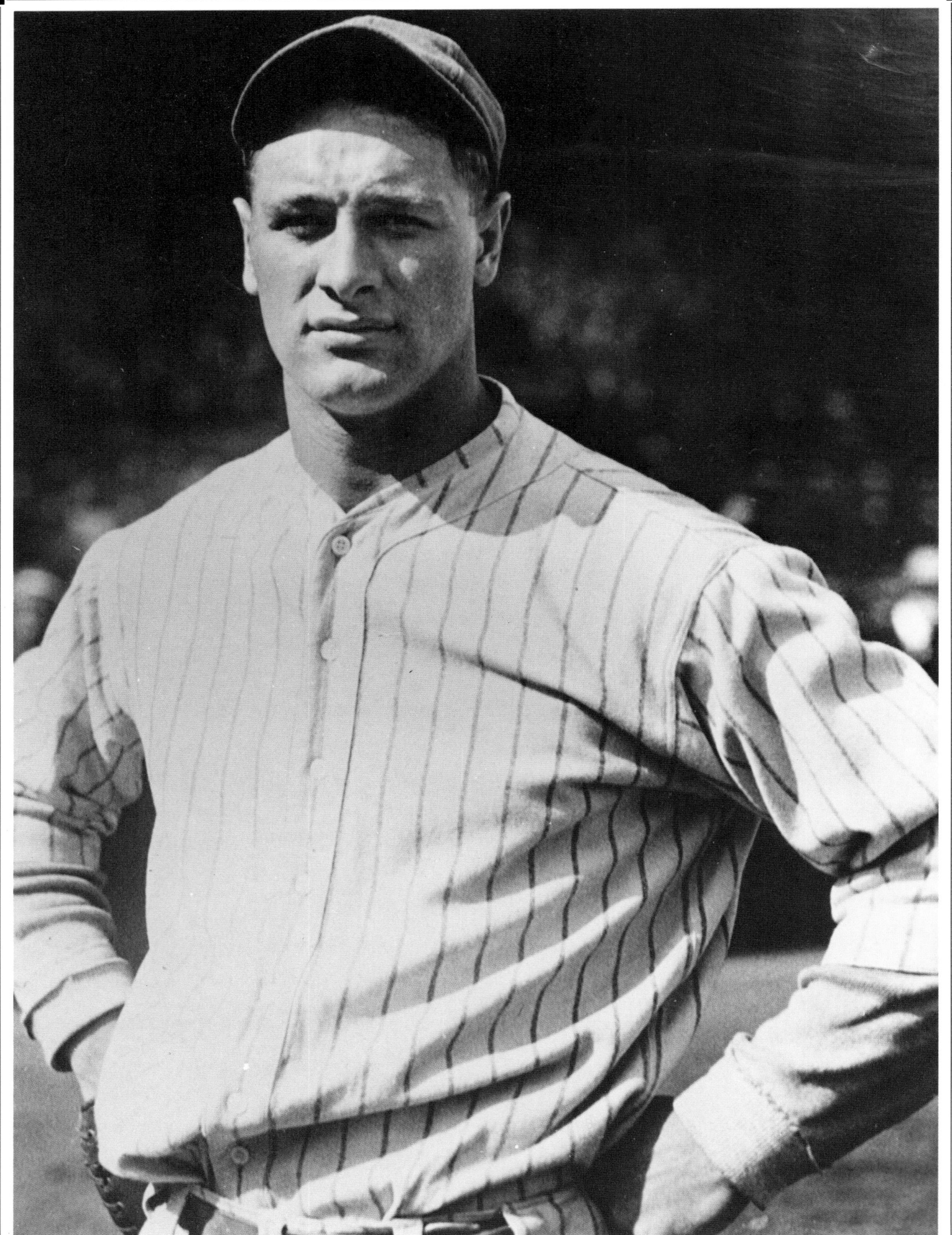

ACKNOWLEDGMENTS

NO MAN IS an island, particularly when it comes to putting together an illustrated biography. For their help in locating written and visual material, I would like to thank: Katie Beltramo and Holly Haswell of Columbia University's Low Memorial Library; Shelly Plutowski of the Mayo Clinic in Rochester, Minnesota; Paul Lasewicz of the Aetna Insurance Company in Hartford, Connecticut; Jacqueline Dace of the Missouri Historical Society; Joe Nathan and Steve Gietschier of the *Sporting News*; Ray Collins of Brown Brothers; Darci Harrington of the National Baseball Library; and Mark Rucker of Transcendental Graphics. Thanks also to Raymond Gonzalez of the Society for American Baseball Research for sharing some of his statistical research on Lou Gehrig; Kathie Johnson, who rummaged through the Hillerich and Bradsby corporate archives at the University of Louisville; and Mike Opipari, who expertly reproduced many of the images seen on these pages.

Over the last several years, I have had the good fortune to talk about baseball in general, and Lou Gehrig in particular, with a number of people in and out of the game. Although some have since moved on to seats with better sight lines, I would be remiss for not acknowledging all of them for their reminiscences and insights: Eldon Auker, Eddie Batchelor Jr., Charles "Rip" Collins, Roger "Doc" Cramer, Frankie Crosetti, Harry Danning, Edwin Diamond, Rick Ferrell, Ray Fisher, Milt Gaston, Charlie Gehringer, Ernie Harwell, Edgar Hayes, Tommy Henrich, Art Herring, Elon "Chief" Hogsett, Willis "Ace" Hudlin, Bill Kennedy, John Kimbrough, Eddie Mayo, Barney McCosky, Marv Owen, Billy Rogell, Stanley Roginski, John Sturm, George Uhle, Eddie Wells, and Bill Werber.

Finally, a tip of the cap to the folks at Taylor Publishing, who thought the subject of Lou Gehrig worthy of another book.

Chapter One

Yankee Doodle Days

LOU GEHRIG: I'll get my working papers. I'll quit school.
MOM GEHRIG: Quit school? How can you say that? How many times have I told you I want you to go to school...and high school...and college. Look at your Poppa. Look at me. We didn't go to school. And what are we? A janitor. A cook. I want you to be somebody.
LOU: Sure, Mom, sure.
MOM: Like your Uncle Otto, Louie. He went to university. He graduated. Don't you see, Louie, that's why I am cooking at Columbia. So you can go there someday and be an engineer like your Uncle Otto.
LOU: But, Mom, maybe I ain't cut out to be an engineer.
MOM: What do you want to be?
LOU: I wanna be...I don't know, Mom.
MOM: You've got to know. In this country, you can be anything you want to be. Don't you want to be an engineer like your Uncle Otto? Don't you?
LOU: Sure, Mom, sure. Whatever you want me to be.

—The Pride of the Yankees

"WHATEVER YOU do, kid," George M. Cohan once advised a young actor, "always serve it with a little dressing."

The country's premier showman, the creator of such electrifying tunes as "You're a Grand Old Flag" and "Give My Regards to Broadway," believed in practicing what he preached. Indeed, no one embodied America's muscular age of steam shovels, flying machines and horseless carriages better than this brash, wisecracking, foot-stomping, flag-waving offspring of Irish immigrant stock. The actor-playwright-composer had been born on the Fourth of July and made a career out of bragging about it.

"What makes the Americans so proud of their country?" one of his characters asked in the hit play, *Little Johnny Jones.*

"Other countries" was the smart-alecky reply.

Cohan understood that vaudeville was more flash than substance; it wasn't the material, but the performance that mattered. So on those rare occasions when the audience was sitting on its hands, he was apt to grab Old Glory, storm across the stage, and belt out a number sure to get everybody's red, white, and blue juices flowing:

I'm a Yankee Doodle Dandy,
A Yankee Doodle, do or die;
A real live nephew of my Uncle Sam,
Born on the Fourth of July.
I've a Yankee Doodle sweetheart,

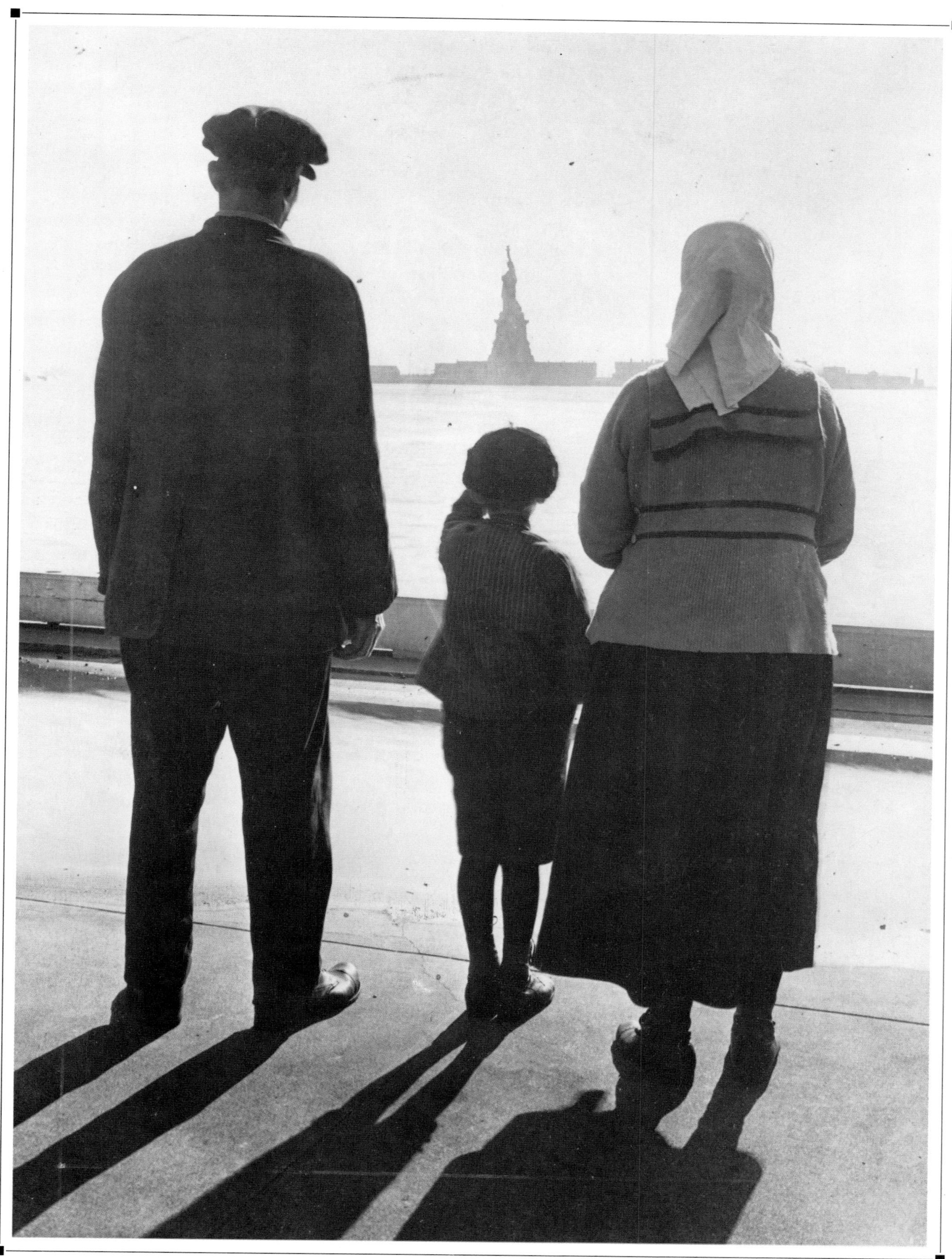

Between 1880 and 1920 nearly 24 million immigrants poured into America, among them Heinrich Gehrig and Christina Flack, Lou Gehrig's parents.

She's my Yankee Doodle joy.
Yankee Doodle came to London just to
ride the ponies —
I am the Yankee Doodle Boy.

Lou Gehrig as an infant. He weighed a husky fourteen pounds when he was born in 1903.

In 1903, America was as robust and unabashedly optimistic as one of George Cohan's song-and-dance numbers. In Washington, ex-Rough Rider Teddy Roosevelt used his big stick to carve out a new country called Panama. In North Carolina, the Wright brothers made like gulls in the tricky ocean breezes. In Detroit, an eccentric lighting engineer began taking orders for his "Fordmobile." In Boston and Pittsburgh, young men in tobacco-stained knickers crossed bats in the first modern World Series. And in the Yorkville section of New York City, Heinrich Ludwig Gehrig hoisted a stein of beer at his favorite German saloon.

The thirty-six-year-old art-metal mechanic wasn't toasting the dawn of the American Century, though he gladly would have, had someone thought of it and offered to pay for the drinks. Though life in a new land hadn't quite panned out as advertised, the German immigrant still clung stubbornly to threads of the American dream, as did most of the other one million foreign-born then living in the world's fastest growing city.

Heinrich, born in Baden in 1867, had emigrated when he was twenty-one. After spending some time in Chicago, he settled in New York, where he met blond-haired, blue-eyed Christina Flack, fourteen years younger than he and stout as a keg. Christina, a native of Schleswig-Holstein, had practically stepped right off the boat, arriving in New York Harbor in 1899. She was a Lutheran, like Heinrich. They married in 1900 and celebrated the birth of a daughter, Anna, in 1902.

If not exactly a Yankee Doodle Dandy, Heinrich Gehrig was now cel-

A Fourth of July parade in New York City, circa 1910. The juvenile flag-wavers had nothing on George M. Cohan, who was born on July 4, 1878, and made a career out of jingoism. A baseball fanatic, America's favorite song-and-dance man often hired actors based on their ability to fill a position on the teams he organized after work.

ebrating, for the second time in little more than a year, being a Yankee Doodle *daddy*. On the sticky evening of June 19, 1903, Christina had given birth to a baby boy inside the family's cramped and airless apartment on Manhattan's upper east side. The predominantly German neighborhood, which also contained Hungarian and Jewish families, was known as Yorkville. The chunky, blue-eyed boy, who weighed in at almost fourteen pounds, was named Heinrich Ludwig after his father. Americanized, that was Henry Louis, or simply "Lou," as the stocky boy came to be called.

Lou at age four. About this time, the Gehrigs moved from the Yorkville section of Manhattan to Washington Heights.

Just thirteen months after delivering Lou, Christina gave birth again to another girl, whom they named Sophie. Hardworking and optimistic, Mom Gehrig anticipated the best for her three young children. After all, this wasn't the old country where young men sometimes chopped off their trigger fingers to avoid serving in the imperial army. In America, went the familiar refrain, you were free to be whatever you wanted to be.

Not that the Progressive Age didn't have its dark side. Most people fleeing poverty and persecution in the Old World found the promised streets of gold lined with garbage, prostitutes, and dead horses. Nonetheless, a hard kernel of truth lurked in the literature that steamship companies circulated overseas, enough to keep thousands of strange faces streaming through Ellis Island each day until a European war turned the spigot off. With toil, thrift, and a bit of luck, one could gain a precious foothold in this polyglot maelstrom. "Do not take a moment's rest," one popular guidebook for newcomers preached. "Run, do, work, and keep your own good in mind."

The new Americans took this advice to heart. Turn-of-the-century Yorkville alone produced such classic success stories as Bert Lahr, the Marx Brothers, and a budding song-and-dance man named Jimmy Cagney (who also was the catcher of the neighborhood's Original Nut Club baseball team). Even those with less vigor or talent considered the disillusionment and bouts of homesickness a fair exchange for the new country's open, unpretentious lifestyle.

"My grandfather took great pleasure in the simplicity of American ways, the casual manners, the lack of pomp," recalled Marie Jastrow, whose family emigrated from Germany to Yorkville about the time Lou was born. "I remember that he liked to take off his coat, tie, and collar and sit by the window reading the *Staats-Zeitung*. If visitors came to the door, he welcomed them in his shirtsleeves and suspenders. That would be unthinkable in the old country."

Fuzzy memories of such "good old days" obscure the fact that the world was a more dangerous place then. Death in the workplace and the birth bed was so commonplace that the average life span at the turn of

The Team at the Top of the Hill

Lou Gehrig and the team he helped make famous both arrived in the Big Apple within weeks of each other. On the balmy afternoon of April 30, 1903—just seven weeks before Lou was born—the New York Yankees, then known as the Highlanders, played their first American League home game, defeating Washington, 6-2, at Hilltop Park. The park, a hastily built wooden structure, was located on the highest ground in the city, a section of upper Manhattan called Washington Heights. To mark the Highlanders' debut, more than 16,000 attendees—including the country's premier showman, George M. Cohan—waved tiny American flags as the 69th Regiment Band marched across the grass playing Cohan's signature tune, "Yankee Doodle Dandy."

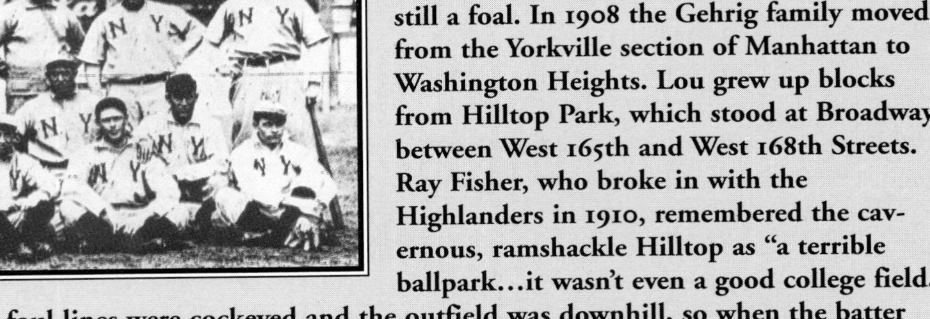

The 1909 New York Yankees, then known as the Highlanders.

The Iron Horse's symbiotic relationship with the Yankees began when he was still a foal. In 1908 the Gehrig family moved from the Yorkville section of Manhattan to Washington Heights. Lou grew up blocks from Hilltop Park, which stood at Broadway between West 165th and West 168th Streets. Ray Fisher, who broke in with the Highlanders in 1910, remembered the cavernous, ramshackle Hilltop as "a terrible ballpark...it wasn't even a good college field. The foul lines were cockeyed and the outfield was downhill, so when the batter hit one out there it actually rolled down towards the fences."

On those occasions when young Lou was able to get inside (or peek through a knothole in the distant outfield fences), he watched some capable performers including pitchers Fisher and Russ Ford, outfielder Birdie Cree, and the enigmatic Hal Chase, the finest fielding first baseman in history when he wasn't fixing the game's outcome for gamblers. Gehrig might even have caught a glimpse of his future college coach, Andy Coakley, then closing out his career on Hilltop's mound.

Although the Yankees have won more games than any team in the history of the American League, they weren't a charter member of Ban Johnson's circuit. In fact, it was quite a battle to establish a team, and then a loyal fan base, in the city. But from the moment the junior circuit declared itself a major league in 1901, it was clear to Johnson that a healthy New York franchise was vital to its success.

However, Manhattan's representative in the senior circuit, the haughty and successful National League Giants, blocked all American League attempts to place a franchise anywhere near its home turf, the Polo Grounds. The storied, bathtub-shaped park sat beneath Coogan's Bluff in the north Harlem section of Manhattan, on Eighth Avenue between 157th and 159th Streets. The Giants owners' ties to the city's corrupt Democratic machine were so strong that no one doubted their threat to run a streetcar line through the site of any prospective American League park.

After two years of war, the two leagues reached a truce in 1903. They agreed to end their expensive player raids and to stage an annual World Series beginning that October. Territories were established. In return for Ban Johnson's promise not to install an American League team in Pittsburgh to compete with the National League Pirates, he was allowed unimpeded access to New York. Giants owner John T. Brush was the only National League owner to vote against this compromise. In a snit, he refused to allow his team to participate in the 1904 Series.

From the beginning the established Giants looked down their noses at the American League upstarts, referring to them as the "invaders." The Giants leader was the two-fisted, acid-tongued, roundly reviled John J. "Mugsy" McGraw, who had been the manager of the American League's Baltimore franchise until it was sold for $18,000 and transferred to New York to become the Highlanders. Run out of the American League by Ban Johnson, McGraw displayed nothing but contempt for Johnson, the junior circuit, and the Yankees.

Hilltop Park was located on the highest ground in Manhattan. In the background is the Hudson River.

After boycotting the 1904 postseason, the Giants magnaminously agreed to play Philadelphia in the 1905 World Series. Behind Christy Mathewson's three shutouts, they easily dispatched the American League representative in five games, which made the Giants and their followers that much more insufferable. "The wham-bam style of those early-day Giants, their cocky, aggressive manners on the diamond, brought the wrath of fans in rival towns down around their ears," wrote Jack Sher. "McGraw instigated this and loved it."

Despotic but brilliant, McGraw "was wise enough to realize that hate is as strong an attraction as love," continued Sher. "Cops were called in Cincinnati, Pittsburgh, and Chicago to keep the Giants from being mobbed on their way to the ballpark. McGraw would cart his players to the park, not in an ordinary bus, but in gilded carriages with banners proclaiming them World Champions. They were belted with eggs and stale fruit, assaulted and defiled, but the fans followed them right through the gate."

The Giants were accustomed to dominating the society pages, sports columns, and turnstile counts. Featuring such stars as Mathewson, Rube Marquard, Jeff Tesreau, Josh Devore, Larry Doyle, George Kelly, Ross Youngs, and Frankie Frisch, they produced a string of championships, winning 10 pennants and three World Series between 1904 and 1924. Just for the heck of it, they also played the Highlanders in a pair of postseason city series, winning handily in 1910 and again in 1914.

The Polo Grounds sat beneath Coogan's Bluff.

The feud subsided when, after the Polo Grounds was nearly destroyed by a fire in 1911, Highlanders owner Frank Farrell offered the Giants the use of Hilltop Park until their own park was repaired. In 1913 the Giants returned the favor, inviting the Highlanders into the newly rebuilt Polo Grounds after their lease at Hilltop had expired.

Shortstop Roger Peckinpaugh, who joined the Highlanders that first summer in the Polo Grounds and stayed nine seasons, recalled that the team "was what we used to call a joy club. Lots of joy and lots of losing. Nobody thought we could win, and most of the time we didn't. But it didn't seem to bother the boys too much. They would start singing songs in the infield right in the middle of a game. There wasn't much managing to do outside of selecting the starting pitcher and hoping we didn't get beat too badly."

John J. McGraw, manager of the Giants from 1903 to 1932.

The joint tenancy figured to last only as long as the Highlanders remained the Giants' poor relations. However, by 1915 the Highlanders had officially changed their name to the Yankees and permanently adopted their now-famous pinstriped uniforms (a fashion that several teams, including the Giants, had been experimenting with since 1909). The cosmetic changes didn't rankle the Giants, but the Yankees' climb up the standings soon did. That year brewery owner Jacob Ruppert and millionaire engineer Colonel Tillinghast Huston bought the Yankees for $460,000 and made immediate efforts to improve the team.

The new owners purchased pitcher Bob Shawkey and first baseman Wally Pipp, and enticed third baseman Frank "Home Run" Baker out of retirement with a fistful of dollars. In 1918, Miller Huggins was hired as manager, and the first of many deals with the financially strapped owner of the Boston Red Sox, Harry Frazee, was struck. For $15,000 and four players the Yankees got outfielder Duffy Lewis and pitchers Ernie Shore and Dutch Leonard. Next to come were submarine pitcher Carl Mays and pitcher-turned-outfielder Babe Ruth. The pair cost Ruppert and Huston a combined $165,000 cash and a $350,000 loan to Frazee (which was guaranteed by a mortgage on Boston's Fenway Park).

Ruth, who turned the world on its ear his first season in pinstripes by hitting more home runs (54) than any other team in the majors, was responsible for the Yankees setting a big-league attendance record in 1920 that lasted more than a quarter century. Folks packed the Polo Grounds, hoping to catch a glimpse of Ruth's next moon shot. Meanwhile, the Giants unhappily watched their own attendance fall off, even though they fielded competitive teams. The Yankees were served notice that they should shop around for another park.

Ruppert and Huston's next brainstorm was to hire Red Sox manager Ed Barrow as their general manager at the end of the 1920 season. Combative and tight fisted, Barrow was the architect of what would become the Yankees dynasty. Aided by chief scout Paul Krichell, whom he hired, over the next two decades Barrow signed or traded for the likes of Waite Hoyt, Joe Bush, Tony Lazzeri, Herb Pennock, George Pipgras, Earle Combs, Bill Dickey, Joe DiMaggio, Phil Rizzuto, and of course, Lou Gehrig. During Barrow's stay in the front office, the Yankees would win 14 pennants and 10 world championships.

After a decade of middle-of-the-pack finishes, the Yankees improved to third place in 1920. The following year they won their first pennant and took on the Giants in the World Series. This meant the entire best-of-nine tournament would be played in the Polo Grounds. McGraw, who considered wearing the visiting team's gray uniform in his own backyard an insult, was damned if his old-school style of ball was going to be overshadowed by the wildly popular long-ball style that the Yankees favored. He was particularly put off by Ruth. McGraw, Ty Cobb, and every other disgruntled disciple of the scientific game of place hitting and base stealing blamed the Sultan of Swat for the advent of "sloppy," go-for-the-fences baseball.

The Yankees won the first two games of the 1921 "Subway Series" by 3-0 scores and had a four-run lead in the third game before the Giants stormed back. McGraw's troops rebounded to win game three, 13-5, and went on to capture the

Series, five games to three. While Mugsy chortled, Yankee supporters pointed to Ruth's absence (he had missed most of the last three games because of an infected arm and bad knee) as the reason behind the collapse. McGraw, always happy to antagonize the opposition, retorted that the big guy should have played hurt. And, he continued, the result proved the superiority, not only of the New York Giants, but of gray matter over brawn.

The two teams met again in the 1922 Series, and this time the Giants swept the Yankees, four games to none. In five games (the second contest had ended in a 3-3 tie), Ruth was held to a puny .118 average and no home runs. Afterwards, he admitted that he had been discombobulated by the Giants' nonstop razzing, which was expertly orchestrated by McGraw.

"Hey, Ruth, your mother was a nigger!" was one of the gentler nuggets tossed in Ruth's direction. Obviously flustered, he and teammate Bob Meusel charged the antagonists' dugout after the first game, looking for a fight. The Giants disdainfully turned their backs. A couple of days later, the Sultan of Swat was roundly booed even by Yankees fans for needlessly bowling over Giants third baseman Heinie Groh, the smallest man on the field. Humbled, Ruth left immediately after the Series on a barnstorming trip out west—"beyond the reach of the echoes of the recent strife at the Polo Grounds," noted John Kieran.

Over the winter Jacob Ruppert finally settled a long-standing feud with Colonel Huston by buying out his partner's interest in the Yankees for $1.5 million. He spent another $2.3 million building a new showcase for his team, Yankee Stadium. The huge 74,000-seat, concrete and steel structure stood just across the Harlem River, about a quarter mile from the Polo Grounds. From that distance the Giants could almost make out the Yankees thumbing their noses at them.

Christy Mathewson and son. The Giants' handsome, college-educated pitcher was the idol of most youngsters growing up in turn-of-the-century New York.

Ruth hit the first home run at Yankee Stadium when it opened for business on April 18, 1923. Sportswriter Fred Lieb immediately dubbed the sports palace "The House That Ruth Built." For the third straight year, the Yankees' season ended with a pennant and a showdown with the Giants. Before the World Series began, McGraw bragged, "I've said it before, and I'll say it again—we pitch to better hitters than Ruth in the National League."

But what goes around comes around. This time out Ruth helped propel the Yankees to their first world championship, hitting .368 with three booming home runs as the Giants fell in six games. "The Ruth is mighty," wrote Heywood Broun afterwards, "and shall prevail." Most of McGraw's comments couldn't be published.

A corner was turned with the 1923 Series. The team that had dominated baseball in New York for decades had been eclipsed by its one-time boarder. Not only would the Giants never win another World Series against the Yankees (in 1936, 1937, and 1951), they would flee the Polo Grounds for the West Coast after the 1957 season, citing poor attendance as the reason. Meanwhile, the team that had once teetered precariously on the top of a hill was securely perched on the top of the heap—a lofty position that, with a total of 22 world titles since 1923, it has yet to step down from.

Like most city kids, Lou grew up playing stickball on New York's streets.

the century was about twenty-five years lower than what it is today. Such highly communicative diseases as tuberculosis, diptheria, cholera, pneumonia, scarlet fever, and whooping cough led to an appallingly high infant mortality rate, especially in the drafty, congested, unclean tenement houses where immigrant families like the Gehrigs lived. Couples typically had several children, with the unspoken expectation that one or two would die young.

The Gehrigs were victims of this morbid math. Sophie died of diptheria on March 27, 1906, at twenty months of age. Within a year, illness took Anna away. A second boy, his name lost to time, also died shortly after his birth. Grief-stricken Christina, having buried three children before she was thirty, understandably focused all of her love and attention on Lou.

"He's the only big egg I have in my basket," she explained. "He's the only one of four who lived, so I want him to have the best."

Immigrant families discovered that though there were several ways to die, there was but one way to live: close to the vest. The Gehrigs got by on probably no more than three or four hundred dollars a year. Part of the problem was work-shy Heinrich, who either was unable or unwilling to hold a steady job. His trade, which consisted of hammering intricate patterns into sheet metal, paid well enough. But Pop Gehrig preferred the camaraderie of the neighborhood saloon where he could quaff beer and play pinochle. Years of health problems didn't help matters.

When Lou was about five, the family moved from Yorkville to Washington Heights, an area of upper Manhattan. If the drab and threadbare living conditions weren't quite Dickensian, they were close enough. Nonetheless, years later Mom Gehrig bristled when reporters tried to portray her son as having grown up in a slum.

"I don't pretend Lou was born with a silver spoon in his mouth," she said. "But he never left the table hungry, and I can say he had a terrible appetite from the first time he saw daylight. Maybe his clothes were torn, dirty, and rumpled after playing baseball and football, but he was always clean and neatly dressed when I sent him off to school."

To make ends meet, Mom Gehrig tackled the arduous, thankless tasks that were the purview of most poor and ill-educated women of the

George Herman "Babe" Ruth shared Lou's background. He was born of impoverished German-American parents, but rose to become a household name. Here he is as a member of the Boston Red Sox, which he joined as a nineteen-year-old pitcher in 1914.

In 1917 Lou posed inside a studio for his grade school graduation photo. "He was average in every sense of the word," Jack Sher wrote of Lou's childhood, "almost pitifully so."

period. She took in laundry, baked and cooked for outsiders, cleaned their apartments—anything to help pay the rent and put food on the table. Because everyone else in the neighborhood was nearly as bad off as the Gehrigs, she had to find her clients in more affluent parts of the city. (Perhaps Mom's most celebrated employer was bootlegger Owney Madden, whose apartment she cleaned. Not much is known of the arrangement, except that it couldn't have continued past 1915. That's when Madden was sent to Sing Sing for murder.) The travel made the tasks more time consuming and, because of trolley fares, more expensive.

By the time Lou was seven, he too was contributing to the family's welfare. He took streetcars to pick up and deliver the laundry his mother washed and ironed. He ran errands around the neighborhood, racing home afterwards with his balled-up fists at his sides. Inside were the pennies and nickels he turned over to his mother.

That often was all she needed to concoct a meal. At the time, milk cost four cents a quart, eggs were ten cents a dozen, and chickens could be had for about sixteen cents a pound. Big-hearted butchers threw in the lung and heart for free. Penny-conscious cooks like Christina could make a tasty, protein-rich meal out of these extras. Cut up the lung and heart, then smother the meat with onions browned in chicken fat. Add a cup of chicken soup, salt, and plenty of paprika, put rice or noodles on the side, and—bingo!—a family of three was enjoying a dinner of lung goulash for only a few cents. Mom Gehrig was an excellent cook, as evidenced by the many ballplayers, including Babe Ruth, who would one day make her kitchen a favorite postgame stop. She specialized in authentic German fare: pickled eels, roast duck, sauerbraten, and pig knuckles.

In most ways, including the grinding poverty, Lou's childhood was no different from that of tens of thousands of other children then growing up in the city. He attended Public School 132 at 183rd Street and Wadsworth, a chunky kid wearing hand-me-down kneepants and an earnest but friendly expression.

Lou and his adolescent mates played games in the park across the street from where the Gehrigs lived; stole bananas and potatoes from

At the turn of the century, *turnvereins* were an integral part of the German-American community. Their emphasis on traditional German gymnastics gave plump adolescents like Lou Gehrig a chance to build muscles and coordination.

vegetable stands; called each other "Mick," "Krauthead," and "Hunky," depending on the victim's ethnicity; and dreamed up 101 forms of minor mischief.

Shy and lacking self-confidence, Lou never was a ringleader. He was content to follow. On hot summer days their path led to the foot of 181st Street and the Hudson River, a favorite swimming hole. The boys would swim buck naked in the dirty water or dive off the steep cliffs. One day when he was eleven, Lou—perhaps acting on a dare or a taunt—swam the mile-wide river clear across to the other side in New Jersey.

Such stunts were dangerous, which is why Pop Gehrig, by most accounts a disciplinarian, boxed his son's ears after he heard of it. (Jimmy Cannon, seven years Lou's junior and himself a product of New York's congested neighborhoods, remembered a Polish lad who did a swan dive into the river—and disappeared. Later, as the victim's mother stood on the pier and screamed hysterically, police brought her young son to the surface. His head was jammed into a giant milk can that had been standing upright on the river bottom.)

Lou was stocky and ungainly ("all belly and ass," recalled one adolescent friend), but Pop Gehrig knew of a way to burn off the baby fat. Outside of the neighborhood beer garden, the favorite social institution of German-American men was the local *turnverein.* Equal parts community center, political forum, and gymnasium, *turnvereins* actually were in decline when Lou began making regular visits as a twelve year old. But to a die-hard group of printers, cigarmakers, brewers, and other workingmen, they remained freestanding outposts of German culture, where one could argue current affairs and work up a sweat, both in the mother tongue.

Turnvereins stressed traditional German gymnastics. Lou, who regularly attended the one at 156th Street in the Bronx, built up his coordination and strength using rings, horses, and the parallel bars. He also worked heavily with dumb bells, medicine balls, pulleys, and Indian clubs. Today, weight training is universally accepted and practiced by athletes in all sports. In Gehrig's time, however, the science of body building was primitive. Even great athletes looked ordinary when stripped in the locker room. Thus Lou's muscular physique—massive thighs, bowling-pin calves, bulging biceps, arching pectorals, and a washboard stomach—inspired considerable awe and comment as he and his body matured.

It was also the source of the extraordinary power he displayed on the sandlots whenever he wasn't going to school or doing odd jobs. Because of his powerful legs, Lou was a soccer standout, booting the ball like a cannon shot past his amazed playmates. He also was ideal for the rugged sport of football, would-be tacklers clinging to his back and legs like fleas hitching a ride on an elephant. The sport he was to gain most renown in, however, was baseball.

A passion for most Americans, baseball has long been romanticized by lumpy-throated writers for its pastoral roots. But the game didn't really take off until it was adopted by the soot-stained masses in the country's growing factoryvilles. By 1903, the year of Lou's birth, eleven major urban areas contained all sixteen big-league clubs: New York, Pittsburgh, Chicago, Detroit, St. Louis, Cincinnati, Cleveland, Boston, Philadelphia, Washington and Brooklyn. These teams would stay put for the next fifty years, an unparalleled stretch of continuity that helped reinforce the narcissistic belief that baseball was more than a mere game, it was life itself.

George Cohan, for one, was smitten by the magic of ball hitting bat. When he was a boy, his father took him to a professional game in New Jersey. "Son," he said, "this is a game I want you to love."

Baseball became the showman's only passion away from the theatre. When he could pull himself away from rehearsals, he visited the Polo Grounds to watch John McGraw's powerful National League Giants. Or he journeyed to Hilltop Park, home of the American League's woeful Highlanders. At either park he'd sit, hat pulled low to ward off recognition, and follow the stars that Lou knew from the baseball cards that came inside Pop Gehrig's packs of Sweet Caporal cigarettes: Christy Mathewson, Ty Cobb, Heinie Zimmerman, Smokey Joe Wood, and (Lou's favorite) Honus Wagner, the gifted, awkward-looking shortstop of the Pittsburgh Pirates and son of German immigrants.

Although the Gehrigs eagerly sought to be known as Americans,

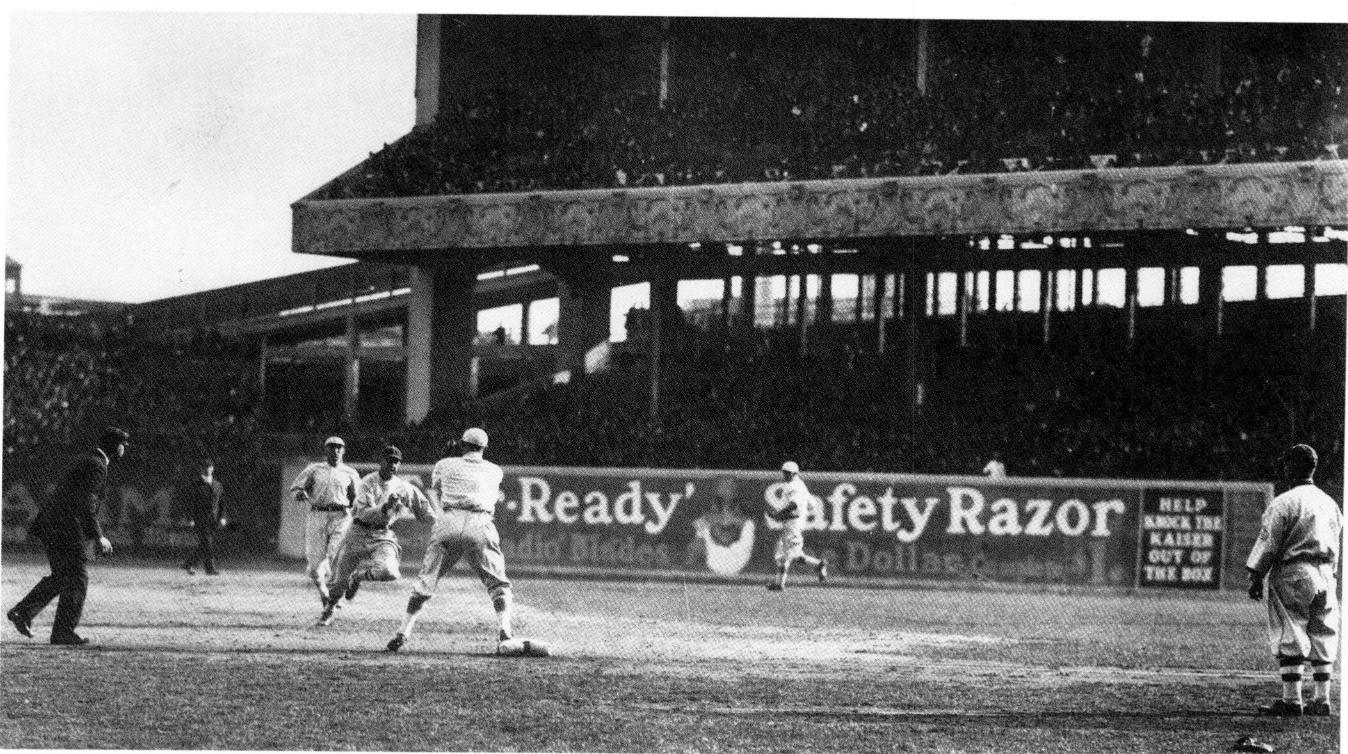

A World Series game played between Chicago and New York at the Polo Grounds in the fall of 1917 after the United States had formally entered the war. Heinie Zimmerman, the Giants third baseman about to put the tag on Eddie Collins, undoubtedly felt a little uneasy about the anti-German hysteria gripping the country. (Notice the sign to the right.) He requested that, for the duration of the war, he be called Henry.

when alone or among their ethnic brethren the family spoke mostly German, a potentially dangerous decision after World War I broke out in the summer of 1914. Before that, most Americans viewed the saber rattling in faraway Europe as another example of Old World rivalries getting out of hand. There was plenty of criticism to spread among Great Britain, Russia, and the continental powers.

But after German troops marched through neutral Belgium and a U-boat torpedoed the *Lusitania* off the coast of Ireland in 1915, with a loss of 1,198 lives (including several hundred Americans), public opinion turned violently against the Gehrigs' native land. President Woodrow Wilson vigorously attempted to keep America out of the bloodbath, but he could do nothing to stem the rising tide of anti-German sentiment in the States. It didn't help matters for New York's German community when saboteurs blew up a dock in New Jersey, an act of terrorism that brought the European war frightingly close to home. National heroes like former president Teddy Roosevelt stoked the fires of prejudice, declaring that those "hyphenated Americans" who attempted to be "both German and American" were "not Americans at all, but traitors to America and tools and servants of Germany against America."

The "bloody Hun" stories making the rounds of street corners and playgrounds did more than make German-Americans uncomfortable; they placed them directly in harm's way. Indiscriminate beatings and job dismissals became widespread. Universities cancelled courses in German language, literature, and history. Practically overnight, sauerkraut became "liberty cabbage," and German measles were called "liberty measles." The Germania Life Insurance Company of New York became the Guardian Life Insurance Company, while the citizens of Berlin, Michigan, thought it prudent to change the town's name for the dura-

Commerce High's championship baseball team of 1920. Lou sits third from right in the middle row. "But then, who was Gehrig?" classmate Lincoln Werden rhetorically asked after joining the sports department of the *New York Times*. "One of thousands of the city's youngsters who poured into the gray buildings daily, whose parents like those of the rest of us were hardworking, struggling folk hoping their sons some day might become businessmen."

tion. Fewer than ten percent of New York's population admitted to having German blood, a percentage that continued to shrink as more and more sought to distance themselves from the image of a German soldier, baby impaled on his bayonet, that loomed menacingly in the public imagination.

After the war, a rich and concerned American sent an emissary to Belgium. His mission was to find those children whose hands had been lopped off by the invading Germans and bring them back to the United States where they could receive proper medical treatment and an education. Alas, after much searching the emissary was unable to find a single child. The reason? The stories of mutilated Belgian children, like that of crucified Canadian soldiers and bayoneted nurses, were lies, part of a propaganda campaign orchestrated by Great Britain and aided immeasurably by the gullible American press.

The revelation came too late for those on the receiving end of the abuse. The Gehrigs, who still had an emotional attachment to Germany, experienced their share of anguish during the war years. Unfortunately, they didn't enjoy the safety of numbers in ethnically mixed Washington Heights that their former neighbors in the German stronghold of Yorkville did. The anti-German hysteria led to taunts of "dumb Dutchman" directed at Lou. Even those who knew better got in on the act. When Mom found a job cooking at Columbia's Sigma Nu fraternity house, students pegged her son, who often helped her out, "Little Heinie." Whether the nickname was used with affection or derision, it stung this teenager, who retreated further into his shell.

On April 6, 1917, as Lou was finishing his final year of grade school, the United States finally entered the war it had been trying for so long to ignore. George Cohan, for one, was so excited by the news that he immediately locked himself into the study of his Manhattan apartment and didn't emerge until the following morning. Then, with a tin pan for a helmet and a broom for a rifle, he marched, arm swinging, in front of his dazzled wife and children, singing a song he had written to honor America's great crusade:

Over there, over there,
Send the word, send the word over there,
That the Yanks are coming, the Yanks are coming,
The drums rum-tumming everywhere.

So prepare, say a prayer,
Send the word, send the word to beware.
We'll be over, we're coming over,
And we won't come back till
It's over, over there.

The wildly popular song (Cohan modestly maintained that he had simply "dramatized a bugle call") pricked a jingoistic nerve. Young men packed recruiting stations. While German books were pulled from library shelves and mobs forced bewildered German-Americans to recite the pledge of allegiance at gunpoint, the American Expeditionary Force sailed for France, led by John J. "Black Jack" Pershing. Most people didn't know that the general's family name back in Prussia had been Pfoerschin.

The national pastime was affected along with the rest of the country. Major-league baseball, termed "nonessential" to the war effort by the U.S. government, contributed 144 American Leaguers and 103 National Leaguers to the various branches of the military. Those who stayed behind played a curtailed 1918 season and performed close-order drills before games, using bats as rifles.

One of the steel-hatted doughboys "over there" was Sergeant Robert Troy, who had been born in Germany in 1888 and later immigrated with his family to America. Raised in Monessen, Pennsylvania, the oldest of five children, the 6-foot-4, 195-pound pitcher ignored the whistle of the local steel mills and heeded instead the siren call of the diamond. As a young man he moved around

Opera star Madame Schumann-Heinck had sons fighting on both sides, a not uncommon dilemma for many "hyphenated Americans" during the First World War.

THE FOOTBALL SQUAD, 1920. ..
Standing left to right: Wiener, Navarro, Kulick, Horvath, Levine (Captain-elect), Sternbach, Gherig, J. Atheneos, Iannitti, Manager Rosen, Captain Wiedman, Miehoffer, Sesit, Ashley, Kaplan, Parker, Asst. Manager Guala, Wilson, Bunora, Yates, Solomon, Golden, B. Atheneos.

Lou, standing seventh from the left, was a jarring fullback and a very capable punter on Commerce High's football team. Best friend Mike Sesit, six players to the right of Gehrig, often accompanied him to a *turnverein* at 85th Street and Lexington Avenue. While hanging on the horizontal bars, Lou complained of sharp pains in his back and legs—a foreshadowing, perhaps, of the disease that would claim his life. "His body behaved as if it were drunk," recalled Sesit.

the country and up through the professional ranks, finally emerging for one brief fling in the major leagues with the Detroit Tigers.

One Sunday afternoon in 1912, Troy took the mound at Navin Field against Walter Johnson and the Washington Senators. To the unexpected joy of several thousand fans, including his family, the rookie exchanged goose eggs with the game's greatest pitcher until things finally blew up on him in the seventh. The Tigers lost. The scatter-armed Troy never really found his control, and so his first big-league appearance turned out to be his last. He drifted into the minors, dreaming of another shot at the big leagues until the day he exchanged his knickers for khakis and was shipped to France as a sergeant with Company G, 319th Infantry Regiment.

An armistice ending hostilities was signed November 11, 1918, but that proved five weeks too late for Sergeant Troy. One day during the Meuse offensive, a German soldier shot him through the chest. Troy died a short while later in an evacuation hospital, after which he was wrapped in a shroud and a blanket and buried under a simple cross near the village of Senoncourt. Troy thus joined Eddie Grant, an infielder on four big-league clubs between 1905 and 1915, and Alex Barr, an outfielder who had played one game for the Yankees in 1914, as the only former major leaguers to be killed in the war.

Stored deep in the bowels of the National Archives in Washington, D.C., is an exchange of several letters between the War Department and Troy's mother, Bertha. In late 1919, the department responded to Mrs. Troy's request for information concerning the whereabouts of her son's body. "My dear Mrs. Troy," private secretary Ralph Hayes wrote:

> The War Department, as you know, has taken steps to direct the return of bodies of our soldiers who are buried in countries other than France; but in France, and in a relatively small portion of that

country, are buried the dead of many nations. In the early stages of post-bellum reconstruction and rehabilitation, the French Government is fearful of the effect upon its population of the disinterment and transport through France of these millions of bodies. The American Government and the War Department eventually will arrange for the return of our dead from France, and the matter is now a subject of negotiation between the two Governments.

Your application for the return of your son, Robert Troy, is being placed on file here, in order that proper action may be taken when the necessary international arrangements for the return of these bodies have been completed.

Blowing the dust off these letters is more instructive than intrusive. No one could ever doubt the loyalty and sacrifice of thousands of hyphenated Americans after reading Bertha Troy's repeated requests to have her dead son brought home — "home," the Troys' adopted country and not the land of their birth. After nearly three years of officious and impersonal correspondence with the War Department, Sergeant Troy's remains finally were disinterred, neatly boxed, and sent on the long voyage back to the States, from Antwerp to Hoboken by ship and then on to Monnessen by rail. Had Bertha Troy and Christina Gehrig somehow known each other, they undoubtedly would have shared something deeper than a common ethnic heritage. A mother's love for her son, they would have commiserated, is a wonderful thing.

It is also severely tested as the son grows out of knickers. Lou characteristically bought his first pair of long pants with his own earnings. Mom Gehrig undoubtedly wished he would have put off this universal rite of passage a little longer. Her worshipful, obedient son was growing up too quickly to suit her.

Lou graduated from grade school and turned fourteen just a couple of months after the U.S. entered the war. Relatively few boys completed high school in those days; instead they got their working papers and joined the labor force. By now Pop Gehrig was fifty years old, sickly, and often unable to work, causing Lou to offer to ditch education for a job.

Mom Gehrig would not hear of it. She announced for probably the ten thousandth time since Lou was born that her son would be more than a mere muscle worker, even if she had to work 'round the clock to support the family. Her much-discussed plans for Lou's future were always vague. But she was adamant that he would continue his education and become something—an architect, perhaps, or an engineer, like his uncle back in Germany. In the fall of 1917, Lou dutifully entered Commerce High School.

Commerce High, located at 155 West 65th Street, was a dreary-looking all-boys school that specialized in preparing its students for the business world. Lou was an average student who earned better-than-average grades through hard work and diligence. "He could hit a baseball without missing a stroke," remembered his typing teacher, Miss Mollie Silverman, "but his thick fingers just couldn't seem to find the right keys on the typewriter."

Classmates marveled that Lou never missed a day of school. Even in the coldest weather, he rarely wore a topcoat or hat—a habit, borne of financial necessity, that he continued even after he had become a major leaguer.

Between hitting the books and augmenting the family income with odd jobs at the local butcher's shop and grocery store, Lou still found time for play. High school sports, however, were more organized and competitive than the sandlot variety to which he was accustomed. Big and shy, he needed a push.

"Some of the kids had told my bookkeeping teacher that I could hit the ball a mile in the park," Lou later recalled. "The teacher ordered me to show up for a school game. I went up to the stadium on a streetcar. When I got there and saw so many people going into the field and heard all the cheering and noise, I was so scared I couldn't see straight. I turned right around and got back on the streetcar and went home. The next day the teacher threatened to flunk me if I didn't show up for the next game. So I went."

Lou was not a natural athlete. In fact, his early reputation in baseball left a lot to be desired. "Gehrig, our first sacker, can certainly field," the school paper remarked in May 1919, "but he is woefully weak at the bat."

By his junior year, 1919-20, Lou's physique was developing impressively. Having sprouted three inches in four months, he wasn't far from filling out to his adult size of six feet and 200 pounds. He was a three-sport man, playing football, baseball, and soccer and helping Commerce High to three straight championships in soccer. He'd previously played hockey, wrestling, and basketball, but a physical exam in his sophomore year revealed "a bad heart." What Lou had was a small heart, which we now know can actually be an asset to athletes, since it pumps blood more efficiently. Alarmed by the doctor, however, he decided to concentrate on the gridiron and the baseball diamond.

Late in the spring of 1920, Commerce High's baseball team was selected by the *New York Daily News* to represent the city in a special "national championship" game with Chicago's top high school team, Lane Tech, which featured a star shortstop named Freddie Lindstrom (who went on to a Hall of Fame career with the New York Giants). The game was scheduled for June 26 at Wrigley Field in Chicago.

Lou, who played first base when he wasn't putting the fear of God into batters with his unpredictable fastball, was excited about the upcoming trip but uncertain that his parents would give him permission to go. At dinner, he told them of the team's invitation to Chicago. *Chicago?* they said. *What kind of foolishness was this?*

"You would have thought I was going to Borneo or Zanzibar," Lou said, recalling the moment years later.

"This baseball is a waste of time," argued Mom. "It will never get you anywhere." Pop, who generally was more sympathetic to Lou's sporting activities, didn't understand the game any better than his wife. One Christmas he had bought Lou a right-handed catcher's mitt, not realizing his son was a southpaw. The matter was debated well into the night before Mom and Pop finally caved in.

Only nine players and the coach made the train trip to the Windy

City. It was a memorable journey: sleeping in Pullman berths, eating in an elegant dining car, and spending their time in Chicago in clean, spacious hotel rooms. En route, the wide-eyed, fuzzy-cheeked lads from Commerce High were treated as kings. Former president Howard Taft stopped by to wish the boys luck, and comic Joey Frisco told jokes and did a little soft-shoe for their entertainment. The thought that this was the way major leaguers were treated must have crept into Lou's mind. It sure beat being a bookkeeper.

Come game day, some ten thousand people were on hand to watch Commerce carve out an 8-6 lead over Lane Tech at the end of eight innings. In the top of the ninth, a pair of walks and an error filled the bases for Lou.

Gehrig had gone hitless in five trips to the plate. This time, however, he got hold of the pitcher's second offering and sent it rocketing toward right field. It kept on going, sailing over the wall and landing on the front porch of a house on Sheffield Avenue.

The mammoth grand slam not only dramatically sealed a 12-6 victory for the out-of-towners, it set sportswriters afire. Someone batting the ball out of the park—any park—was still an unusual sight (although the Yankees' phenom, Babe Ruth, was in the process of revolutionizing the game that summer with an unheard of 54 round-trippers). After all, the previous major-league season had seen the Chicago Cubs and their visitors combine for just 18 home runs total at Wrigley Field, many of them of the inside-the-park variety. "Gehrig's blow would have made any big leaguer proud," reported the *Chicago Tribune*, "yet it was walloped by a boy who hasn't yet started to shave."

Lou and his teammates returned home the following morning. Five thousand people and the Hebrew Orphan Asylum band waited at Grand Central Station for the Twentieth Century Limited to pull in, at which point they mobbed their conquering heroes. A grand march and some speechifying followed, after which the players went home to their respective tenements to glow in the treatment the local dailies gave their exploits.

Commerce High's budding slugger, who had just turned seventeen three weeks earlier, was singled out for special attention. This Gehrig boy, the New York newspapers proclaimed, was "the Babe Ruth of the schoolyards."

CHAPTER Two

—A BUMMER'S BUSINESS—

To many immigrants, finding any games at all here, never mind which ones, must have been a revelation. To see so much arable land turned over to people at play must have seemed almost unnatural, if not un-European. The freedom to frolic is seldom listed among our basics, yet what gift has done more to shape the happy-go-lucky, take-on-anything Yankee character that foreigners so goggle at?

—Wilfred Sheed

ALTHOUGH MOM Gehrig knew next to nothing about baseball, she was sufficiently impressed by the commotion surrounding Lou's performance in Chicago to stash newspaper accounts of it into a dresser drawer. She would use this convenient repository for the next thirteen years, until Lou married and his wife spent months sorting and pasting the exasperating jumble of headlines, boxscores, pictures, and game accounts into thick albums that modest ballplayers such as Lou disparagingly called "fathead books."

The cavalier manner in which Christina preserved her son's athletic heroics is not surprising, given her expectations. She had always planned that Henry Louis Gehrig's name would be writ large where it really counted: on a university sheepskin. She was convinced that his greatest achievements would come in a true profession, perhaps one that German-Americans were making a name in, such as engineering. Better that the Babe Ruth of the schoolyards be known as the Charles Steinmetz of the schoolyards, she reasoned.

Charles P. Steinmetz—now *here* was someone to look up to, in a manner of speaking. A crippled German immigrant barely four feet tall, he had arrived in the United States with ten dollars, no job, and no command of the English language. Yet his genius in mathematics and electrical engineering was responsible for many of the great advances in electricity at the turn of the century. The General Electric Company was built around Steinmetz, who had some 200 patents to his credit when he died in 1923.

Lou was no Steinmetz, but he was no dim bulb either, possessing intelligence slightly above average. He was a fair student, one who might have done better scholastically if he hadn't conducted most of his studying during streetcar rides to and from school, practice, and work.

Lou Gehrig of Columbia: "the best college player since George Sisler."

As indestructible on the gridiron as he was on the diamond, Gehrig (third from left in the front row) helped the Columbia Lions win five of their nine games in 1922.

Ultimately it was his physical prowess, not his classwork, that got him into college.

One afternoon in the fall of 1920 when Lou was a high school senior, the Commerce football team played a rival at Columbia University's South Field, just off Broadway at 116th Street. Scouting on the sidelines were Columbia's football coach, Frank "Buck" O'Neill, and Bobby Watt, the former president of Phi Delta Theta. Watt had returned from service in France to become Columbia's graduate manager of athletics.

Watt was familiar with the Gehrigs. He had hired Mom as a cook on fraternity row a few years earlier. Mom, in turn, was able to get Pop a job as a janitor and handyman, although he often missed work because of illness. Lou—"Little Heinie" to Watt's patronizing frat brothers—helped out his parents on campus: cleaning, washing dishes, serving

Gehrig played one season of football at Columbia, alternating between the line and the backfield. After Lou ran for two touchdowns in the 1922 opener against Ursinus, Paul Gallico wrote: "Gehrig is the beef expert who has mastered the science of going where he is sent, for at least five yards. His plunges seemed to carry force."

meals. Once he had arrived late for practice, his face smudged black with coal dust. Embarrassed, he admitted that he had had to fill in for his ailing father in the furnace room.

Little Heinie had grown up since Watt went off to war. This afternoon the fullback with the boxcar build gained his eye. Lou's line plunges were of locomotive force, and his punts practically scraped the clouds. Watt was incredulous when told that the phenom's name was Lou Gehrig. "That kid—the little fat boy—that's him?"

Afterwards Watt visited with Lou and his parents to talk about obtaining a football scholarship to Columbia. Mom was ecstatic, though it wasn't going to be easy—not that anything ever was for the Gehrigs. After Lou graduated from Commerce High in February 1921, he had to undertake several months of arduous study in Columbia's extension program to meet the school's scholastic requirements. The effort paid off. He passed the entrance exam and was awarded a football scholarship for the fall of 1921.

Meanwhile, a worm appeared in Lou's shiny apple. In the spring of 1921, although not yet a full-time student, Lou received permission from

Columbia University, originally chartered as King's College in 1754, moved to Morningside Heights in 1897. The first Columbia student to make a name in professional baseball was Eddie Collins, who played six games as "Sullivan" for the Philadelphia Athletics in 1906 while still a student. The indiscretion, which forced Collins to forfeit his final year of college eligibility, didn't keep the gifted second baseman out of the Hall of Fame.

Columbia baseball coach Andy Coakley to work out with the varsity team. On April 5, Columbia played an exhibition game against the Hartford Senators of the Class A Eastern League. Hartford won, 4-3, but it was Gehrig's performance that wowed Hartford manager Art Irwin. In his only two trips to the plate, Lou socked two long home runs off pitcher Alton Durgin.

"When he came up again in the third inning," reported the *Hartford Times*, "Durgin ... was all set for revenge. He got a strike on Gehrig, but the next one he threw Gehrig leaned on, and it went sailing out of the enclosure past a big sundial and almost into the School of Mines. It was a mighty clout and worthy of Babe Ruth's best handiwork."

Not long afterwards, Irwin and Art Devlin, a scout for the New York Giants, arranged a tryout at the Polo Grounds. Lou worked out for several days, but he failed to impress the Giants' mercurial, sawed-off manager, John McGraw, who was in a foul mood over his team's losing streak.

"Get this fellow out of here!" McGraw finally screamed one morning after watching the nervous hopeful let a simple grounder roll between his legs. "I've got enough lousy players without another one showing up!"

Andy Coakley pitched nine seasons in the big leagues before becoming baseball coach at Columbia. His best effort was 18 wins for the Philadelphia Athletics in 1905, a season more notable for a costly wrestling match with the irrepressible Rube Waddell. The horseplay injured Waddell's shoulder and forced the Athletics' ace to miss the World Series, which was won by John McGraw's Giants.

Devlin tried to plead Gehrig's case, citing the half dozen balls he had blasted into the seats in batting practice. Baseball's "Little Napoleon" waved him off. The clumsy looking youngster was told not to come back.

Not one to easily give up, Devlin offered Lou an opportunity to play with Hartford, which had a working arrangement with the Giants. Hartford being a professional team, of course, meant Lou would be paid for playing ball—a violation of collegiate rules. Irwin and Devlin assured Lou that his anonymity, and thus his scholarship, would be safe.

Lou wasn't as gullible as his admirers later liked to portray him. Amateur athletes playing for pay under assumed names was a widespread practice. Some, including former Columbia standout Eddie Collins (who

Gehrig moves into a pitch at South Field on Columbia's main campus. A student cramming for an exam remembered the commotion Lou's clouts regularly caused: "I looked out of the window just in time to see a ball bouncing off the top of the sundial, maybe some 450 feet from home plate. And there was Lou standing there in his baggy knickers grinning from ear to ear."

went on to star for the Philadelphia Athletics and Chicago White Sox), had been caught and punished. Most, however, went undetected.

Lou had first become a baseball wage earner a couple of years earlier, earning five dollars a game pitching and catching for the Minquas, a neighborhood team sponsored by the local Democratic club. "I don't understand baseball," Mom Gehrig had said of the welcome contribution to the family coffer, "but I can understand five dollars!"

So could Lou, though this time the stakes were much higher. If he was caught playing organized ball, it could cost him his college eligibility and his athletic scholarship, without which it would be much harder to pay his tuition. Nonetheless, on June 2 newspapers announced that "Lefty" Gehrig, described as "a hard-hitting semipro from Brooklyn," had signed to play first base for Hartford. The assumption was that the former high school star had decided to forsake college for a professional career.

Lou's first game in organized ball was the following day against the Pittsfield Hillies. By now the papers had been tipped off. In print, the new recruit was referred to as "Lou Lewis."

Batting sixth, Lou Lewis went hitless in three official at-bats and contributed a sacrifice as Hartford won, 2-1. The youngster "appeared to be a bit nervous," reported the *Hartford Courant.* "After he gets used to surroundings he may develop. They seldom fail to make the grade with Irwin teaching the ways of baseball."

The next afternoon Lou clouted a triple his first time up as Hartford won again, 5-3. Two more hits the following afternoon caused local sportswriters to trot out what had become almost shopworn comparisons to Ruth.

Unlike Ruth (who would hit an ungodly 59 round-trippers that summer for the Yankees), Lou Lewis hit not a single home run for the Senators during his two-week stint. But his presence was felt. As of June 15, he was batting a commendable .261 with two triples and a double, and Hartford had won eight of thirteen games to climb into first place. After that date, however, mention of Lou Lewis disappeared completely from the sport pages.

The reason was a visit from Andy Coakley, who had found out about Lou playing under an assumed name and hustled the 130 miles from New York to Connecticut to lay down the law to Lou and, presumably, Irwin. Lou, just short of his eighteenth birthday, was homesick as well, so the decision to return to New York was an easy one to make. (A strange addendum to the story was that one month later, the 63-year-old Irwin either jumped or fell off the steamer *Calvin Austin* and drowned in the Atlantic.)

For the rest of his life, Lou would bristle with anger whenever John McGraw's name came up. McGraw and his pals, Lou insisted, had misrepresented the consequences of him going to Hartford, consequences that included a one-year ban from playing sports at Columbia.

Lou, who entered Columbia in the fall of 1921, was contrite and ashamed. Later, however, he was guilty of milder violations that biographers have unaccountably overlooked. It was common knowledge during Lou's lifetime that he played in 1922 and 1923 with the Morristown club in New Jersey as Lou Long. The thinly disguised pseudonym was inspired by the name of teammate Mike Bowe's fiancée, Catherine Long.

The semipro team, which played Sunday afternoons in Morristown, also competed on Sunday mornings as the Westinghouse team at Weidenmayer's Park and the Asylum Oval in Newark. How much Lou earned is unknown. Evidently, no one in Columbia's athletic department caught on to the charade. Or perhaps because playing semipro for a few dollars on weekends was considered not nearly as egregious an offense as signing a contract in organized ball, department officials decided to wink at the infraction.

At any rate, Lou's athletic suspension was lifted at the start of his sophomore year, allowing him to plant his cleats on South Field's gridiron for his one and only college football season.

College football was evolving into a wildly popular spectator sport in the twenties, but for the game's hardy participants it was still a brutal, smash-mouth affair, long on line plunges and quick kicks, and short on passing. Often playing without helmets, these iron men were expected to tough out the entire sixty minutes of play. Lou, one of the most punishing members of

Lou Gehrig in 1923, his sophomore season at Columbia.

the Columbia eleven, alternated between the backfield and the line in the autumn of 1922. He also did most of the punting.

"They stomped all over Lou," recalled one teammate, "but they could never crush his grin or spirit. And anyone who ran into him head-on never felt quite the same afterwards."

Iron-headed Lou was a standout on an average team. He ran for a pair of touchdowns in Columbia's season-opening rout of tiny Ursinus College. The following Saturday his plowlike rushes helped Columbia blow past Amherst, 43-6. Wesleyan and New York University fell by baseball-like scores of 10-6 and 6-2, respectively, boosting the Lions' mark to a perfect 4-0 and raising the hopes of alumni and students.

But then Williams hung a 13-10 defeat on the undefeated Lions, and the season degenerated after that. Columbia squeezed in a 17-6 win against Middlebury between a 56-0 drubbing by Cornell and a 28-7 loss to Dartmouth.

Lou's final football game was a Thanksgiving Day contest with Colgate, which crushed Columbia, 59-6. Despite separating his right shoulder, he scored the Lions' only points on a 40-yard pass reception. He also ran in a muffed punt for another score, but the touchdown was called back because of a penalty. Throughout the long afternoon, Lou ignored his injury and the hopelessness of the cause and, true to his nature, battled to the final whistle.

Sportswriter Grantland Rice watched the slaughter from the press

After losing a year of collegiate eligibility when he was caught playing professionally with Hartford as Lou Lewis, Gehrig took another risk playing semipro ball with a New Jersey nine. This time around Gehrig (third from left in back row) chose another uninspired moniker: Lou Long.

This drawing, part of a series of advertisements created by the Aetna Life Insurance Company in the 1950s, depicts the scene on April 28, 1923, immediately after Gehrig had pitched and batted Columbia past New York University. His performance prompted scout Paul Krichell to offer him a contract to play for the Yankees.

box. Afterwards he brought Colgate coach Dick Harlow home with him. Harlow was full of praise for the injured Gehrig.

"His right arm and shoulder were useless," Rice said of Gehrig. "But he stuck to his job."

It soon evolved that a job—a real, paying job—was what Lou desperately needed. His parents were ailing and the bills were mounting.

Then there was the matter of school itself. Studying was difficult enough, but the manner in which Lou was treated only compounded his sense of inferiority and shame. To many of his better-off fraternity brothers, the stocky and unsophisticated student stood out as an oaf in his nondescript secondhand clothes. Habitually broke, scared to death of the opposite sex, ill equipped to parry snickers and smug putdowns, Lou had to wonder at times just what he was doing in this environment. Columbia has since taken great pride in claiming Lou Gehrig as one of its own, the Phi Delta Theta fraternity even establishing an annual award in his name. The truth is that Lou was treated so shabbily he had practically nothing to do with Columbia or the fraternity after he left both for the Yankees.

In the spring of 1923, Lou prepared for his first—and only—season of competition in Columbia's blue-trimmed flannels.

Gehrig starred on the mound and at the plate. When he wasn't pitching, Coakley installed him at first base or the outfield to keep his bat in the lineup. "Lou was a fair outfielder, a first baseman without any glaring weaknesses, and a good pitcher" was the coach's assessment. "In the outfield he covered a lot of ground, got most of the drives hit his way, and got the ball away fast with his strong arm. As a pitcher, he didn't have much stuff, but he did have a better fastball than most college pitchers. Some days no college team could beat him."

"Columbia Lou" was a sensation, "the best college player since George Sisler," observed the *New York Times.* As a moundsman, he compiled a 6-4 record in 11 starts. In five outings he reached double digits in strikeouts. In a losing effort against Williams on April 18 (the same day brand-new Yankee Stadium opened in the Bronx), he struck out 17 batters, a school record for nearly a half century.

But it was his long-ball hitting—tremendous drives that disappeared into the treetops at Rutgers and Cornell—that had Coakley slapping his forehead in amazement and the stands abuzz. For the season Lou compiled the following numbers:

Games	*AB*	*R*	*H*	*BA*	*SA*	*2B*	*3B*	*HR*	*RBI*	*SB*
19	63	24	28	.444	.937	6	2	7	—	5

Watching one day was Paul Krichell, chief scout of the New York Yankees. He could barely contain his excitement when reporting to New York general manager Ed Barrow. Barrow, who had come over from the Boston Red Sox to the Yankees, calmed Krichell down. Have another look, he advised.

Krichell did. On April 28 he took in Columbia's game against New York University. Lou pitched a six-hitter and struck out eight, but the highlight of the Lions' win was another spectacular home run—the longest yet seen at South Field. Stepping up in the fifth, Lou practically knocked the cover off the ball, which cleared 116th Street, bounced off the library steps, and just missed hitting the college dean, who looked around in astonishment.

After the game Krichell hurried into the Lions' dressing room and introduced himself. The following morning Lou and Andy Coakley were sitting in Ed Barrow's office, listening to an offer of $3,500—which included an immediate $1,500 signing bonus—for Lou's signature to a professional contract.

The money was tempting, to say the very least, but Lou took time to mull it over.

He was almost twenty years old with a minimum of two more years of college to go. His aging parents were simply worn out from a lifetime of struggling. Pop, an epileptic, needed an operation, and Mom's lingering cold had developed into double pneumonia. The family was in arrears in rent and doctor bills. And faculty members, most of whom liked Lou and were sympathetic to his earnest attempt to gain an education, worried about his ability to handle the increasingly rigorous course work. Unlike modern college athletes, who frequently major in general studies or phys. ed, the student athletes of 1923 were cut no slack in the classroom.

"Lou, you've been in my class for almost a year," a business professor gently said when asked for his advice. "I think you better play ball."

Lou had always derived an elemental joy from athletic competition, that almost intoxicating satisfaction that surrounds the completion of a muscular task done well. Outside of his own home, an athletic field was the only place where he felt truly comfortable. Plus, America was one of the few countries where a man could actually get paid handsomely for something he had been doing for the pure love of it since he was a kid. For all of the effort spent chasing his parents' rather fuzzy dreams to "be something," a hard life had taught Lou to be practical.

He signed with the Yankees.

"Mom and Pop have made enough sacrifices for me," he explained. "Mom's been slaving to put a young ox like me through college. It's about time that I carry the load and take care of them."

Mom Gehrig, who had cried when her son had been accepted into Columbia, wept when he left it. To many foreign-born parents who had sacrificed knees and knuckles to give their children an opportunity they never had, a career in professional athletics—"a bummer's business"—seemed to be a poor substitute for a real profession. Although Lou's parents learned to be proud of his athletic accomplishments, Mom never fully accepted the notion of education being secondary to games. Even after her son had become one of the most famous and recognizable athletes in America, she would proudly remind reporters that Lou Gehrig had once been a college man.

CHAPTER Three

WALLY PIPP'S HEADACHE

The boy picked up a bat—one of Ruth's, by some curious chance—and advanced to the plate. He was obviously nervous, missed the first two pitches, then bounced one weakly over second base. Then he hit one that soared into the right field bleachers, high up, where only Ruth had ever hit a ball . . . He hit another ball in there—another—still another. His nervousness had slipped from him now.

"That's enough," Huggins cried. He turned to his players. "His name's Gehrig," he said, and walked slowly behind the hulking figure of the youngster toward the dugout. The players looked after them in silence.

—Frank Graham

WHEN LOU Gehrig joined the Yankees after school let out in June 1923, he had no way of knowing that he was getting in on the ground floor of what would one day become the most storied sports dynasty in America. The team was coming off two straight World Series losses to its crosstown rival, the Giants. But beginning that fall, when they finally beat the Giants for their first championship, the Yankees would bludgeon their way to twenty World Series crowns in forty seasons (1923-1962), including six sweeps. Their domination would be so complete that the cry "Break up the Yankees!" would become a mantra around the big leagues, and writers would seriously suggest that the Bronx Bombers be given a one-strike handicap when they came to the plate.

"Man, we were always in awe when we met the Yankees," recalled Eddie Wells, a collegiate pitcher from Ohio who started his career with Detroit the same week Gehrig reported to the Yankees. "There was just a certain air about them, like they were different from other ballplayers. We looked at them as being double big leaguers."

The architects of the Yankees' dynasty were general manager Ed Barrow, owner Jacob Ruppert, and the biggest drawing card in the game—a moon-faced man-child named George Herman "Babe" Ruth.

Ruth's story was already as familiar then as it is today. In time-honored Horatio Alger fashion, the saloonkeeper's son had moved from an orphanage's sandlot to a starring role with the Boston Red Sox. Switched from the mound to the outfield to take advantage of his thunderous bat, Ruth had revolutionized the game with prodigious pokes into the stands. In 1920, Ruppert got Ruth for $125,000 (and a $350,000 loan) from Boston owner Harry Frazee, who desperately needed the money to keep his theatrical productions going.

In his first three years in pinstripes (1920-1922), Ruth had averaged

Yankee Stadium opened on April 18, 1923, just a few weeks before Lou Gehrig joined the team.

The house that Ruth built was actually paid for by Yankees owner Jacob Ruppert, who inherited his father's brewery business and fortune. Ruppert tried to rename the Yankees after his best-selling beer Knickerbocker. The public bought the brew, but not the name change.

49 home runs, 143 RBI and 141 runs scored—and this despite missing a chunk of the 1922 season after he and teammate Bob Meusel were suspended for defying baseball commissioner Judge Landis's ban on barnstorming. His gaudy slugging percentages of .847 in 1920 and .846 in 1921 not only set new standards, they remain the highest of all-time. Before he retired in 1935, Ruth would lead the league in home runs and slugging a dozen times each, capture six RBI crowns, and set a passel of single-season and career batting records.

Ruth's versatility was astounding. He was a fine defensive outfielder whose throwing arm for years was widely considered the majors' best. He ran the bases aggressively but intelligently, six times scoring 150 or more runs in a season and stealing 123 bases (including 10 steals of home) during his career. And who knows what he might have accomplished had he remained a pitcher? As it was, he compiled a lifetime 94-46 won-lost record (including 23- and 24-win seasons) with a 2.28 ERA. What other man could have led the league in ERA (1.75 for Boston in 1916) and eight years later win a batting championship (.378 for the '24 Yankees)? Who else could have been an integral member of seven world championship teams—three as one of the game's top southpaw pitchers, four as its greatest hitter? If one was to name the all-time superman of sports history, Babe Ruth would be it, hands down.

The numbers, of course, can't begin to describe Ruth's remarkable persona. No one kept statistics on how many scotches he downed, how many women he bedded, how many autographs he signed, how many twenty-dollar tips he dispensed, how many names he forgot, how many children's heads he rubbed, how many winks he gave as he circled the bases. The public Ruth was crude but lovable, a loud, gregarious, warm-hearted, bulb-nosed Santa Claus who filled up a room like no one before or since.

"If you weren't around in those times, I don't think you could appreciate what a figure the Babe was," marveled Richards Vidmer, then a writer for the *New York Times* and *Tribune Herald*. "He was bigger than the President. One time, coming north, we stopped at a little town in Illinois, a whistle stop. It was about ten o'clock at night and raining like hell. The train stopped for ten minutes to get water, or something. It couldn't have been a town of more than five thousand people, and by God, there were four thousand of them down there standing in the rain, just waiting to see the Babe."

Ruth's popularity kept the turnstiles spinning at the Polo Grounds, which the Yankees had shared with the Giants since 1913. In 1920, the club drew 1,289,422 fans, a major-league record that would stand until 1946.

But the best chapters in the Yankees' story were still to be written that sunny June morning when Gehrig, his glove and spikes wrapped inside a newspaper, took a nickel subway ride from his home to Yankee Stadium. In the clubhouse, a historic first meeting took place when Ruth, who was tying his shoes, was tapped on the shoulder by trainer Doc Woods.

"Babe," said Woods, "I want you to meet Lou Gehrig, from Columbia."

Babe looked up from his shoes. Whether he was being introduced to a five-year-old orphan or the King of England, his response was always the same. He flashed a smile, stuck out a meaty mitt and boomed: "Hiya, keed!"

A small group of players—Ruth, Everett Scott, Aaron Ward, and Wally Pipp—was milling around the batting cage, getting in a little extra work, when Gehrig, accompanied by manager Miller Huggins, walked out on to the field a couple of minutes later.

"Hey, Wally!" Huggins yelled at Pipp, who was settling in for some batting practice. "Let the kid hit a few, will ya?"

Lou grabbed the first bat at hand, which just happened to be Ruth's favorite—a forty-eight ounce wagon tongue that even a strongman like Gehrig might have trouble swinging.

Lou nervously dug the toe of his left foot into the dirt, then jerked the heavy bat around at the first few offerings. The ball dribbled off the bat. He missed a couple of others. From the seats behind the home dugout came shouts of encouragement from a few college friends who had come along for moral support.

"Show that big guy, Lou," someone yelled. "He's not the only one that can hit it out of the park."

Lou quickly found the range. The batting practice pitcher served the ball right down the middle and—*craaackk!*—it reversed direction faster than a bug trapped in a jar and landed in the right-field bleachers, dubbed "Ruthville" because of all the home runs Babe hit there.

A half-dozen more smashed balls followed. The veterans watched in silence while Lou's private cheering section went nuts. "Attaboy, Lou! Babe knows he's got company now!"

Afterwards, Lou worked out a spell at first base. Raw and ungainly, one observer judged him as "one of the most bewildered recruits anyone had ever seen." But he had a future as neatly laid out as tomorrow's wardrobe, if only Huggins could figure out where to play him.

Gehrig made his major-league debut on June 16, 1923, replacing Pipp at first base in the ninth inning against St. Louis. Two days later he was called to bat for Aaron Ward in the ninth inning of a losing effort against Detroit. Facing him was a right-

Wally Pipp was the Yankees first baseman from 1915 to 1925 before finishing up his career with Cincinnati. He hit .281 over 15 seasons and led the American League with 12 round-trippers in 1916 and 9 in 1917. The two home-run titles were just one less than Gehrig would win after replacing him in the lineup.

Hartford manager Paddy O'Connor poses with Lou in 1924, the year Gehrig tore apart the Eastern League.

hander, Ken Holloway. If he was nervous about his first big-league at-bat, it wasn't readily apparent. He hit a hard line-drive foul past first before finally striking out.

Except for a handful of cameo appearances, Lou just sat on the bench. The inactivity puzzled his parents, who came to Yankee Stadium expecting to see their hard-working son earning his wages.

"They pay you to be a bummer," said Pop. "You do nothing. What kind of business is this?"

Lou soon found out. On July 19 he collected his first hit, swatting a ninth-inning pinch single off the Browns' Elam Vangilder at Sportsman's Park. A few days later he was optioned to Hartford, which now had a working agreement with the Yankees. Managing the team was Paddy O'Connor, who had been a career minor-league catcher and one-time coach under Huggins.

Lou's first two weeks at Hartford were miserable. Whether it was homesickness, disappointment over being sent down, or falling in with the wrong crowd on the team, his performances at bat and in the field were so bad Ed Barrow finally ordered Paul Krichell to Hartford to find out what was going on.

A major lack of self-confidence was at fault. Although hardly unique to even veteran .300 hitters (who, after all, fail seven out of every ten times at-bat), a young man away from home and struggling to live up to advance billing is particularly vulnerable to self-doubt.

Gehrig's roommate was Harry Hesse, the man he had replaced at first base. Hesse, who moved to the outfield, was shocked to discover that Lou had come to Hartford with nary a dime. He had used his bonus money to pay for his parents' medical bills. After they were well, he sent them on the first real vacation they had ever had. From the moment he started drawing a biweekly paycheck from professional baseball, Mom and Pop Gehrig never worked another day in their lives. Lou thought that supporting them was the least he could do to express his appreciation and love.

"He didn't have money for clothes," said Hesse. "He looked like a

The architect of New York's dynasty was their volatile but brilliant general manager, Ed Barrow, who served in the Yankees front office from 1921 to 1945. Considered one of the greatest judges of talent ever, during his long, colorful career Barrow discovered Honus Wagner, switched Babe Ruth from the mound to the outfield, and built the Yankees' farm system.

tramp. When he was in that first slump, I've never seen anyone suffer so much. He took everything to heart. He was a guy who needed friends, but didn't know how to go about getting them. He'd get low and sit hunched over and miserable, and it was pretty tough to pull him out of it."

Like all good baseball men, Krichell and O'Conner had to be part amateur psychologists. They worked on easing Lou's fear of failure and reminded him of the rewards waiting for him.

"You have a wonderful career ahead of you," said O'Connor, "but you have to accept the good with the bad. Nothing can stop you, except Lou Gehrig."

Lou was told to concentrate on improving his skills, particularly in fielding.

"You can wind up a rich man from this game," continued O'Connor. "Six months of work, six months of ease, all for two hours of hustle each afternoon for 154 games."

Lou never completely lost his fear of failure, the nagging notion that

Lou's Amazing Feet

When discussing the game's top base runners between the wars, names such as Max Carey and Ben Chapman come to mind. Lou Gehrig was no speed merchant, but he was aggressive, which made him a far greater threat on the basepaths than commonly thought. In fact, one of the most astounding but little-known feats of Gehrig's career is that he stole home 15 times. To put this in perspective, realize that another, far more fleeter Lou—Lou Brock—accomplished this only twice in 938 career steals. Interestingly, Gehrig never successfully stole home after the month of July. Evidently, the dog days of August and September made his piano legs even heavier.

Of Gehrig's 103 lifetime stolen bases, 23 of them (including all of his steals of home) were the result of a double steal. This offensive maneuver, typically employed with runners on first and third, is not normally associated with the hard-hitting Yankees teams of the twenties and thirties. But New York used it to great advantage, with Gehrig and fellow burglars Ben Chapman, Bob Meusel, Tony Lazzeri, and Babe Ruth (who himself swiped home nine times in a Yankee uniform) among the chief practitioners. Even Joe DiMaggio, who rarely attempted to steal a base (he had just 30 in his career), pulled off a couple of successful double steals with Lou.

Listed here are each of Gehrig's steals of home, including date, opponent, inning, and his double-steal partner.

Date	Opponent	Inning	Partner
June 24, 1925	Washington	7	Wally Schang
April 13, 1926	Boston	1	Babe Ruth
July 24, 1926	Chicago	3	Babe Ruth
June 11, 1927	Cleveland	5	Tony Lazzeri
June 29, 1927	Boston	8	Bob Meusel
July 30, 1927	Cleveland*	3	Bob Meusel
July 19, 1929	Cleveland*	2	Cedric Durst
June 7, 1930	St. Louis	6	Bill Dickey
April 15, 1931	Boston	8	Tony Lazzeri
July 28, 1931	Chicago	5	Ben Chapman
April 12, 1932	Philadelphia	9	Ben Chapman
June 20, 1933	Chicago	6	Tony Lazzeri
June 28, 1933	Detroit	9	Ben Chapman
June 2, 1934	Philadelphia	1	Jack Saltzgaver
May 15, 1935	Detroit	7	Tony Lazzeri

*First game of doubleheader

Miller Huggins played thirteen years as a big-league second baseman, but he is best remembered for his dozen years (1918-1929) as manager of the Yankees. Only 5-foot-4 and 140 pounds, Huggins refused to back down from disciplining the team's biggest offender, Babe Ruth. When Ruth stayed out late three nights in a row in 1925, Huggins fined him $5,000—ten times more than any player had ever had to cough up. Conversely, Huggins treated Gehrig like a son. "There was never a more patient or pleasant man to work for," Lou said when the tiny manager died unexpectedly of blood poisoning in 1929.

he would wake up one day to discover that his unusual ability to hit a baseball had somehow mysteriously vanished. Even as a big-league star, mild slumps would lead him to take hours of extra batting practice and approach bewildered (if flattered) .200-hitting scrubs for advice.

His insecurity manifested itself at contract time. Although Lou became a holdout a couple of times late in his career, for the most part he skipped the haggling and immediately signed whatever offer was mailed to him. "I always wondered every year whether the Yanks would sign me again," he admitted.

"No matter what his achievements," his wife said many years later, "he was dogged by a sense of failure and a need, constantly, to prove himself. Success brought Lou no sense of attainment, no relaxation. It was like something ephemeral to be clutched with both hands. He was afraid if he loosened his grip for a moment, everything he had struggled for would slip away."

This inner propulsion produced a remarkable first season at Hartford: a .304 batting average and 24 home runs in just 59 games. To this day, no one in the Eastern League has ever hit home runs at a greater pace. Forty-five of his 69 hits went for extra bases, further evidence of his power. He even took a turn on the mound, beating New Haven, 6-4.

By the time Lou was recalled to the parent club in early September, he had pulled out of his emotional funk. His roommate had even arranged a date for Lou—the first time, Hesse suspected, that the shy goliath had ever gone out with a member of the fairer sex.

Everett Scott, baseball's original iron man, was a man of extremes. The durable but light-hitting shortstop played 13 big-league seasons, at one time going 2,401 at-bats without a home run. The Yankees captain's 1,307-game playing streak ended May 5, 1925, when Miller Huggins tried to put some punch into the Yankees' Ruth-less lineup. Scott always insisted the daily grind was no chore. "The lively ball ended my string," the career .249 hitter said, "not bad legs."

As the Yankees waltzed to their third straight pennant (they would eventually finish 16 games ahead of second-place Detroit), Miller Huggins worked Gehrig into several games. Not everyone was pleased. Bullet Joe Bush, a grizzled veteran looking to nail down his second straight 20-win season, openly bitched about having the rookie first baseman start a game he was scheduled to pitch against Washington.

"Don't put that damn clown out there at first," Bush told Huggins. "This game may not mean anything to the team, but it means a lot to me. That guy will gum it up."

Maybe Bush had a psychic connection. Sure enough, in an early inning Lou botched a bunt, allowing a run to score. In full view of thousands of fans, Bullet Joe let Lou have it with both barrels. "Ya stupid college punk!" he screamed. "Where's your brains, dummy?" Embarrassed, holding back tears, Lou just stared at the ground.

Trailing 5-2 in the eighth, the Yanks staged a comeback. With two on, Washington manager Donie Bush opted to intentionally walk Ruth and pitch to Lou. Left-hander Ray Francis was brought in to pitch.

Although platooning was a relatively new strategy in 1923, Bush and others on the bench expected Huggins to go with the percentages and substitute a right-handed batter for Gehrig. Ignoring Bush's protests, Huggins said, "Go on up there and hit that ball."

Lou, always respectful of authority, did exactly as he was told. He pulled Francis's first offering to right field for a double that cleared the sacks and tied the score. A few seconds later he came home on a single to give the Yankees a 6-5 victory. "Look, kid," said Bush in the dugout, "you may not be so hot with the glove, but you can pound that ball." For Bush, that was tantamount to a public apology.

During his thirteen games in pinstripes, Lou hit a sparkling .423, with four doubles, a triple and his first big-league home run included among his 11 hits. The four-bagger came on September 27 in Boston. In a preview of history's most devastating one-two punch, Ruth banged out a run-scoring triple off Bill Piercy and then trotted home when Lou followed with a liner over the fence.

With Pipp hobbled by an injured ankle, Huggins tried to insert his hot-hitting rookie into the World Series against the Giants. Because he had joined the club too late in the season, the opposing manager had to give his permission for this addition to the active roster. John McGraw said no—a bitter disappointment to a rookie who could not be sure of being this close to playing in a World Series again. Just as bad was the lost opportunity to cash a postseason check.

McGraw's refusal deepened Lou's disdain for the rival manager. He

Babe and friends, 1922. "He was a circus, a play, a movie, all rolled into one," recalled a teammate. "Kids adored him. Men idolized him. Women loved him. There was something about him, something with men like that who come along once in a while, that made him great."

Ruth gives rookie Gehrig some pointers in 1923. "Almost any batter that has it in him to wallop the ball is swinging from the handle of the bat with every ounce of strength that nature placed in his wrists and shoulders," ***Baseball Magazine*** **reported in 1921, the year of Babe's 59 home runs. "He has not only slugged his way to fame, but he has got everybody else doing it."**

had to be satisfied with sitting on the bench and watching the Yankees take the Series in six games, with Ruth's three home runs and Bob Meusel's eight RBI.

The following spring the Yankees trained in New Orleans. Players were not paid until the regular season began six weeks later, but this was hardly a problem for well-paid veterans, especially one just coming off a World Series victory. Lou, however, was so broke—he had arrived with fourteen dollars in his pocket—he wandered the streets after practice looking for a part-time job.

"Things are pretty tough, Dan," he glumly told Dan Daniel, a New York beat writer. "I can't seem to find a job, not even washing dishes."

Daniel was incredulous. "What are you talking about?" he said. "You're a Yankee, a player with the best team in baseball. You're not supposed to go around searching for a job. If you're broke, go see Huggins."

"I just can't do that," said Lou.

Daniel went to Huggins and told him of this conversation. The manager took Lou aside and gave him a $100 advance. "Now please stop looking for a job," he pleaded.

Gehrig in 1925, the year he finally cracked the starting lineup.

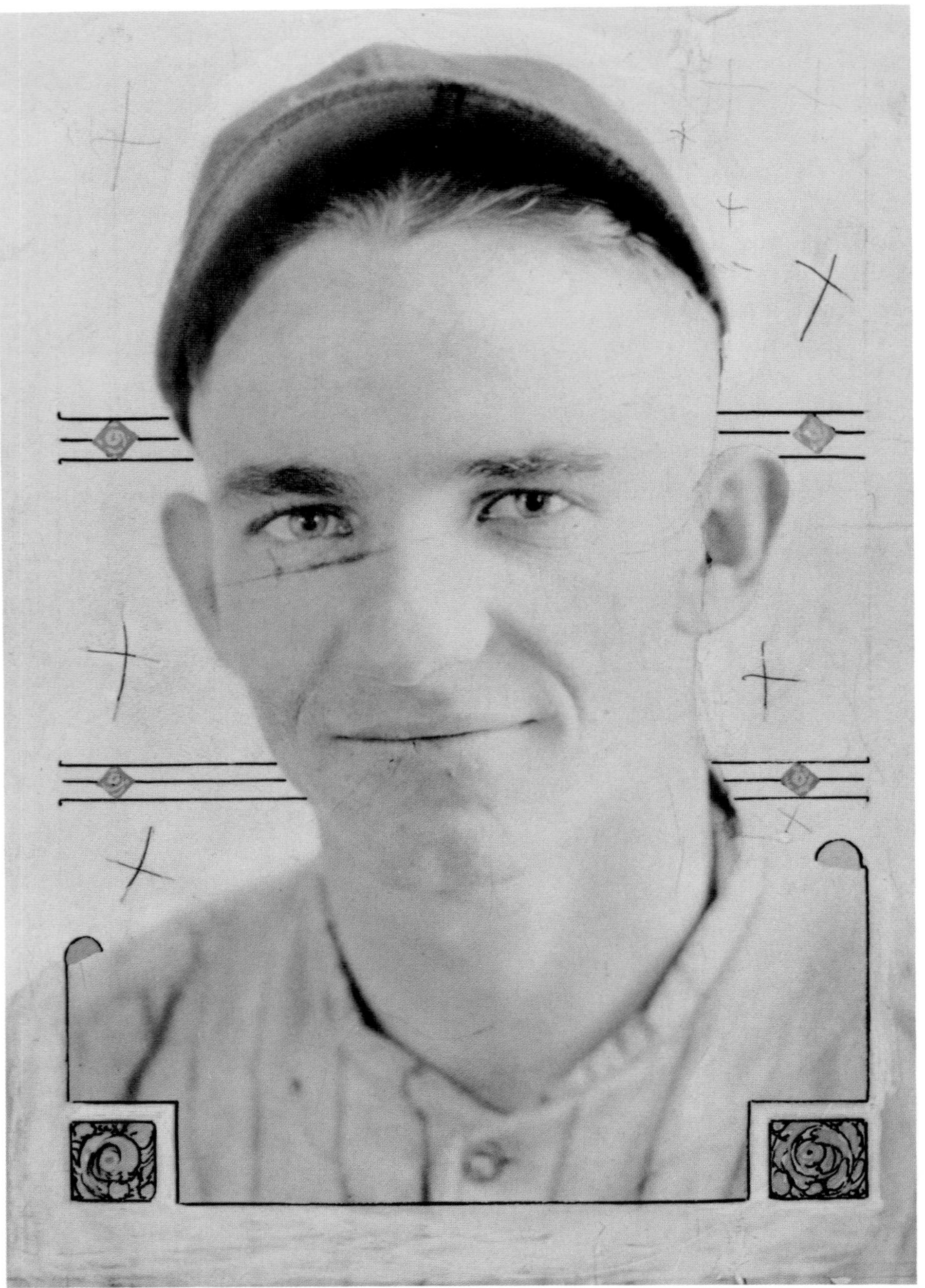

Paul "Pee Wee" Wanninger was with the Yankees for just one season, but he played a role in ending one streak and starting another.

The money, which barely tided him over until camp broke, couldn't disguise Lou's social ineptitude. The veterans went out to dinner every night, chased women, knew where to find the best bootleg scotch, and left generous tips in their wake. On a team filled with Broadway flash, all top hats and tails, Gehrig was a pair of old brown shoes. His uncommunicative, straight-arrow ways turned off more sophisticated teammates like Pitcher Waite Hoyt and Meusel, and made him the butt of practical jokes. Carl Mays was particularly cruel, to the point that one day in the locker room Lou challenged the crusty pitcher to a fight. Mays wisely backed down. But the petty hazing, which included bats sawed into pieces, continued all spring.

Gehrig spent most of the 1924 season in Hartford, where he once again hung up some eye-popping numbers. In 134 games he hit 37 home runs, scored 111 runs, and stroked the ball at a .369 clip. On June 17 against Worcester he hit his only minor-league grand slam, then he asked Paddy O'Connor for permission to go home to spend his twenty-first birthday with his parents. Mom had written, explaining that it "would be very nice" if the three Gehrigs could get together to celebrate.

O'Connor said it was Lou's decision, but he'd prefer the league's top slugger spend his birthday snuffing out the opposition instead of some candles. "We're in a damned hot pennant race," he reminded him. On June 19 Gehrig banged out a double, triple, and home run in a 9-8 win

Lou put some muscle in the Yankees' batting order, clubbing 20 home runs in 1925, his first year as a regular.

Earl Whitehill raised Lou's ire by tucking a fastball under his chin during a 1925 game. Gehrig waited for the small but pugnacious Detroit pitcher after the game and started a brawl that ended up with Lou slipping and knocking his head on a concrete stanchion. "Who won?" he groggily asked when he regained consciousness. Teammates considered Lou's foolish overreaction much ado about nothing, and he soon learned to accept the occasional brushback as a sign of respect and not an act of aggression.

over Worcester, then grabbed a train the following day—an open date—to celebrate a belated birthday with his folks.

The Yanks, having learned their lesson the previous season, recalled Lou in late August so as to have him available for postseason action. On September 4 against Philadelphia, he replaced Ruth (who had a sore left arm) in the outfield and contributed two hits to the cause. Otherwise, he was used mostly as a pinch-hitter down the stretch as Washington outlasted the Yankees to capture the pennant.

On September 21 at Detroit, Lou experienced another major-league first: his first ejection. It came after he singled in two runs in the eighth inning off Earl Whitehill. Lou was caught between first and second and tagged out, cause enough for Ty Cobb to take his place in the third-base coaching box in the bottom of the inning and direct a stream of vile commentary toward Lou sitting in the visitors' dugout. The Tigers' playing manager was an old hand at agitating, and Lou snapped at the bait. When he rushed from the dugout to confront Cobb, he was thumbed out of the game.

Lou batted .500 (6 for 12) in limited action, notice to Miller Huggins that, come 1925, he had to find a way to insert him into the regular lineup. But where? In the first month of the season Lou played a half dozen games in left field and right, made a few pinch-hitting appearances, and continued to work out mornings at first base. There was even idle talk about putting Lou on the mound. An errant batting practice pitch thrown to Wally Pipp would finally end all of the speculation and indecision.

The 1925 campaign was a failure from the get-go. Babe Ruth's physical collapse on the trip north from spring training—the "bellyache heard around the world" wrote W. O. McGeehan—set the tone for the club's season-long woes. Injuries, old age, bickering in the clubhouse, and Ruth's open defiance of manager Huggins (Babe eventually was suspended by the club and fined a whopping $5,000) accounted for their fall to seventh place.

On June 1 Ruth played his first game of the season. The contest with Washington at Yankee Stadium was a front-page event whose real significance wouldn't be understood for some time. In the eighth inning, Lou was inserted as a pinch-hitter for Paul "Pee Wee" Wanninger. Pee Wee had replaced Yankees captain Everett Scott at shortstop on May 6, bringing Scott's record streak of 1,307 consecutive games to a halt. Having ended one iron-man performance, the weak-hitting Wanninger would now be instrumental in seeing another, far more substantial streak begin.

In the 17th and final pinch-hitting appearance of his career, Lou failed to get around on one of Walter Johnson's fastballs and flied to Goose Goslin in left. Lou would never again appear in a boxscore as anything other than a regular. The following day Miller Huggins told him that he was replacing Wally Pipp as the Yankees' first baseman.

For many years afterwards the words "Wally Pipp" enjoyed wide currency among foremen and parents as a sort of shorthanded warning of the dire consequences that awaited would-be malingerers: *You're not going to work? Don't you remember what happened to Wally Pipp when he had a headache and decided to take the day off?*

The facts are a bit kinder to Pipp, who actually was as dedicated and durable a player as his replacement. The 32-year-old veteran, then in his 12th season in the majors, was a better-than-average hitter (who had led the league in home runs in 1916 and 1917), a fine glove man, and a team player who didn't feel threatened helping Lou improve his fielding in practice.

But on the morning of June 2, 1925, it was his misfortune to get in the way of a wild fastball thrown by a batting practice pitcher, Charlie Caldwell Jr. Pipp went down like a shot hog. The semiconscious player wound up spending two weeks in the hospital.

"I just couldn't duck," Pipp would explain for the rest of his life. "The ball hit me on the temple. Down I went. I was too far gone to bother reaching for any aspirin tablets, as the popular story goes." After the season, Pipp was traded to Cincinnati where he showed his real stuff by playing in 155 games.

Lou takes his cuts during batting practice. It wasn't until Wally Pipp was sold after the 1925 season that Lou truly felt he had made the grade. "That was the greatest thrill of my career," he said, "the knowledge that I was the regular first baseman of my hometown team. At last I could go to my parents and tell them that I had regular work at good pay so long as I could hit the ball and hustle."

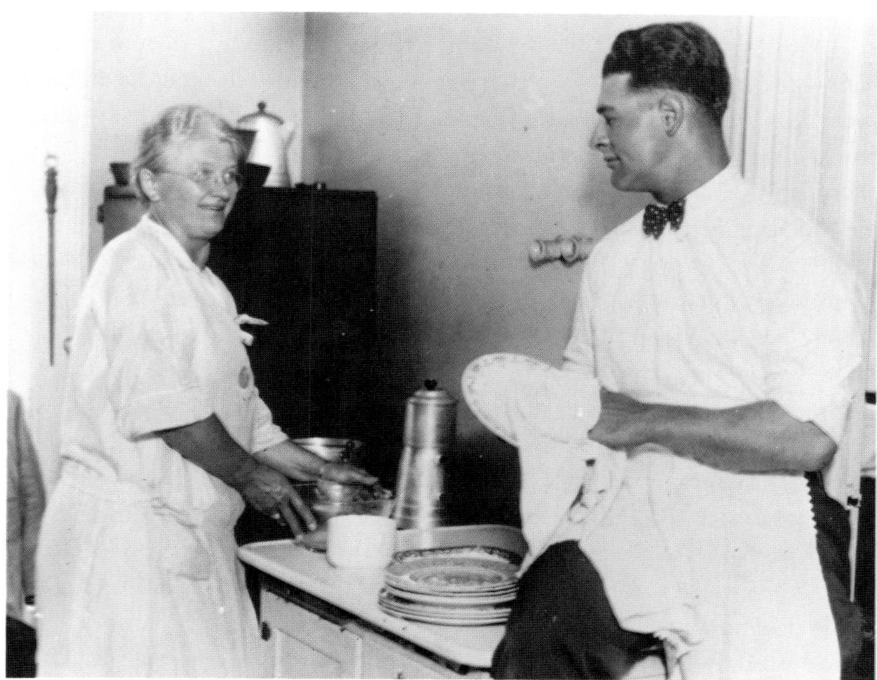

This was no publicity photo. Lou, who lived with his parents until he was thirty years old, always helped his mother with the dishes.

Lou batted cleanup behind Ruth during most of 1926, which helped account for 107 RBI, his first of a record 13 consecutive seasons of 100 or more RBI.

Placed sixth in the order, behind Meusel and clean-up hitter Ruth, Lou banged out hits his first three times at bat against Washington's southpaw, George Mogridge. Before the game, Huggins had come up to Lou in the clubhouse and dramatically announced, "You're my first baseman today. Today—and from now on." Huggins had no way of knowing that before it was all over, "now on" would grow to an eventual 2,130 games.

Gehrig wasn't a ball of fire at first. He was pinch-hit for six times over the next several weeks, sometimes as early as the fourth inning, and was less than graceful around the bag. But he toiled and showed steady improvement in both areas. "In the beginning, I used to make one terrible play a game," he told a writer in 1935. "Then I got so I'd make one a week, and finally I'd pull a bad one about once a month. Now, I'm trying to keep it down to one a season."

At the end of the year, Gehrig had a .295 average—not spectacular (the league average was .292), but still third best on the squad behind Earle Combs and part-timer Ben Paschal. He hit 20 home runs, including a shot off Washington's Firpo Marberry on July 23 that was the first of an eventual 23 career grand slams. Demonstrating surprising base-running ability, he scored 73 runs—the last time until 1939 that he would be under the century mark in that category. He also swiped six bases, including a steal of home on June 24 that was his first big-league stolen base.

With the club in apparent disarray and the Senators coming off a second straight pennant, few experts were brave enough to predict a flag for New York in 1926. But that's what happened, thanks to Herb Pennock's 23 victories, a new middle infield (shortstop Mark Koenig and second baseman Tony Lazzeri), and a return to form by Babe Ruth (.372, 47 homers, 155 RBI). Only a flurry of hits by the Tigers' Heinie Manush kept Babe from capturing baseball's Triple Crown.

Gehrig, still making himself comfortable, weighed in with a .313 average and a league high of 20 triples. His 16 home runs and 107 RBI were notable: In this transitional period between place hitting and swing-from-the-heels slugging, only four other American Leaguers (Ruth and Lazzeri were among them) had reached double figures in homers while driving across 100 runs. But Lou's home run and RBI counts would actually be the lowest full-season totals of his career.

On August 13 Lou belted a pair of four-baggers off Walter Johnson, joining Jack Fournier as the only players ever to take the legendary speedballer deep twice in the same game. Unlike Fournier's twin blows, which were of the inside-the-park variety, Gehrig's blasts carried out of cavernous Griffith Stadium. Considering that during his fabled 21-year career "the Big Train" surrendered a paltry 97 home runs in nearly 6,000 innings pitched, Lou's feat was indeed impressive.

Gehrig's earnestness, however, grated on many of his grizzled teammates, who like war-horses in all professions took great pride in acting as if they'd seen it all. Once Lou openly sobbed in the dugout after failing to drive in an important run—truly a rare sight on a big-league bench. On other occasions he happily brought some of Mom Gehrig's home-cooked goodies into the clubhouse, for there was nothing like a jar of pickled eels or a plate of pig knuckles to keep up the boys' strength.

Miller Huggins admired Lou's old-school dedication as much as he despised Ruth's lack of self-discipline. "Lou has become an influence to the entire team," he told the press at the beginning of the season. "You get a player with that kind of spirit, and it spreads like a contagion to the other players."

Well, maybe not all players. While "pep" was a staple of collegiate diamonds, Lou's infield chatter irritated some moundsmen. "Let me provide my own inspiration, would ya, kid?" Waite Hoyt shot back one day.

Mike Gazella, a utility player trying his best to hang on in the majors, could appreciate Lou's giving every play the ol' college try. Though Lou

In 1926 Rogers Hornsby (right) batted .317 and managed the St. Louis Cardinals to a World Series win over New York. His crosstown rival, first baseman George Sisler, was photographed at the Series that year with George, Jr.

Before the '26 Series began, Lou took time to pose with agent Christy Walsh's newborn baby.

It's October 2, 1926, and the stands at Yankee Stadium are jammed to overflowing for the opener of the Cardinals-Yankees World Series. Among the crowd were Mom and Pop Gehrig, who proudly watched their son knock in both runs of the Yankees' 2-1 win. It was Lou's first of an eventual 34 World Series games.

kept his mouth shut around the veterans, Gazella had no compunctions about being the big guy's surrogate mouthpiece. After New York lost its fourth game in a row to Cleveland in a late September showdown for first place, the tiny infielder ripped the team's complacency.

"You fellows have been kidding me about the old college spirit ever since I have been on this ball club," Gazella yelled. "If you gutless sons of bitches had a little of it, you wouldn't have quit as you did out there this afternoon."

As inspirational speeches go, Gazella's probably doesn't rank up there with Knute Rockne's plea to win one for the Gipper, but it had the desired effect. The Yanks edged the Indians by three games for the pennant.

Huggins's heavy hitters met the St. Louis Cardinals in a World Series best remembered for Grover Cleveland Alexander's bases-loaded strikeout of Tony Lazzeri in the deciding seventh game. But there were thrills aplenty leading up to that moment.

The biggest thrill for Lou was just being there. On October 2, a crowd of 61,658 fans—including Mom and Pop Gehrig—were on hand as Lou ran onto the field for his first World Series game. Lou was nervous. But the curtain of noise, the acres of colorful bunting, and the exploding flashbulbs all proved more invigorating than intimidating. In his first at-bat, Gehrig tied the game with a groundout. Then in the sixth inning he won it, singling to right to score Ruth.

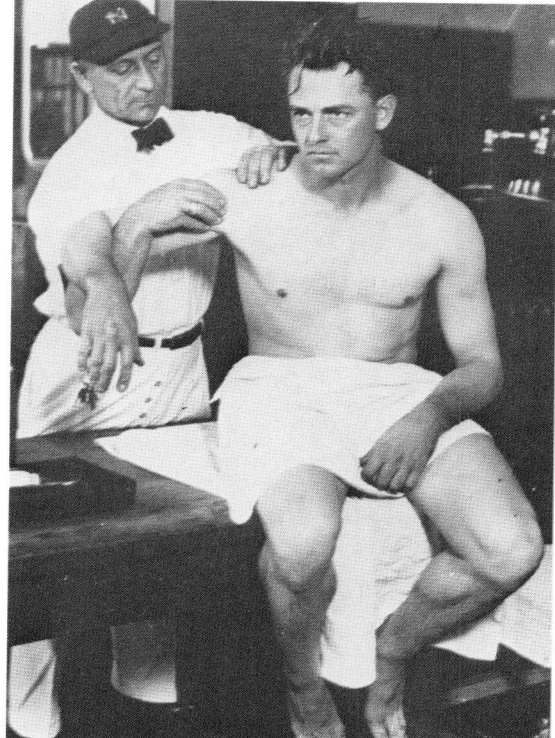

"The secret of success is to pitch for the New York Yankees," said Waite Hoyt, seen here getting a rubdown from trainer Doc Woods. The son of a vaudevillian, "Schoolboy" was signed by the Giants when he was fifteen years old but gained most of his 237 career victories in pinstripes. The future Hall-of-Famer won 22 games in 1927 and led the league in ERA, then followed up with 23 victories in 1928. He pitched the Yankees into six World Series and won six of nine postseason decisions.

In one of baseball's most dramatic moments, thirty-nine-year-old Grover Cleveland Alexander moseyed in from the bullpen to strike out Tony Lazzeri with the bases loaded and two outs in the final game of the 1926 fall classic. What few remember is that before fanning, the Yankees' rookie second baseman lined one of Alexander's pitches into the left field seats, just missing a grand slam by a couple of feet. "Anybody can strike out," Miller Huggins said in his defense, "but ballplayers like Lazzeri come along once in a generation."

The Cardinals rebounded to win the next two games, but then the Yankees pounded five St. Louis pitchers in a 10-5 rout in the fourth contest. In this game Ruth slammed three home runs, the first time anybody had ever done it in postseason play. The teams split the next two games, setting up a game seven showdown at Yankee Stadium. The championship boiled down to one dramatic moment in the seventh inning.

The Cardinals were leading by a run, 3-2, when the Yankees put runners on first and third with two out. Gehrig, batting fifth in the Series, was intentionally walked to get to Tony Lazzeri. Manager Rogers Hornsby then called time, walked out to the mound, and called for Ol' Pete—Grover Cleveland Alexander—to come out of the bullpen.

According to legend, at the time the thirty-nine-year-old Alexander—who suffered from alcoholism, epilepsy, and recurring nightmares from his army days in France—was sleeping off an all-night drunk after pitching his second complete-game win of the Series the day before. But he hitched up his trousers, walked out into the gathering darkness, and struck out Lazzeri on four

Ol' Pete Alexander won a lot (373 games) and drank a lot during his two decades in the game, but he played on just one world championship team, the '26 Cardinals. The down-and-out pitcher wound up reenacting the Lazzeri strikeout with a flea circus and drinking his wife's perfume for the alcohol before dying alone in a rented room when he was sixty-three.

Warming up at Yankee Stadium are (from left) Bob Meusel, Mark Koenig, Babe Ruth, Lou Gehrig, and Earl Combs. "In the daytime you sat in the dugout and talked about women," recalled Waite Hoyt. "In the night time you went out with women and talked about baseball." Small wonder Hoyt often exclaimed, "It's great to be young and a Yankee."

pitches. That bit of high drama closed out the inning, not the game (as a popular movie starring Ronald Reagan would later portray).

The real end was almost anticlimatic. With two outs in the bottom of the ninth, Ruth drew a walk. Then, with the dangerous Meusel at bat and Gehrig on deck, Babe unaccountably took off for second. The throw down got him easily. Ruth's fruitless dash sent a jubilant St. Louis team roaring into the clubhouse while stunned Yankee fans stood there wondering, *Wha' happened?*

The loss to the underdog Cardinals stung. But Lou had performed admirably in his first World Series. He had outhit Ruth, .348 to .300, and driven across just one run fewer than Babe. Mourners in the Bronx could take heart. For the rest of the twenties and all of the thirties, it would be the only Series the Yankees would ever lose with Lou Gehrig on the team.

Chapter Four

BUSTER AND BABE

> Babe wanted to go on the town when he could. Lou wanted to build a home for his folks in the suburbs and get home to them just as soon as the ball game was over. Babe hated authority. Lou accepted it as just and right. Babe loved people. Lou was a loner, his early shyness replaced by suspicion that came with success.
>
> Who knows who was right? Surely Babe was ridiculous when he left a ten-dollar tip where fifty cents would have been generous. But Lou's dimes were just as silly.
>
> —Claire Hodgson Ruth, *Babe and I*

IF BABE RUTH was the man who built Yankee Stadium, by 1927 Lou Gehrig was its major subcontractor. That year Ruth broke his own record by ripping 60 home runs, but for most of the summer he actually trailed Gehrig, whose own 47 round-trippers were more than any other man besides Ruth had ever hit. It's often been stated that Ruth's output exceeded that of any other American League team, but it's never mentioned that his less flamboyant teammate outhomered Boston, Chicago, Cleveland and Washington himself. To pitchers, it hardly mattered which of the two was wagging the bat. On their lips the names practically blended into a single four-syllable simile for devastation that, befitting their mutual Germanic background, had a certain Teutonic ring to it: *Ruthandgehrig.* If one didn't get you, the other probably would.

At this stage of Lou's career, sportswriters were still trying to pin an appropriate nickname on him. He was most frequently called "Columbia Lou" in press accounts, then later dubbed "the Crown Prince." Players experimented with a couple of their own inventions. One was "Biscuit Pants," a reference to his broad beam and the oversized, custom-fitted knickers that covered it. Another was "Buster," which perfectly suited his awkward, boyish, sock-'em-off-the-fences image.

Buster and Babe. From their personalities to the way they hit the ball, they were as different as any two men could be. Ruth's picturesque corkscrew swing produced arcing moon shots that lingered attractively against the blue sky before dropping into the seats like gifts from some benevolent baseball god. Gehrig's flat, explosive swing sent howitzer shells that threatened to knock the bricks loose from the outfield walls.

"They were both tremendous hitters, of course," recalled longtime

Gehrig and Ruth in 1927

The greatest team ever? The '27 Yankees won 110 games, then swept the Pirates in the World Series. A half century later, a computerized tournament matched a half dozen all-time great squads. The finale pitted the Yankees of Ruth and Gehrig against the '61 Yankees of Maris and Mantle. Murderers Row won—thanks to Gehrig's two-run homer off Whitey Ford in the tenth inning.

Detroit second baseman Charlie Gehringer. "Ruth hit the ball so far and so high…He had that uppercut swing, so he never hit a hard grounder. Gehrig would knock your legs off, but Ruth, the only thing he hit hard would be in the air. I don't even remember him ever hitting a double play ball. He wouldn't hit it hard enough. It'd have that top spin and dribble along. But Gehrig? He'd hammer 'em."

Although Babe and Lou were friendly, their differences became more evident once they rolled down their stirrups. Pete Sheehy, the Yankees' longtime clubhouse manager, was once asked what he remembered most about America's national hero. He thought hard for a minute, then replied, "Ruth never flushed the toilet." Sheehy wasn't quizzed about Gehrig. But it's a good bet that Lou not only flushed, but put the seat back down as well.

John Drebinger joined the staff of the *New York Times* in 1923 and covered Big Apple baseball for the next 37 years. "Gehrig idolized the Babe," he said, "and the Babe was very fond of Lou. But Gehrig could never forget he had been a poor boy. He was always worried he was going to lose his money.

"Gehrig envied the careless way the Babe tossed his money around. We used to play poker on the trains with the Babe. Five-card stud. The Babe would bet like the devil, just taking wild gambles. He wouldn't drive you out, but he never folded. Always played down to the last card. Most of the time we'd clean up on him. Gehrig would be sitting across the aisle, watching the game. The Babe would be throwing his dough around in this fine style, and Lou would look at him and say, 'My God, isn't that wonderful.'"

The Yankees' infield in 1927. From left: first baseman Gehrig, second baseman Tony Lazzeri, shortstop Mark Koenig, and third baseman Joe Dugan. "Jumpin' Joe" was a raconteur and night owl, but also a flashy fielder and capable hitter. "Fellows like Ruth and Gehrig can ruin an ordinary ballplayer," he said. "They win so many games by their individual efforts that you wonder why you are in the lineup."

Everywhere Ruth went, he was mobbed by admirers and well-wishers. The consummate showman (many thought he would have made a great comedic actor), he was quick with a quip or a tip. He'd happily oblige any photographer's request, no matter how outlandish.

"See, Babe got most of the publicity," said catcher Benny Benbough. "Lazzeri hit a couple of home runs one day and Babe hit one, and it came out in the papers, BABE RUTH HITS HOME RUN. But nothing was said about Lazzeri—except down in the little print. And they used to kid about it. They'd say, 'Geez, I hit two home runs, I get nothing. He gets one, he gets all the headlines.'

"Of course, that's what Babe was getting paid for. You were under a shadow when you had a fellow like that because he was the one they were paying the money to. He was the one drawing the crowds. Even Gehrig when he was going great, he never got the publicity Babe did. See, Babe was such a colorful figure. Not just the homers, but the things he did. He was always in a jam. He was always good copy."

Schoolboy Hoyt on Babe Ruth: "His homeliness was classic. No one failed to recognize Ruth, no matter where he was. He was the cartoonists' dream. . . ." On Gehrig: A "smooth-faced Atlas, an all-American type, a typical first-boy-in-the-seat in Sunday school."

Lou, conversely, was ill at ease in most social situations, especially

Count the number of fish on each man's line. Even when it came to posing for staged shots like these, Lou came out second best to Babe.

Wilcy Moore was "cool as a cake of ice," said Miller Huggins. In 1927 Moore unexpectedly won 19 games and a $300 bet from Ruth, who claimed that the thirty-year-old rookie, "the lousiest hitter in history," wouldn't get three hits. According to legend, Moore used the money to buy two mules for his Oklahoma farm. He named one "Babe," the other "Ruth."

when Babe, arm thrown around his teammate's shoulders, would pull tongue-tied Lou into the spotlight. As a result, many reporters and fans thought Lou standoffish. The truth of the matter, Lou confided to a reporter, was that he usually was so scared of saying the wrong thing that "I would just about shit in my pants."

Unlike Lou, who had an excellent memory for names and faces, Ruth was notorious for butchering or forgetting names. Benbough, who customarily warmed up with Ruth before games, was "Googles." Waite Hoyt, his after-hours companion for many years, was "Walter." Ruth even got his first wife's name wrong in his autobiography! After hitting his 58th home run off the Red Sox in 1927, a man came into clubhouse and asked Babe to autograph the ball.

"I wonder who that guy was," Babe said after the man left. "I'm pretty sure I've seen him someplace."

"You sure have," replied a teammate. "That was Hod Lisenbee, the pitcher who threw you that home run ball today!"

To compensate for his poor memory, most people Ruth came in contact with were called "Kid." There were exceptions. Young women were "Sister," while older folks became "Mom" or "Pop."

This suited Mom and Pop Gehrig, who regularly had Ruth over to their place, just fine. Lou and his parents and their famous guest would converse fluently in German while Babe enjoyed one of Mom's delicious ethnic meals. Ruth even gave Mom a pet Chihuahua, whom she named "Jidge," a corruption of Ruth's real name, George. Benbough, Bob Meusel, Joe Dugan, Tony Lazzeri, and Mark Koenig also regularly feasted on Mom's stuffed pig, turkey, or goose with all the trimmings. They were known as "Mom's Boys."

Although Lou was never a big drinker, beer was always available to wash down a good meal. Prohibition, the law of the land since the Volstead Act officially took effect on January 1, 1920, was no deterrent to good times. (One New York writer maintained that he could summarize the entire history of the United States in eleven words: "Columbus, Washington, Lincoln, Volstead, two flights up and ask for Gus.") Several of the Yankees were enthusiastic members of the speakeasy subculture, making the rounds of nightclubs, brothels, and blind pigs when they could get out from under Miller Huggins's thumb. Ruth, as might be expected, was one of the ringleaders, although his status meant he often moved in circles far removed from his less famous and poorer-paid teammates.

When Ruth was around, however, he picked up most of the tabs. And why not? In 1927 Babe made $70,000—more than the rest of the starting lineup combined (and more than the president of the United States). Third baseman Dugan and left fielder Meusel made $12,000 each, while center fielder Earle Combs and shortstop Koenig were paid $10,500 and $7,000, respectively.

Gehrig's $7,500 salary was slightly less than the $8,000 that

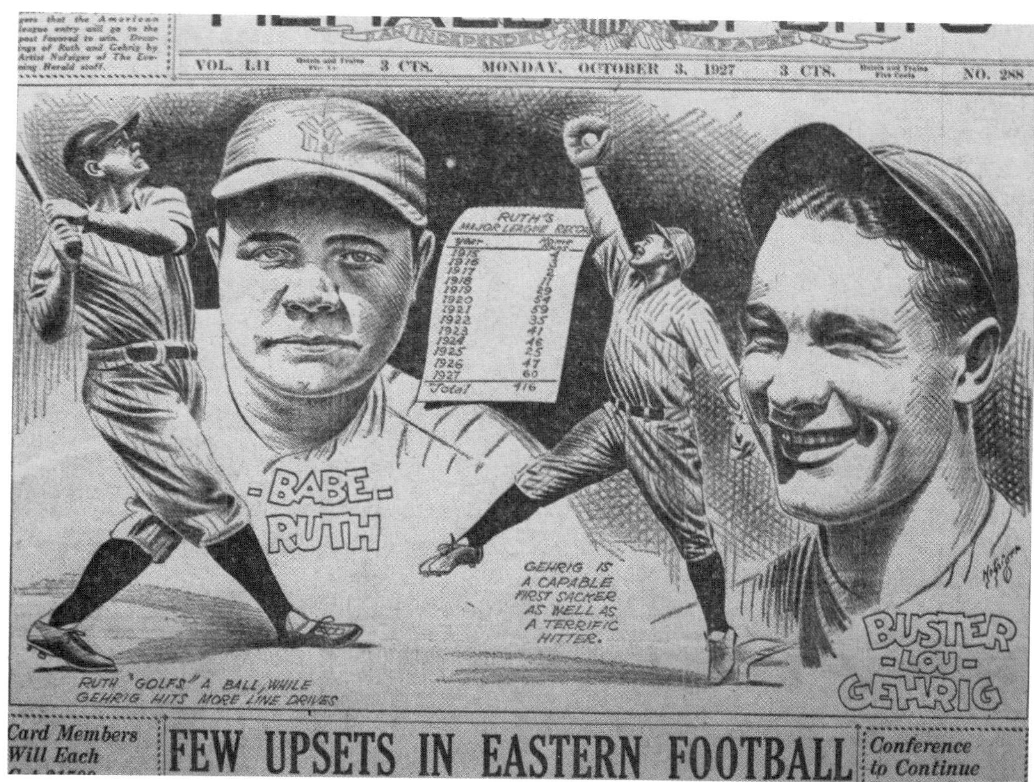

gers that the American League entry will go to the post favored to win. Drawings of Ruth and Gehrig by Artist Nufziger of The Evening Herald staff.

VOL. LII 3 CTS. MONDAY, OCTOBER 3, 1927 3 CTS. NO. 288

Card Members Will Each

FEW UPSETS IN EASTERN FOOTBALL

Conference to Continue

Babe and Buster. The Yankees' twin sluggers were polar opposites in nearly everything, from their personalities to the way they hit the ball. While Ruth's soaring home runs caressed the clock, Lou's line drives defied time, exiting the park faster than a dentist suddenly remembering a four o'clock appointment.

Benbough and Lazzeri made. Herb Pennock was the highest paid pitcher ($17,500), while the rest of the staff ranged from $2,500 to $13,000. Reserve infielders and outfielders were paid between $1,800 and $7,000. Jacob Ruppert's entire payroll probably didn't exceed $170,000.

Whatever they were paid, the men surrounding Ruth and Gehrig in the lineup were more than spear carriers that summer. Combs batted .356 and led the circuit in base hits and triples. Lazzeri hit .309 and finished third behind Ruth and Gehrig with 18 round-trippers. His 102 RBI were one behind Meusel's total. Long Bob also hit .337 and finished second in stolen bases, swiping 24 without getting caught once.

The pitching was a surprise, with seven hurlers accounting for all but five of the team's victories. The mound corps was led by Waite Hoyt, whose 22 wins and 2.63 ERA topped the league's charts. Herb Pennock won 19, Urban Shocker chipped in with 18, and a refugee from the Carolina League, Wilcy Moore, had the one great season of his career. The 30-year-old rookie right-hander shuttled between starts and the bullpen, winning 19 games (13 in relief) and saving 13 more, tying Garland Braxton of Washington in that category. The staff's 3.20 ERA

Herb Pennock was one of nearly a dozen former Red Sox players that populated the Yankees' roster during the 1920s. The slightly built curveballer won 240 games during his twenty-two-year Hall of Fame career, half of which was spent in Yankee pinstripes. Blending smarts with pinpoint control, Pennock also won all five of his World Series decisions. "If you were to cut that bird's head open," Miller Huggins said, "the weakness of every batter in the league would fall out."

was almost a full run off the league average and remained the game's best until 1942.

Lots of stories have been told about the '27 Yankees, most of them true. There was the time when the team arrived in Detroit just thirty minutes before game time. This was after an especially grueling overnight train trip from Boston. To make matters worse, the dining car had been taken off. With bleary eyes and grumbling stomachs, the players piled into cabs and followed a police escort to Navin Field. There was no time for fielding or batting practice. But New York's window-smashers—some stuffing hot dogs with sauerkraut down their throats as they dressed—raced out onto the diamond for the 3:35 start and bombed the Tigers, 19-2.

The Yankees' attack—dubbed "Five O'Clock Lightning" because so many of their late-inning rallies occurred about that time—actually made Paul Gallico edgy in the press box.

"It was like when I was a kid, and there used to be a lot of blasting going on down on Park Avenue where they were digging out the cut for the New York Central tracks," he reflected. "There would be a laborer with a box with a plunger handle, and they would spread the mats and get ready to dynamite. There would be a nerve-wracking suspense and what seemed like an interminable wait. But then there would be one hell of a big boom, and chunks of Park Avenue would go flying through the air. Well, it was just like that with the 1927 Yankees. You never knew when that batting order was going to push the handle down."

September 30, 1927: Ruth launches number 60.

During a game at Cleveland, the Indians decided to pitch the Yankees' left-handed hitters outside—a strategy that almost cost their third baseman, Rube Lutzke, his life. First, Ruth drilled a shot off Lutzke's shoulder, knocking him down. Gehrig

Babe was never lacking female companionship. Once, when he noticed an attractive young lady who cradled an infant and stared at him, he said, "You'd better watch out, or I'll put one in the other arm too."

then toppled Lutzke with a smash off his shins. Finally, Meusel drove the ball straight into Lutzke's stomach, knocking the wind out of him. Cleveland players rushed to the aid of their fallen teammate.

"Are you hurt, Rube?" they yelled.

"Hurt?" responded the groggy Lutzke, looking skyward. "Hell, a guy was safer in the World War!"

The Yankees made a shambles of the pennant race, piling up an American League record 110 wins, including 21 victories in 22 outings against the St. Louis Browns. The only other team with a realistic chance at the flag, Washington, checked into Yankee Stadium for an important Independence Day doubleheader riding a 10-game winning streak. They left nursing their wounds after getting drubbed, 12-1 and 21-1.

"These guys not only beat you," said one demoralized Senator, "they tear your heart out. I wish the season was over."

It soon was. The only real excitement during the second half of the season was the home run duel between Ruth and Gehrig. In a year where papers were filled

Kentuckian Earle Combs joined New York in 1924 and held down the center-field spot for the next eleven years. "We'll call you 'The Waiter,'" Miller Huggins told his leadoff man. "When you get on base, you wait for Ruth or Gehrig or one of the other fellows to send you the rest of the way." Combs hit .325 lifetime and led the league in triples in 1927, 1928, and 1930. He also hit .350 in World Series competition. Tough as concrete and a gentleman who disapproved of swearing and drinking, Combs ended his Hall of Fame career prematurely when he fractured his skull, crashing into the outfield wall in St. Louis.

Double Devastation

Babe Ruth and Lou Gehrig, the most feared home-run tandem in baseball history, connected in the same game 74 times, including two World Series contests. Here is a complete listing of each of them, including date, opponent, inning, and the number of men on base.

Date	Opponent		Inning	Men On	Pitcher
September 10	Philadelphia	Ruth	4	0	Sam Gray
1925		Gehrig ...	4	0	Sam Gray
September 12	Philadelphia	Gehrig ...	4	0	Rube Walberg
1925[a]		Ruth	9	0	Rube Walberg
May 10	+Detroit	Gehrig ...	5	1	Sam Gibson
1926		Ruth	5	0	Sam Gibson
June 29	Philadelphia	Gehrig ...	1	1	Sam Gray
1926		Ruth	3	1	Sam Gray
August 14	+Washington	Gehrig ...	1	1	Dutch Ruether
1926[a]		Ruth	3	0	Dutch Ruether
September 11	Detroit	Gehrig ...	2	1	Lil Stoner
1926		Ruth	9	2	Lil Stoner
September 19	Cleveland	Ruth	7	1	Dutch Levsen
1926		Gehrig ...	7	0	Dutch Levsen
September 25	St. Louis	Gehrig ...	3	0	Milt Gaston
1926[b]		Ruth	6	1	Win Ballou
		Ruth	9	0	Joe Giard
April 23	Philadelphia	Ruth	1	0	Rube Walberg
1927		Gehrig ...	1	0	Rube Walberg
May 1	+Philadelphia	Ruth	1	1	Jack Quinn
1927		Gehrig ...	6	1	Jack Quinn
		Ruth	8	0	Rube Walberg
May 23	Washington	Ruth	1	0	Sloppy Thurston
1927		Gehrig ...	1	0	Sloppy Thurston
May 31	Philadelphia	Ruth	1	1	Jack Quinn
1927[a]		Gehrig ...	3	0	Jack Quinn
June 7	+Chicago	Ruth	4	0	Tommy Thomas
1927		Gehrig ...	4	0	Tommy Thomas
June 16	+St. Louis	Ruth	1	1	Tom Zachary
1927		Gehrig ...	1	0	Tom Zachary
June 30	+Boston	Gehrig ...	1	2	Slim Harriss
1927		Ruth	4	1	Slim Harriss
September 2	Philadelphia	Ruth	1	0	Rube Walberg
1927		Gehrig ...	1	0	Rube Walberg
		Gehrig ...	2	1	Rube Walberg
September 6	Boston	Gehrig ...	5	0	Tony Welzer
1927[a]		Ruth	6	2	Tony Welzer
		Ruth	7	1	Tony Welzer
September 27	+Philadelphia	Gehrig ...	4	0	Jack Quinn
1927		Ruth	6	3	Lefty Grove

May 12 1928	+Detroit	Gehrig ...	3	1	Owen Carroll
		Ruth	6	0	Lil Stoner
May 17 1928	+St. Louis	Gehrig ...	4	0	Hal Wiltse
		Ruth	5	0	Hal Wiltse
May 22 1928	+Boston	Gehrig ...	5	2	Slim Harriss
		Ruth	6	1	Slim Harriss
May 29 1928	+Washington	Gehrig ...	3	0	Milt Gaston
		Ruth	4	0	Lloyd Brown
		Gehrig ...	4	0	Lloyd Brown
		Ruth	7	0	Lloyd Brown
June 7 1928	Cleveland	Ruth	9	2	Joe Shaute
		Gehrig ...	9	0	Joe Shaute
June 12 1928	Chicago	Gehrig ...	1	1	Grady Adkins
		Ruth	5	1	Grady Adkins
		Gehrig ...	6	1	George Cox
June 17 1928	St. Louis	Ruth	7	0	John Ogden
		Gehrig ...	9	1	General Crowder
July 15 1928[b]	+Cleveland	Ruth	1	1	George Grant
		Gehrig ...	5	0	Dutch Levsen
September 30 1928	Detroit	Ruth	5	1	Vic Sorrell
		Gehrig ...	7	0	Vic Sorrell
April 18 1929	+Boston	Ruth	1	0	Red Ruffing
		Gehrig ...	6	0	Milt Gaston
May 4 1929	Chicago	Gehrig ...	2	0	Red Faber
		Ruth	7	1	Hal McKain
		Gehrig ...	7	0	Hal McKain
		Gehrig ...	9	0	Dan Dugan
May 19 1929	+Boston	Ruth	3	1	Jack Russell
		Gehrig ...	3	0	Jack Russell
July 28 1929	+St. Louis	Gehrig ...	1	1	General Crowder
		Ruth	12	0	Rip Collins
August 11 1929	Cleveland	Ruth	2	0	Willis Hudlin
		Gehrig ...	4	0	Willis Hudlin
August 28 1929	+Philadelphia	Ruth	1	0	Rube Walberg
		Gehrig ...	5	1	Jack Quinn
September 8 1929	+Detroit	Ruth	4	2	Vic Sorrell
		Gehrig ...	6	2	Emil Yde
September 10 1929[b]	+Detroit	Gehrig ...	1	3	Phil Page
		Ruth	9	2	Owen Carroll
September 18 1929[a]	+Cleveland	Ruth	1	0	Walter Miller
		Gehrig ...	3	1	Walter Miller
September 18 1929[b]	+Cleveland	Gehrig ...	7	3	Milt Shoffner
		Ruth	8	1	Milt Shoffner
May 22 1930[b]	Philadelphia	Gehrig ...	1	3	Bill Shores
		Ruth	2	0	Jack Quinn
		Gehrig ...	4	1	Eddie Rommel
		Gehrig ...	7	1	Glenn Liebhardt
May 30 1930[a]	+Boston	Ruth	1	0	Hod Lisenbee
		Gehrig ...	6	0	Hod Lisenbee
June 7 1930	St. Louis	Ruth	1	2	Lefty Stewart
		Gehrig ...	2	0	George Blaeholder
June 15 1930	Cleveland	Gehrig ...	3	1	Milt Shoffner
		Gehrig ...	5	2	Belve Bean
		Ruth	6	0	Belve Bean

June 25 1930[b]	+St. Louis	Ruth	3	0	George Blaeholder
		Ruth	5	0	Herman Holshauser
		Gehrig ...	6	0	Herman Holshauser
July 18 1930	St. Louis	Gehrig ...	4	1	Sam Gray
		Ruth	5	0	Sam Gray
July 20 1930	Cleveland	Ruth	4	0	Milt Shoffner
		Gehrig ...	4	0	Milt Shoffner
		Gehrig ...	5	2	Milt Shoffner
July 21 1930	Cleveland	Ruth	3	1	Walter Miller
		Gehrig ...	8	1	Belve Bean
August 17 1930[a]	+Chicago	Gehrig ...	2	0	Ted Lyons
		Ruth	7	0	Frank Henry
June 19 1931	St. Louis	Gehrig ...	3	1	Sam Gray
		Ruth	5	0	Rolland Styles
June 21 1931[a]	St. Louis	Gehrig ...	1	1	Lefty Stewart
		Ruth	3	2	Lefty Stewart
July 16 1931	+Cleveland	Gehrig ...	6	0	Clint Brown
		Ruth	7	1	Clint Brown
July 22 1931[b]	+Detroit	Ruth	1	1	Tommy Bridges
		Ruth	6	0	Charlie Sullivan
		Gehrig ...	6	0	Charlie Sullivan
July 23 1931	+Detroit	Ruth	3	2	Earl Whitehill
		Gehrig ...	8	0	Earl Whitehill
August 5 1931[b]	Boston	Ruth	3	1	Hod Lisenbee
		Gehrig ...	8	0	Hod Lisenbee
August 14 1931[a]	Cleveland	Gehrig ...	5	0	Mel Harder
		Ruth	9	0	Mel Harder
August 20 1931	St. Louis	Gehrig ...	4	0	Sam Gray
		Ruth	9	3	Wally Hebert
August 21 1931	St. Louis	Ruth	3	1	George Blaeholder
		Gehrig ...	3	0	George Blaeholder
September 7 1931[b]	Philadelphia	Ruth	6	0	Waite Hoyt
		Gehrig ...	6	0	Waite Hoyt
		Ruth	9	0	Waite Hoyt
April 12 1932	Philadelphia	Ruth	1	0	George Earnshaw
		Gehrig ...	3	0	George Earnshaw
		Ruth	4	1	George Earnshaw
May 21 1932[a]	+Washington	Ruth	5	3	Lloyd Brown
		Ruth	6	1	Frank Ragland
		Gehrig ...	6	0	Frank Ragland
June 3 1932	Philadelphia	Gehrig ...	1	1	George Earnshaw
		Gehrig ...	4	0	George Earnshaw
		Ruth	5	0	George Earnshaw
		Gehrig ...	5	0	George Earnshaw
		Gehrig ...	7	0	LeRoy Mahaffey
June 8 1932	Detroit	Ruth	1	1	Earl Whitehill
		Gehrig ...	7	1	Earl Whitehill
June 23 1932	St. Louis	Gehrig ...	4	1	Bump Hadley
		Ruth	7	0	Wally Hebert
July 9 1932[a]	+Detroit	Gehrig ...	3	1	Earl Whitehill
		Ruth	6	0	Earl Whitehill
August 25 1932	+Cleveland	Ruth	6	1	Oral Hildebrand
		Gehrig ...	9	0	Oral Hildebrand

August 26	+Cleveland	Gehrig ...	3	1	Wes Ferrell
1932		Ruth	7	0	Wes Ferrell
September 24	Boston	Gehrig ...	5	2	Ed Gallagher
1932		Ruth	9	0	John Michaels
April 27	Philadelphia	Ruth	5	1	Merritt Cain
1933		Gehrig ...	7	0	Merritt Cain
May 23	+Cleveland	Ruth	1	0	Oral Hildebrand
1933		Gehrig ...	3	2	Oral Hildebrand
June 8	Philadelphia	Gehrig ...	6	1	Tony Freitas
1933		Ruth	7	0	Ray Coombs
August 7	+Washington	Gehrig ...	1	1	Lefty Stewart
1933[b]		Ruth	8	0	Lefty Stewart
September 23	Boston	Gehrig ...	1	1	Lloyd Brown
1933		Ruth	4	2	John Welch
May 28	St. Louis	Gehrig ...	6	0	Ivy Andrews
1934		Ruth	7	1	Jack Knott
		Gehrig ...	7	0	Jack Knott
June 3	Philadelphia	Gehrig ...	4	1	Merritt Cain
1934		Ruth	8	0	Merritt Cain

World Series

October 9	St. Louis	Ruth	4	0	Bill Sherdel
1928	Cardinals	Ruth	7	0	Bill Sherdel
		Gehrig ...	7	0	Bill Sherdel
		Ruth	8	0	Pete Alexander
October 1	Chicago Cubs	Ruth	1	2	Charlie Root
1932		Gehrig ...	3	0	Charlie Root
		Ruth	5	0	Charlie Root
		Gehrig ...	5	0	Charlie Root

[a] First game of doubleheader [b] Second game of doubleheader
+ Game played at Yankee Stadium

with news of Lindbergh, Capone, and Sacco and Vanzetti, the Crown Prince's attempt to unseat the undisputed home-run king captured its share of the public imagination.

By August 15, Lou had outhomered Babe, 38 to 36. But then Ruth caught fire. While Lou would hit only nine more in the last six weeks, Babe smashed 24 in 42 games—an astonishing pace that would have produced about 90 over a full season. Number 60 came on the second-to-last day of the season, when Babe golfed a curve ball from Washington left-hander Tom Zachary into the right-field bleachers.

Only ten thousand were on hand that afternoon at Yankee Stadium. Although many spilled out of the stands to congratulate Ruth after the game, there was nowhere near the hysteria that would accompany Roger Maris's chase of Ruth's single-season record thirty-four years later. In 1927, most people reasonably assumed Babe would just hit more the

next year. Maybe 70 or 75? Who knew? Lou, far from displaying any jealousy over Babe's accomplishment, watched from on-deck with a combination of awe, pride, and hero worship. For years he considered his biggest thrill in baseball to be the day he shook Babe Ruth's hand at home plate after number 60 had landed in the seats.

It was an even bigger thrill than receiving that year's Most Valuable Player Award, as voted on by the league's sportswriters. Lou led the league in total bases (447), doubles (52), and set a record with 175 RBI. He also finished second in batting (.373), hits (218), runs (149), triples (18), walks, and home runs. In recognition, he received 56 votes, 21 better than runner-up Harry Heilmann, who had won his fourth batting title in seven years for the Tigers. Many criticized the selection process, which made previous winners ineligible. The general concensus was that Ruth, who had won the award in 1923, probably would have outpolled Lou had he been allowed on the ballot.

In 1954, Cleveland broke New York's record with 111

San Francisco native Mark Koenig quit school at sixteen to play ball. He became the Yankees starting shortstop in 1925 and a regular nocturnal companion of Babe Ruth. "When I think of all the wasted hours, my God!" he once lamented. "What somebody with brains could have done with them, you know? I mean, the hours you kept. You could go to bed at three o'clock in the morning because you wouldn't have to be out until one o'clock. You could sleep until eleven. All those wasted hours."

Lloyd Waner (left) and his brother Paul combined for 5,611 base hits in the major leagues. They're pictured with their parents and sister at the 1927 World Series, which the Pirates lost in four straight. Despite the sweep, they went home to Oklahoma as heroes: combined, they had outhit Ruth and Gehrig in the Series, allowing townspeople to cash in on a large bet.

Ruth and Gehrig flank another pair of immortals: Tris Speaker (second from left) and Ty Cobb. Both outfielders were winding up their careers with the Philadelphia Athletics.

victories, but then was upset in the World Series by the Giants. Murderers Row, on the other hand, capped the glorious summer of '27 by dismantling a very good Pittsburgh team in October.

Legend has it that the Pirates were spooked before the Series even began when they watched the mighty Yankees pound the ball in a batting practice display orchestrated by Miller Huggins. Knowing that several Pirates were in the stands observing them, the Yankees' skipper had instructed Waite Hoyt to just feed the boys fat pitches, which Lou, Babe, and the rest of the starting lineup obligingly deposited into the far-off reaches of spacious Forbes Field.

Paul Waner, a slightly built Oklahoma farmboy who starred in the Bucs' outfield with his brother Lloyd, always insisted that the story just wasn't so. Paul may have said something to the effect that "They sure are

Mom and Pop Gehrig.

Babe and Buster on the sidelines with Notre Dame coach Knute Rockne.

big, aren't they?"—a remark overheard and embellished by New York writer Ken Smith. But the Pirates, who after all had been world champions just two years earlier, weren't awed or nervous. They were simply humiliated.

"The one thing I remember best about that Series is that I didn't seem to actually realize I was really playing in a World Series until it was all over," Paul Waner said later. "The first time we came to bat in the first

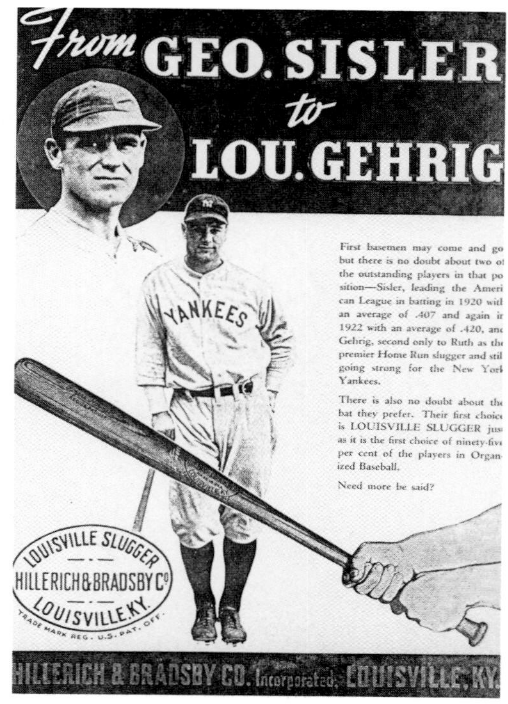

Lou's three home runs in a 1928 game against the Chicago White Sox prompted Hillerich and Bradsby to showcase one of its more satisfied customers in national ads like these.

Even champions can make mistakes. In 1928 Murderers Row lined up in support of presidential candidate Al Smith. Smith lost, but the Yankees continued to win.

game, Lloyd singled and I doubled, and from then on the two of us just kept on hitting like it was an ordinary series during the regular season."

Unfortunately, the Yankees had the same philosophy. Despite a power outage—Ruth accounted for New York's only two home runs of the Series—they treated the Pirates as if they were the St. Louis Browns. In Lou's first at-bat of the first game, he tripled in a run when Paul Waner missed a shoestring catch of a short fly to right. Behind Hoyt and Wilcy Moore, New York won, 5-4. Lou knocked in what proved to be the winning run with a sacrifice fly in the fifth inning.

George Pipgras went the distance the following afternoon in an easy

Gehrig steadily improved as a fielder during his career. In this 1928 game against St. Louis, he nips the Browns' Gene Robertson at the bag.

The St. Louis Cardinals provided the competition in the 1928 World Series. From left to right: Jim Bottomley, Frankie Frisch, Tommy Thevenow, and Walter "Rabbit" Maranville. Unlike the Cardinals and other big-league clubs, the Yankees—on the orders of owner Jacob Ruppert—wore freshly laundered uniforms each game.

Willie Sherdel helped pitch the Cardinals into two World Series against the Yankees, but then lost all four of his starts against them. Gehrig hit .500 (5 for 10) with a home run and five walks off the little left-hander.

6-2 victory. The Series then moved to Yankee Stadium. Lou smacked a booming triple to the wall in left-center field his first time up. It produced two runs, the only ones needed in the Yanks' 8-1 rout.

The Series ended twenty-four hours later. Facing elimination, Pittsburgh gamely fought back with a pair of tallies in the seventh off Wilcy Moore, knotting the game at three runs apiece. In the bottom of the ninth, the Yankees loaded the bases with none out. Lou had a chance to be the hero, but Johnny Miljus struck him out. Miljus then fanned Meusel. Then, with one strike on Lazzeri, Miljus uncorked a wild pitch that sent Earle Combs scampering across home plate with the run that won the game and brought the Series to an abrupt, anticlimactic finish.

Paul Waner stood stunned on the outfield lawn and thought, "Gee, I've just played in a World Series." But just barely. Not only was it the first time an American League team had ever swept the fall classic, it was the shortest Series ever played. From first pitch to last, it had lasted all of 74 hours and 15 minutes—a little more than three days in real time. The lightning-like sweep cemented boasts that the 1927 Yankees were the greatest team ever assembled.

The understated end contrasted with Lou's emotional state at the time. Towards the end of the regular season, Mom Gehrig had fallen ill, and Lou was beside himself with worry. After each afternoon's game he would rush to the hospital, where he would stay at her side until she dozed off to sleep.

"I'm so worried about Mom that I can't see straight," he told a favorite reporter, Fred Lieb. "If I lost her I don't know what I would do."

Distracted, his production fell off, allowing Ruth to pass him in home runs and cutting into his RBI pace, which in early September seemed certain to reach an unbelievable 200.

Lou actually thought of sitting out the Series, but neither Miller Huggins nor his mother would hear of it. She came off the critical list during the Series and so did her doting son, who wound up hitting .308 against the Bucs.

BASEBALL
MAGAZINE
"Sunny" Jim Bottomley, Slugging First Baseman of the St. Louis Cardinals, Who is Having a Record Season.
Oct.
20¢
THE ART OF MAKING HARD PLAYS EASY—Tris Speaker
THE MASTER COACHES—F. C. Lane
STAR ROOKIES OF 1928—J. M. Gould
WHEN FACTS AND FIGURES DISAGREE—J. Genewich
OVER 500,000 FANS READ THE BASEBALL MAGAZINE

Like Will Rogers, "Sunny Jim" Bottomley never met a man he didn't like. A bottle of booze could always make him smile, too. Between all the smiling and drinking, the Cardinals first baseman found time to knock in plenty of runs—a dozen in one game alone in 1924, still the all-time record. Bottomley was a key ingredient in four St. Louis pennants and two world championships during his career, which culminated in his election to the Hall of Fame in 1974.

Mom's recovery allowed Lou to join Ruth on a barnstorming tour across the heartland of America all the way to California. Arranged by Ruth's agent and ghost writer, Christy Walsh, Babe and Buster were the captains of opposing teams: the Bustin' Babes and the Larrupin' Lous. The month-long tour covered 8,000 miles and attracted 200,000 paying customers. Lou's $10,000 share was about a third of what Ruth got.

"The kid's giving it all to his mother," Ruth told the press when the tour ended. Reporters asked the two how they were going to spend the balance of the off-season.

"I plan to play a lot of basketball," said Lou.

"I ain't doing a thing," boomed Babe, "except you know what!"

Depending on how one viewed his activities, Babe was either a delightful scamp or a trousered ape. Sure, he could affectionately tossle the hair of some starry-eyed, mop-topped, ten-year-old on his way into the park or during one of his countless hospital visits. Babe genuinely loved children; they came down to his level. But if he came across that same kid's older sister in a speakeasy or hotel lobby, all bets were off.

Once Ruth celebrated a pennant-clinching victory by ordering a piano and a case of premium bootleg hooch up to his hotel suite. The place was jammed with young women and players. Babe climbed on top of the piano.

"Anyone who doesn't want to fuck," he bellowed, "can leave right now!"

Baseball Annies weren't Lou's style. Like many men who are close to their mothers, his view of other women was a blend of fear and respect. While Ruth charged through life with his pants around his ankles, Lou was quietly looking around for a partner for life. Not that his teammates were any help. When he'd asked Bob Meusel and Benny Benbough if they knew of any nice girls, they had howled in laughter. You wouldn't know what to do with a woman, they told him.

Lou was no virgin, but he was virtuous. Before he married in 1933, he confided to a trusted friend that he had been with girls, though it's hard to imagine these affairs being of the wham-bam-thank-you-ma'am variety that Ruth and many of his teammates heartily endorsed. Several of them sent a prostitute up to his room once, a gag that heavily embarrassed Lou and kept the team in stitches for weeks. Lou surely ignored recounting the incident in the many letters he wrote his mother from the road.

In 1928, the Yankees threatened to once again take apart the league. They roared to a 39-9 start and at midseason had a 17-game lead over the improving Athletics. But injuries to Meusel, Lazzeri, Benbough, Combs, and Pennock soon brought the team back to the pack.

Caught up in the heat of a pennant race, Lou shrugged off his own aches and injuries and played every game of the schedule for the third

Ruth is greeted by Gehrig and a blizzard of straw boaters as he ends his third home-run trot of the afternoon in the final game of the '28 Series. Gehrig either scored or drove in 14 runs in the four games, but few remembered that he had played.

After the 1928 season, Ruth and Gehrig went on a month-long barnstorming tour that traveled as far as the West Coast, where the rubber-chicken circuit included a football dinner before the Southern Cal-Notre Dame game.

straight season. During a game with Washington, second baseman Bucky Harris dragged a bunt down the first base line and purposely stomped on Lou's big toe. Lou's throw went sailing over the catcher's head, allowing the runner on third to score what eventually proved to be the winning run.

"I've never seen a man look so surprised and hurt," Harris later said. "But he never uttered a word of complaint."

Bustin' Babe and his sidekick, Larrupin' Lou, lassoed some cheers in 1928 at the World Series Rodeo inside Madison Square Garden.

Before a game in Omaha, Nebraska, the captains of the Larrupin' Lous and Bustin' Babes were introduced to Lady Amco, a world-champion, egg-laying hen known far and wide as "the Babe Ruth of chickens." Considering its day-in, day-out dependability, perhaps it should have been known as "the Lou Gehrig of chickens." That morning Lady Amco laid an egg for the 171st consecutive day.

Because teams played each other 22 times each season, Harris fully expected Gehrig to even accounts at some point during the year.

"But Lou never did a thing," Harris said. "Every time after that when I got to first, he just gazed at me as though to ask me how I could do such a thing. I got feeling so ashamed of myself for what I'd done that I finally apologized to him. You should have seen the poor guy light up!"

Philadelphia passed the faltering Yankees, but New York swept a crucial Sunday twin bill at Yankee Stadium on September 9 to reclaim the top spot. There was little celebrating. The team learned that the 38-year-old, veteran pitcher Urban Shocker had died that day of heart disease in a Denver hospital.

Ultimately, the Yankees hung on to win their third straight pennant by two and a half games. Babe kept up his pounding, hitting 54 home runs, double what runner-up Lou managed. Lou finished third in batting (.374), second in runs, hits, and slugging, and tied Ruth for RBI honors with 142. He also tied Heinie Manush of St. Louis with 47 two-base hits.

The beat-up Yankees went into the World Series as underdogs to the Cardinals, who featured Frankie Frisch at shortstop, Jim Bottomley at first, Chick Hafey in left, and a pair of 20-game winners in Bill Sherdel and Jesse Haines. A broken finger kept Combs on the bench and a bum arm rendered Pennock useless.

Waite Hoyt, who had chalked up 23 victories during the regular season, opened the Series with a three-hit gem at Yankee Stadium. Lou started the scoring by doubling in Ruth in the home half of the first. He later added a second RBI in the Yankees' 4-1 triumph.

The following afternoon the Yanks faced Grover Cleveland Alexander. George Pipgras, winner of a league-high 24 games, was asked to shake hands with Ol' Pete before they squared off. Pipgras put his hand out "and I swear he missed it by a foot, he was so drunk," he recalled. "Either that or he had a wicked hangover."

The Yankees wasted no time sobering up their old nemesis. Cedric Durst singled, and after Koenig flied out, Ruth walked on four pitches. Then Lou made his only hit off Alexander in two World Series a typically productive one, thumping the first pitch for a long home run that produced a quick 3-0 lead.

"It was a ball that the center fielder broke in on," Pipgras said, "but it just kept on rising and rising and finally hit the scoreboard. If you know where that scoreboard was in Yankee Stadium, you know what a clout that was." By the end of the afternoon that scoreboard showed the home team winning easily, 9-3.

Smelling an unprecedented second straight World Series sweep, the Yankees traveled west and buried the Cardinals under an avalanche of power. After St. Louis seized a 2-0 lead in the third game, Lou led off the bottom of the second with a booming home run off Jesse Haines that landed on top of the right-field pavilion at Sportsman's Park.

The score was still 2-1, St. Louis, when Ruth rifled a one-out single in the fourth. This brought up Lou, who lined the ball to center. Taylor Douthit foolishly tried for a shoestring catch, but the ball bounded past him to the fence. His muscular plowhorse legs churning, Lou circled around the bases for an inside-the-park home run that gave New York a 3-2 lead they never relinquished.

The wrecking crew liked its 7-3 triumph so much it closed out the Series the following day by the same score. Once again, Lou homered to hand the Yankees a 3-2 lead that was never headed. But once again Larrupin' Lou saw the spotlight stolen by the Babe, who walloped solo home runs in the fourth, seventh and eight innings.

Ruth's second home run was the most dramatic, coming after Sherdel had apparently struck him out on a quick pitch. The maneuver, still used in the National League, had been declared illegal for the Series. After a heated argument, Ruth was awarded new life by the umpire.

Babe settled into the box, all the while exchanging obscenities with Sherdel. As he would so many times during his career, Ruth rose to the occasion and shut up the opposition by poling one into the seats. By the following inning, many of the paying customers were on his side. Straw boaters and seat cushions floated onto the field in celebration of his third round-tripper, which gave Babe a final Series average of .625 (10 hits in 16 at-bats), a record that stands to this day.

On the wild train ride back to New York, Ruth and company celebrated by guzzling champagne and breaking into Jacob Ruppert's private compartment, where Babe and an unlikely accomplice, Lou, ripped the clothes right off Ruppert and his friends. Liquid cheer flowed into the wee hours of the morning. Afterwards, Miller Huggins wandered through the cars, asking if anyone had found his false teeth.

Gehrig's own gaudy .545 average, his four home runs (which equalled Ruth's 1926 record), and his nine RBI (which set a new postseason standard) were lost in the uproar. "Gehrig tied Ruth's record of four home runs in a series," the *New York Times* observed, "yet few knew he played."

For the second-best player in all of baseball, this had become the leitmotif of his major-league career.

CHAPTER Five

—THE HARD NUMBER—

What visions burn, what dreams possess him, seeker of the night? The packed stands of the stadium, the bleachers sweltering with their unshaded hordes, the faultless velvet of the diamond...The mounting roar of eighty thousand voices and Gehrig coming up to bat...

—Thomas Wolfe, *You Can't Go Home Again*

IN 1929 the Yankees wore numbers on their uniforms for the first time. Since no precedent for assigning them existed, it was decided that the single digits, at least, would be handed out according to each player's position in the lineup. Thus, leadoff man Earle Combs was given number 1, third-place hitter Ruth number 3, clean-up batter Gehrig number 4, and so on. Lou's digit was soon known around the American League as "the hard number"—a sign of respect to his awesome production and unrelenting style of play.

It was well-deserved. Lou, who turned twenty-six during the season, was just entering his prime. Although 1929 was a slack year statistically for Lou (.300, 35 home runs, 126 RBI), the following three seasons saw an astounding spurt of power and run production. From 1930 through 1932 Lou averaged 213 hits, 148 runs, 38 doubles, 14 triples, 40 homers, and 170 runs batted in. Although offensive numbers reached unprecedented levels in 1930, the first summer of the depression, only Lou scalded the ball to the tune of 419 total bases, a category he would lead the circuit in the following season as well.

That summer of '31 may have been Lou's best. The *Sporting News* selected him as the league's most valuable player. He set a still-standing league record by driving in 184 runs, established the all-time major league mark for runs produced (runs + RBI - home runs) with 301, and tied Ruth in the home run department with 46, including three grand slams in four days. This kind of hitting convinced a gangly high school star from the Bronx that he would be better off playing first base any place except Yankee Stadium.

"I'd never seen such brute strength," said Hank Greenberg, whom Yankees scout Paul Krichell had been actively pursuing. "'No way I'm going to sign with this team,' I said to myself. Not with him playing first base."

Buster at bat: "He'd hammer 'em."

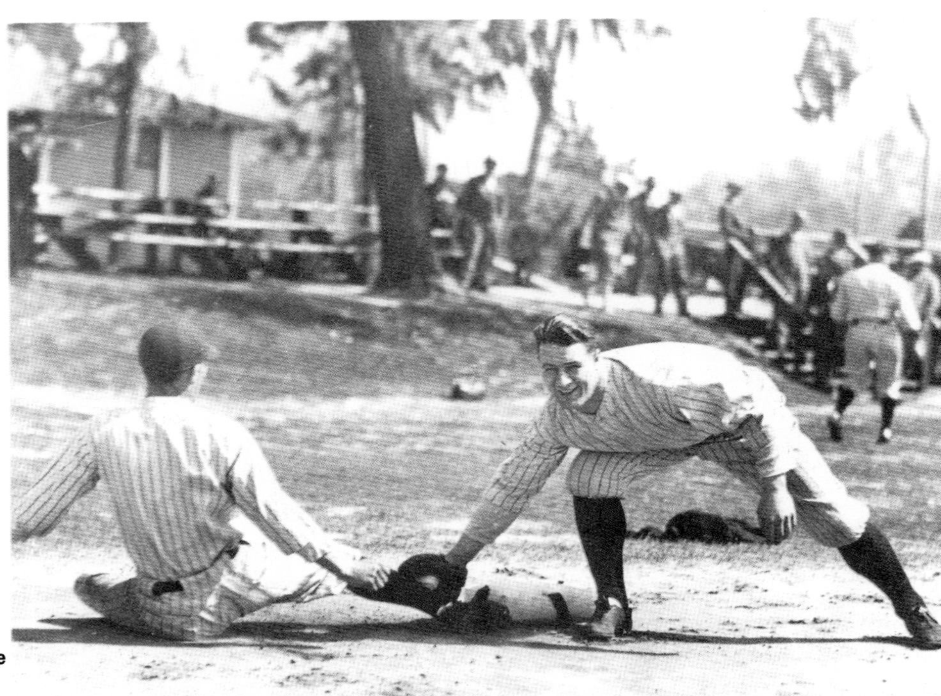

Two views of Lou in spring training in the late twenties.

Greenberg turned down a better offer from the Yankees to sign with the Tigers, a decision he never regretted. "There was a long line of first basemen owned by the Yankee organization who spent their whole careers in the minors waiting for him to leave. I'm just glad I escaped being one of them."

The secret of Lou's power was the solidity of his batting style. The standard practice of the time was to stand loosely at the plate, swing the bat back over the shoulder, then attack the pitch with the back foot on the ground and the front foot in the air. (The Giants' Mel Ott and the Athletics' Al Simmons were extreme practitioners of this "lunging" style of hitting.)

The Guns of October

Gehrig and Ruth were the very picture of consistency in postseason play.

Simmons and Foxx? Aaron and Mathews? Mays and McCovey? Forget 'em. By sheer weight of numbers, Ruth and Gehrig remain the most potent combination in baseball history. In their 10 seasons together in the regular lineup, 1925 through 1934, they combined for 772 home runs and averaged a collective 274 RBI per season. No other one-two punch has ever come close to those numbers.

The Yankees' dynamic duo actually jacked up their production several notches in October, a time when such gifted regular-season performers as Ty Cobb, Ted Williams, Willie Mays, and Barry Bonds have fallen flat on their faces. In the four World Series that Babe and Lou played together (1926, 1927, 1928, and 1932), the pair hit an aggregate .415 with 18 home runs and 47 RBI in just 19 games. Twenty-nine of their 54 hits went for extra bases, producing an unworldly composite slugging percentage of .931. And this was against the cream of National League pitching! With this kind of hitting, it comes as no surprise that the Yankees won 15 of the 19 World Series games in which Gehrig and Ruth were in the lineup, including the last 12 in a row. Here is how their postseason performances together break down:

1926 vs. St. Louis (New York lost, 4 games to 3)

	G	AB	R	H	BA	2B	3B	HR	RBI	SA
Ruth	7	20	6	6	.300	0	0	4	5	.900
Gehrig	7	23	1	8	.348	2	0	0	3	.435
Total	7	43	7	14	.326	2	0	4	8	.651

1927 vs. Pittsburgh (New York won, 4 games to 0)

	G	AB	R	H	BA	2B	3B	HR	RBI	SA
Ruth	4	15	4	6	.400	0	0	2	7	.800
Gehrig	4	13	2	4	.308	2	2	0	5	.769
Total	4	28	6	10	.357	2	2	2	12	.786

1928 vs. St. Louis (New York won, 4 games to 0)

	G	AB	R	H	BA	2B	3B	HR	RBI	SA
Ruth	4	16	9	10	.625	3	0	3	4	1.375
Gehrig	4	11	5	6	.545	1	0	4	9	1.727
Total	4	27	14	16	.593	4	0	7	13	1.519

1932 vs. Chicago (New York won, 4 games to 0)

	G	AB	R	H	BA	2B	3B	HR	RBI	SA
Ruth	4	15	6	5	.333	0	0	2	6	.733
Gehrig	4	17	9	9	.529	1	0	3	8	1.118
Total	4	32	15	14	.438	1	0	5	14	.938

Before becoming an American League umpire, George Pipgras won 93 games in 11 seasons for New York, inluding a league-high 24 in 1928. He also won all three of his World Series starts. Pipgras's daughter, LeMorn, used to get a box of chocolates every birthday from her favorite player, Lou Gehrig, which made Pipgras's umpiring of Lou Gehrig Day in 1939 a particularly bitter-sweet experience.

Gehrig, on the other hand, would first step forward and set himself. At the time he started to bring his bat forward, his thick, muscular legs were planted in the batter's box like a pair of thousand-year-old sequoias. Then his back (left) foot would shove off the ground, his knee acting as a pivot for the savage rotation of his trunk. From his foot, knee, and hips, Lou's power continued to ripple through his shoulders, arms, wrist, and bat before finally exploding against the ball.

Pitchers never did figure a way of getting Gehrig out consistently. Willis Hudlin, a right-handed sinkerballer for Cleveland, pitched against him for fourteen seasons beginning in 1926. In hindsight, he thinks his old adversary handled high balls better than low. "A low ball, you have to lift it," said Hudlin, who admits that in Lou's case, that probably just meant the difference between lining the ball into the power alleys for a triple and pulling one over the right-field fence.

"There's no one way to pitch to great hitters like Ruth, Foxx, Gehringer, Simmons, and Gehrig," said Rick Ferrell, the Hall of Fame catcher who divided his eighteen years in the American League between Washington, Boston, and St. Louis. "You have to keep moving the ball around the plate. A fast ball here, then maybe call for a change-up. But you can't pitch them the same way every time. They adjust. That's why they're great hitters."

Despite his production, Lou was rarely brushed back. He was plunked with a pitch only 45 times during his career, with a high of seven in 1936. While his reflexes and middle-of-the-box stance were partially responsible, his imposing presence made even such notorious barbers as Lefty Grove think twice about administering a close shave.

"Grove never threw much at Gehrig," recalled Roger "Doc" Cramer, Grove's teammate in Philadelphia and Boston. "Didn't want to wake him up, he said."

Lou wasn't somnolent, only monotonous. Unlike Ruth and Jimmie Foxx, who enjoyed yapping with the catcher and the umpire while at bat, Gehrig was all business as he settled into the box.

He waved a heavy bat. When Lou first broke in, he used a Rogers Hornsby model. (Hornsby, incidentally, favored the same flat-footed style of hitting.) The large-barreled bat, which tapered to a medium handle and a small knob, was 35 1/2 inches long and weighed between 38 and 40 ounces. In 1925 he began experimenting with thicker-handled clubs. Then, late in the 1926 season, he sent in an order to Hillerich and

Gehrig was an aggressive base runner. Biscuit Pants stole home 15 times in his career and legged out six inside-the-park home runs, including one in the 1928 World Series.

Bradsby, the famous Kentucky bat manufacturer, for a model he called "number one." Lou's custom-made Louisville Slugger was 35 inches long, weighed 37 ounces, and had a large barrel tapering gradually to a medium handle and a large knob. With some minor modifications (a smaller knob in 1927, a small handle and a medium knob in 1931, and the normal incremental decreases in weight as the season progressed), this was the bat he used most often during his career.

During his first few years, Lou struck out fairly regularly. But as he learned more about pitchers' strengths, weaknesses, and tendencies, the strikeouts dropped noticeably—from a high of 84 in 1927 to just 38 five years later. In 1934, when he hit 49 home runs, he whiffed but 31 times, a remarkably low total for a power hitter.

Lou, not far removed from his gridiron days, could dish out punishment on the basepaths as well as at the bat. He once described how he and Ruth had deliberately knocked out two men on the same play during the 1928 World Series sweep of St. Louis.

"The play was at second base," he said. "I gave Frank Frisch all I had and knocked him kicking. The ball rolled to short center field. Ruth had turned third and was headed for the plate. He hadn't seen me take Frisch out, but he knew I had—that's how we played in those days. Ruth kept heading for the plate, and when he got there he bowled Jimmy Wilson over. The ball had been retrieved by then. Frisch was still sitting back of second rubbing his leg when Ruth reached the dugout. It was dirty baseball, but that was the rule of the day."

Spitballer Urban Shocker broke in with the Yankees in 1916, but gained his greatest fame with the St. Louis Browns, for whom he had four straight 20-win seasons. Traded back to the Yankees in 1925, he won 49 games in three seasons before dying of heart disease towards the end of the 1928 season.

Throughout his career Lou exhibited a fierce will to win, doing whatever it took to put the Yankees in the victory column. At times he could display a considerable temper, especially when dealing with umpires. Generally forgotten is that during his playing days Lou was tossed out of seven games and came close to an early shower on a few other occasions.

He was a team man to the core. But his aggressiveness stopped short of malice. Frankie O'Rourke detailed an incident that occurred in the midtwenties when he was playing second base for the Tigers. Gehrig was perched on first base when Tony Lazzeri hit a ground ball to O'Rourke. "I went over to the bag to pivot on the play," he said, "and I thought a truck hit me."

Umpire Billy Evans immediately signaled a double play because of Lou's interference, but the little infielder was livid.

"I yelled some names at him—strong names, too, which was customary in that time—and Gehrig stopped and started back to me. I figured this was the end, but Harry Heilmann came in from right field and shouldered Gehrig away from me. I never was so glad to see a guy in my life as I was to see Harry. The next day I was at second base in the pregame infield practice for the Tigers, and I happened to look up and there's Lou standing behind first base with his arms folded. He was looking straight at me as though he was going to bore a hole through me. Our bench was on the first base side, and I would have to pass Gehrig to get to it.

"I fielded grounders as long as I could but realized I couldn't stand out there all day, so I finally tossed my glove aside and started for our bench. Gehrig took a few steps to meet me, put out his right hand and said, 'Frank, I'm sorry I went into you so hard yesterday. I shouldn't have done it.'

"I shook his hand as warmly as if he had been the President and said, 'Forget about those names I called you, young fellow.' We were firm friends forever after."

Bob Shawkey, a 196-game winner for the Athletics and Yankees, was New York's manager between the Miller Huggins and Joe McCarthy eras. In 1930, his only season at the helm, he repeatedly warned his first baseman about prematurely pulling his foot off the bag on throws. "One day it's going to cost us a close game," he warned Gehrig. Sure enough, it did, and Lou "sat down on the bench and cried like a baby," said Shawkey. "He was that type. Very sensitive boy. Later on, after he'd had his dinner, he came up to my room and apologized, promised it would never happen again. And it didn't."

The "hard number" was actually a little soft, statistically speaking, in 1929, a year filled with turmoil. Months before overspeculation helped lead to Wall Street's crash, Jacob Ruppert was warning his players to get out of the stock market. The ticker held no interest for Lou, who had invested his World Series shares and barnstorming money into a new nine-room house for his parents in New Rochelle. But another collapse, that of the only manager he had known since joining the Yankees, deeply affected him.

In September, Miller Huggins checked into St. Vincent's Hospital to have doctors examine a giant, beet-red carbuncle growing on the side of his face. Five days later, he was dead of blood poisoning.

"I guess I'll miss him more than anyone else," Lou said sadly. He remembered the tiny manager's constant encouragement, his patient

Lou was far from being a stock-market wizard, preferring to invest his money in a new home for his parents.

instruction, and his advice on matters outside the playing field. "Only Lou's willingness and lack of conceit will make him into a complete ballplayer," Huggins had told the press. "That and those muscles are all he has."

He'd also had Huggins. But now he was gone.

Obviously distracted, Lou saw his batting average drop 74 points from 1928's figure, and only a couple of gift hits kept it from slipping even lower. In the meaningless finale against Philadelphia at Yankee Stadium, the Athletics' slick-fielding third baseman, Jimmie Dykes, played far back on the infield during Gehrig's last two at-bats. Twice Gehrig laid down bunts in the direction of Dykes, who obligingly held on to the ball each time. The two hits gave Lou a final batting mark of .300.

Meanwhile, Dykes and his teammates were celebrating a more substantial achievement. That summer, after several years of playing bridesmaid to New York, the Athletics had finally grabbed the flag, finishing 18 games ahead of the runner-up Yanks. Coming off two consecutive World Series sweeps, the Yankees may have been due for a letdown, but this one lasted three years. During that spell, Connie Mack's Philadelphia Athletics captured three pennants and their last two championships (1929 and 1930), thanks to a powerful, young team centered around four future Hall-of-Famers: Lefty Grove, Mickey Cochrane, Al Simmons, and Jimmie Foxx.

"That was a great ball club," Dykes reflected in his old age. "The '29, '30, '31 Philadelphia Athletics. I always said there may have been clubs as good, but there were never any better. The Yankees were good, but they weren't better. We beat them three years in a row.

"It was a hell of a bunch of guys, too. Great gang. Anything could happen in the clubhouse. Shoes nailed to the floor. Sweatshirts tied into knots. Itching powder in your jockstrap. You're out there in front of 30,000 people and dying to scratch. Christ. Limburger cheese smeared on your hatband on a hot day. You'd damn near pass out. But on the ball field, no fooling."

The heart of the team was its battery of Grove and Cochrane, a pair of firebrands who had broken into the major leagues in the same game back in 1925. "You have Grove pitching and Cochrane catching, and you lose 1-0, you're a little timid about going into that clubhouse," warned Doc Cramer.

Grove, who won 300 games in the bigs, led the loop in strikeouts seven times and in ERA nine times during his career, including each of the Athletics' pennant-winning seasons. During those three years he was a combined 84-19 on the mound, including a remarkable 31-4 mark in 1931. His batterymate, Cochrane, was a high-strung, jug-eared receiver so agile the newspapers described him as "a shortstop in shinguards." The traditional image of a heavy-legged catcher mired eighth in the order didn't apply to Cochrane, a sprightly, spray-hitting lifetime .320 hitter who usually batted third in the order.

Al Simmons, a Milwaukee Pole who had been born Aloysious Szymanski, held down left field and batted clean-up. Simmons was a swaggering, ill-tempered, right-handed batter whose .334 lifetime average included back-to-back batting championships in 1930 (.381) and 1931 (.390). Following him in the order was first baseman Jimmie Foxx, whose "muscles had muscles," opponents liked to joke. The good-

A new major-league attendance record was set in 1930, thanks in no small part to a juiced-up ball. Nine of sixteen teams hit .300 or better. Lou lost the batting title by two points to Philadelphia's Al Simmons (bottom, right), though he led the circuit with 174 RBI.

Lewis "Hack" Wilson, the Chicago Cubs' sawed-off, merry-making outfielder, took advantage of the rabbit ball to knock in 190 runs in 1930, which remains the all-time record. All told, Wilson led the National League in home runs four times (including a league-record 56 in 1930) and runs batted in twice. Aptly described as "a low-ball hitter and a highball drinker," Wilson died a penniless drunk in Baltimore in 1948.

natured "Double X" was a key component of the Athletics' minidynasty, hammering 100 home runs and driving in 343 runs during their three summers of domination. Foxx's best years were ahead of him: 58 home runs in 1932, followed by a trade to the Red Sox and a Triple Crown season in 1933, and 50 homers and 175 RBI in 1938, the year of his third Most Valuable Player Award. Throughout the twenties and thirties, he would be Gehrig's closest competition for the title of the game's top first baseman.

The Philadelphia-New York battles of this period made for great entertainment. Between 1927 and 1932 the two teams divided six pennants, making almost every one of the 133 games they played against each other a crucial matter of league leadership and civic pride. For the

In 1905 the future terror of American League pitchers was still a two-year-old youngster in a sailor suit.

In the early 1930's regional manufacturers distributed these two Lou Gehrig trading cards.

The Goudey Gum Company of Boston was the first national manufacturer of baseball cards after the First World War. In that sense, Goudey's 1933 Lou Gehrig was his "rookie" card although he'd been in the league for ten years at that point. Goudey's 1934 set included a "Lou Gehrig says" tagline that continued on the back of almost every card in the series. Today, either card is worth between $600 (good condition) and $5,000 (near mint).

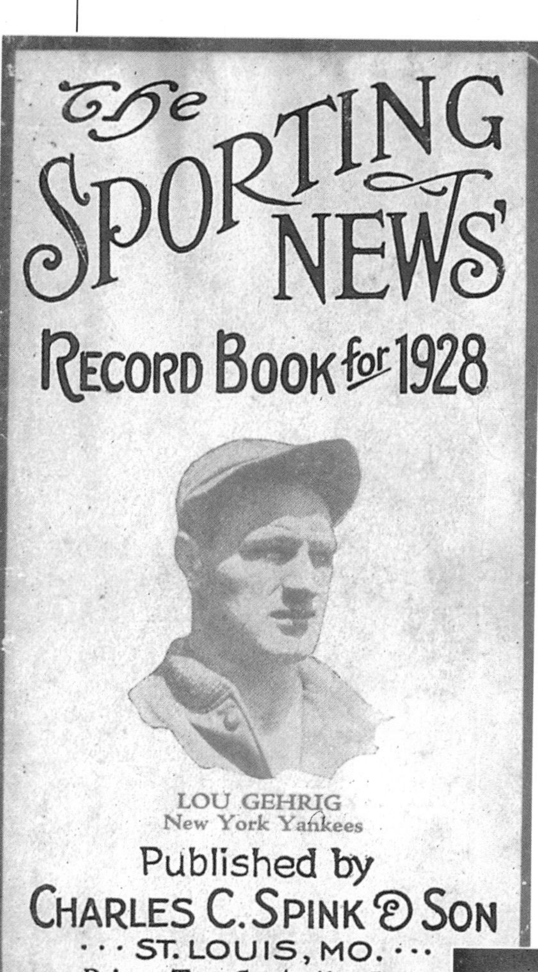

The
SPORTING NEWS
RECORD BOOK for 1928
LOU GEHRIG
New York Yankees
Published by
CHARLES C. SPINK & SON
ST. LOUIS, MO.
Price: Ten Cents the Copy

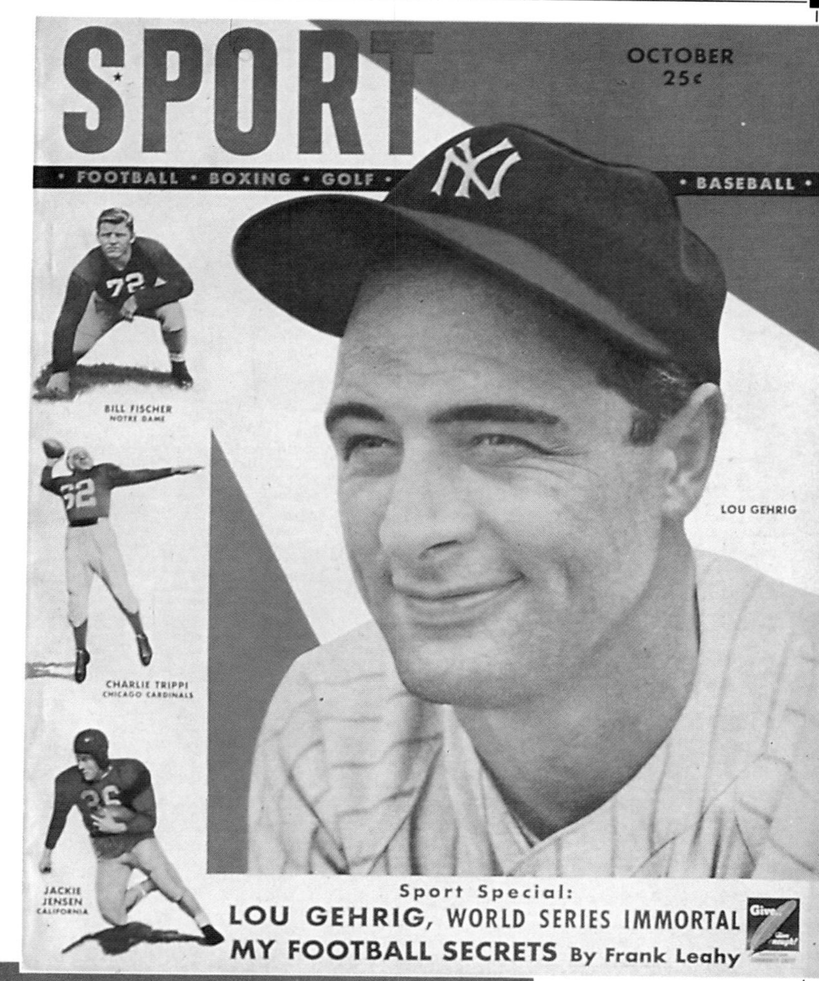

SPORT
OCTOBER
25¢
FOOTBALL • BOXING • GOLF •
• BASEBALL •
BILL FISCHER
NOTRE DAME
CHARLIE TRIPPI
CHICAGO CARDINALS
JACKIE
JENSEN
CALIFORNIA
LOU GEHRIG
Sport Special:
LOU GEHRIG, WORLD SERIES IMMORTAL
MY FOOTBALL SECRETS By Frank Leahy

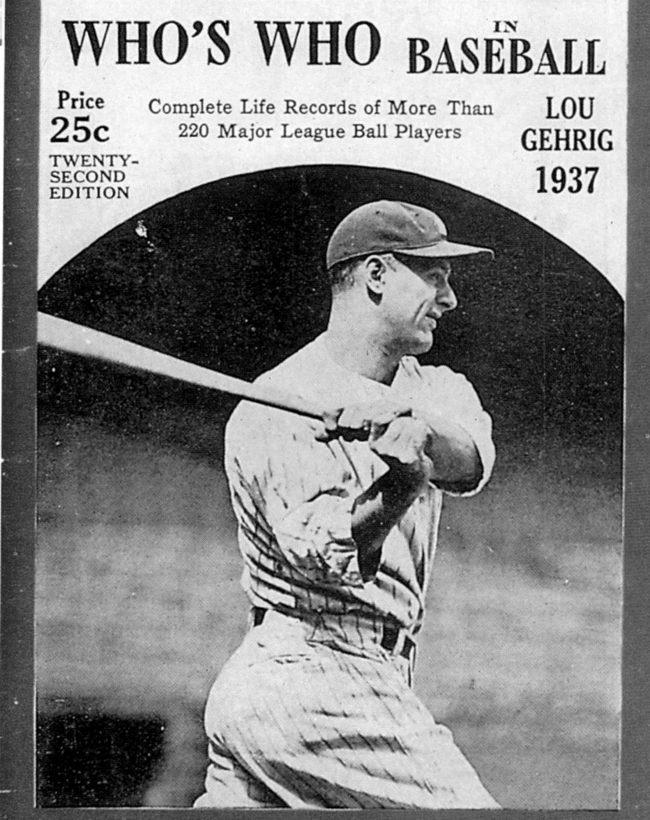

WHO'S WHO IN BASEBALL
Price
25c
TWENTY-SECOND EDITION
Complete Life Records of More Than 220 Major League Ball Players
LOU GEHRIG
1937
Copyrighted by the BASEBALL MAGAZINE CO., 1937

Throughout his career the Iron Horse was a regular cover boy on sporting publications.

As these two rotogravure spreads illustrate, Lou Gehrig was the key link between the Murderers Row teams of the 1920s and the Bronx Bombers of the 1930s.

Members of Lou Gehrig's Knot Hole League of America received free passes to ball games, an honorary Yankees contract, and this patch to proudly wear on their shirt or jacket.

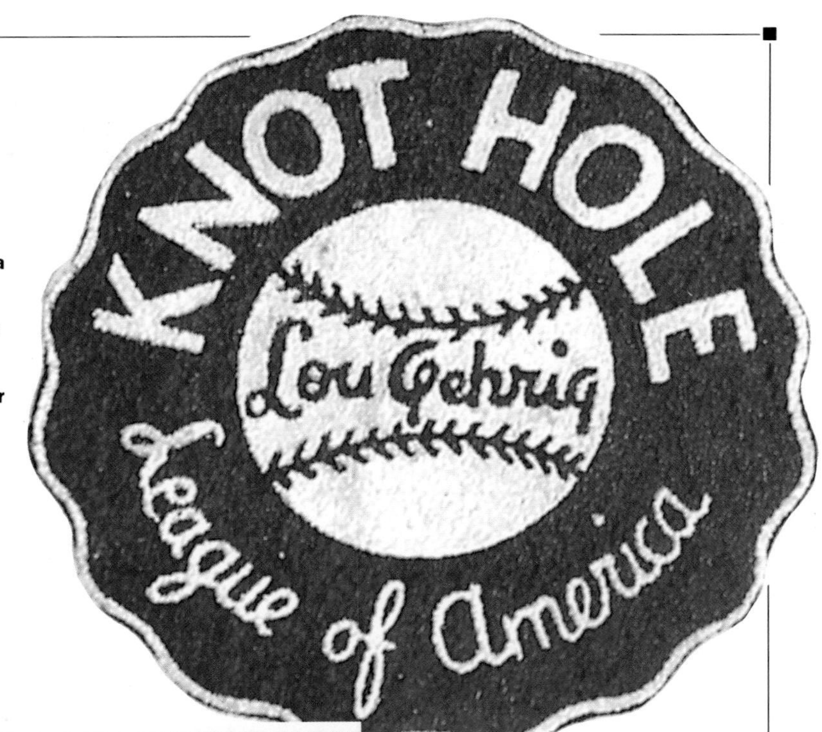

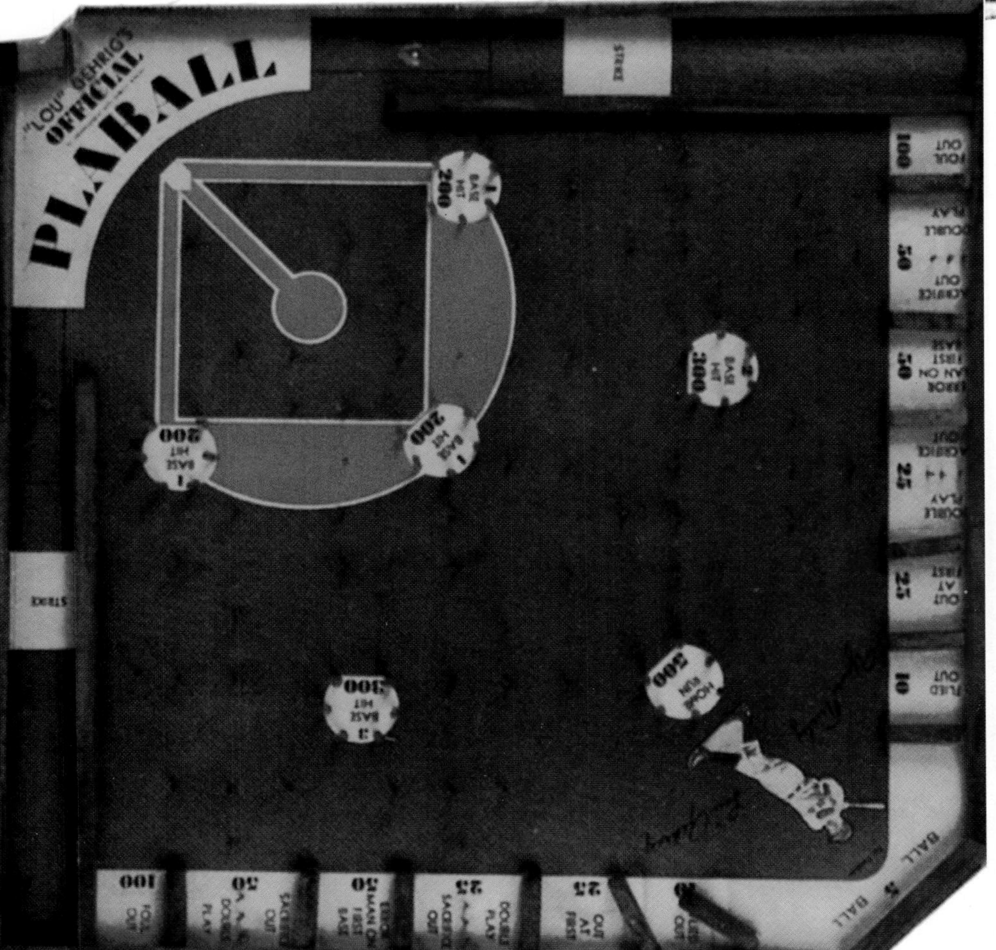

In the early thirties, the Rich Illinois Manufacturing Company of Morrison, Illinois, came out with Lou Gehrig's Official Playball board game.

In 1935 Fred Fisher, a well-known composer and close friend of the Gehrigs, published "I Can't Get to First Base With You," a song dedicated to "Lou Gehrig—Famous First Baseman."

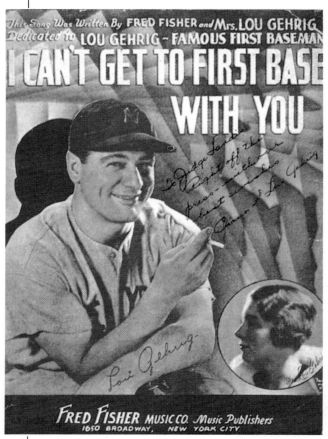

Posters from two movies closely associated with Lou Gehrig: *Rawhide*, the western he starred in, and *The Pride of the Yankees*, his life story.

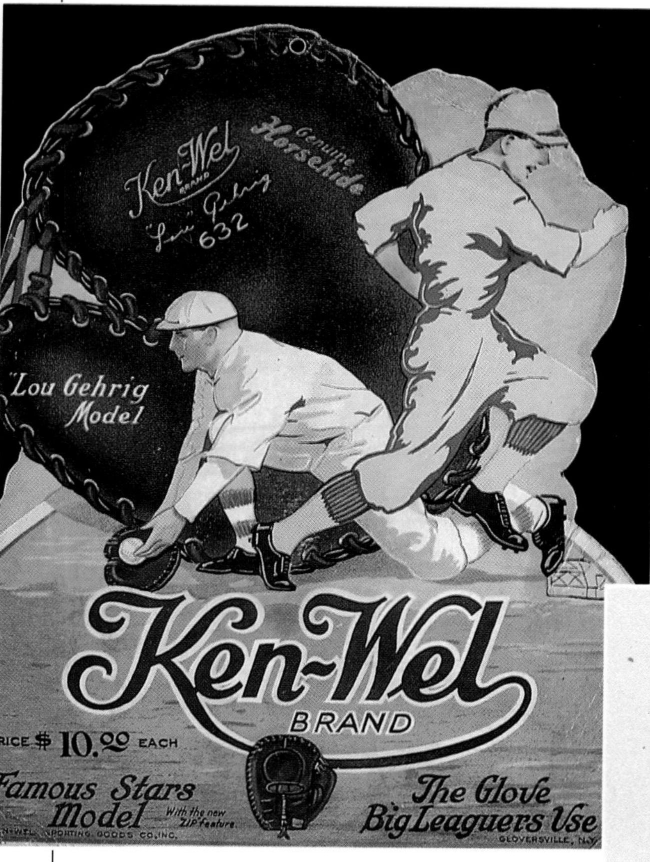

Lou was a spokesman for two brands he actually used: Ken-Wel gloves and Camel cigarettes.

***Lou Gehrig: Boy of the Sandlots*, published by Bobbs-Merrill in 1949, was one of several juvenile biographies to appear after the Iron Horse's death.**

A dozen years after he had played his last big-league game, Lou's distinctive face was still appearing on calendars.

In 1989, Lou Gehrig became the fourth ballplayer (Babe Ruth, Jackie Robinson, and Roberto Clemente were the others) to appear on a first-class stamp.

record, the Yankees won 73 times, the Athletics 59. (There was also a tie in 1927.) Westbrook Pegler described the frenzy accompanying one such contest when 85,265 people elbowed their way into Yankee Stadium for a late-season showdown:

> The crowd was so vast and so wild that the ball game had to be halted several times until the players, the umpires, and the house policemen cleared the ground of old straw hats and drifting papers.
>
> When all was over, the ground and the stands were covered with such debris that the cleaners were still at work loading the litter into hand trucks long after darkness had fallen.
>
> Police lines were set a quarter of a mile from the Yankee Stadium and perhaps 20,000 more customers were turned away after 1:30, half an hour before time of the first game.
>
> Automobiles were parked in solid acres on the regular parking spaces generally sufficient for the stadium trade and thousands more were drawn up in rows on one of the city's undeveloped playgrounds just north of the ballpark, where policemen and racketeers seemed to be partners in the parking business. They must have collected thousands of dollars, for the tariff was one dollar per car.

Murderers Row, 1931 style. From left: Gehrig, Combs, Lazzeri, and Ruth. The Yankees finished third, but scored a record 1,067 runs. Gehrig drove in 184 of them, still the American League standard.

Lyn Lary is the reason Gehrig didn't out-homer Ruth in 1931. The Yankees short-stop was on first with two outs when Lou drove the ball into the stands at Washington. The ball hit the seats so hard it ricocheted into the hands of the center fielder. Thinking it had been caught, Lary trotted into the dugout. Gehrig, running with his head down, was out for passing the runner and awarded a triple. The bonehead play cost Lou the home-run title outright, as he and Ruth wound up the season tied with 46 each.

No World Series games, not even the first ones in Washington, St. Louis, or Cincinnati, where the citizens achieved something rather distinguished in the way of frenzy, ever drew a more frantic crowd. The patrons were so eager to be on the scene that some of them lay flat on the concrete foot-ways leading from tier to tier of the grandstand and peered through gaps in the architecture.

The aisles and the catwalks overhead were packed solid with trade. People sat on the steps, perched or teetered in comfortless places on the railings, and even dangled in festoons from the beams. The roofs of apartment houses three furlongs away were fringed with optimists, and police-men were seen chasing hundreds off the fire escapes lest they tear down the walls with their weight.

The day was hot, dusty, and close, and the air outside the stands just before the game was thick with the fumes of automo-biles gnashing their fenders and bleating angrily in the traffic jams.

Featuring some of the biggest boppers in baseball history, these games were characterized by lots of scoring: on 35 occasions, one team or the other scored 10 or more runs. Overall, the Yankees averaged six runs a game, the Athletics five. But they also were very competitive affairs, with 31 of the 132 decisions determined by a single run and an additional 23 games set-tled by two runs.

Not surprisingly, many of the memories surrounding the rivalry involve home runs. There was the ball Jimmie Foxx drove into the deep-est part of Yankee Stadium's third deck. "It took 45 minutes to walk up there," joked the victim, Lefty Gomez. And then there was the laundry fluttering on the rooftops on Lehigh Avenue, across the street from Shibe Park's right-field wall. Babe Ruth would launch one, and it would bounce among the pillow cases and bed sheets hung out to dry.

Lou continued his custom of excelling in big games. During the height of the New York-Philadelphia rivalry, he led all Yankee hitters with a .353 average. And this against Grove, George Earnshaw, Rube Walberg, and Jack Quinn, all outstanding pitchers. On May 22, 1930, in the second game of a doubleheader at Shibe Park, Lou set a league record by knocking in eight runs in a 20-13 drubbing of the A's. That mark was later eclipsed by teammate Tony Lazzeri. But two years later, Shibe Park was the sight of Lou's greatest day in the majors.

On June 3, 1932, Lou stepped up to the plate in the first, fourth, and fifth innings and hit the ball over the right-field fence each time. All three home runs came off George Earnshaw, no soft touch. The big right-hander had averaged nearly 23 victories over the last three seasons and had tacked on another four World Series wins. But after Lou's third home run, Connie Mack pulled Earnshaw out of the game and replaced him with Leroy Mahaffey. As Mahaffey trudged out to the mound, Mack invited Earnshaw to sit on the bench next to him.

"Sit down here for a few minutes, son," the courtly 70-year-old patriarch in the stiff collar said. "I want you to see how Mahaffey does it. You've been pitching entirely wrong to Gehrig."

So Mack and Earnshaw watched intently as Mahaffey fed Lou a fast ball in the seventh inning. A split second later, they craned their necks and watched it sail over the left-field wall.

"I understand now, Mr. Mack," said Earnshaw. "Mahaffey made Lou change his direction."

Seventeen-year-old Jackie Mitchell, the first woman to ever sign a professional baseball contract, enjoyed a moment of glory in 1931 when she struck out Ruth and Gehrig in an exhibition game between the Yankees and the Double-A Chattanoooga Lookouts. Was it staged? Well, the game was a makeup of a rainout. It had originally been scheduled for April 1—April Fool's Day. In any event, Commissioner Landis, upset by the wide-spread newsreel coverage of Mitchell's outing, quickly declared her contract null and void.

Second baseman Tony "Poosh 'Em Up" Lazzeri got his nickname from a restaurant owner in Salt Lake City who stuffed the young minor leaguer with free dinners and urged him to "poosh 'em up," that is, hit. The pasta paid off. In 1925 the San Francisco strongman had 60 home runs and 222 RBI playing for his hometown in the Pacific Coast League. Lazzeri, actually a notorious clubhouse prankster, came across as quiet and uncommunicative as his partner on the right side of the infield. The reason was his epilepsy, which did not prevent him from averaging 96 RBI a season during his dozen years in New York. Lazzeri was one of several members of the '27 team to die young. When he was forty-two, he had a fit and took a fatal fall down a flight of stairs.

Incredibly, Lou stepped up in the ninth and just missed hitting a fifth home run. This time he drove an Eddie Rommel pitch to the deepest part of center field. Al Simmons ran to the wall and made a desperate last-second leap, snaring the ball before it went over.

Missing out on a fifth round-tripper was disappointing to Lou, especially when it was the hardest ball he had hit all day. Nonetheless, the Yankees had won, and his four blasts had tied a record set by two nineteenth-century players, Bobby Lowe of the Boston Beaneaters in 1894 and Ed Delahanty of the Philadelphia Phillies in 1896. Later, reporters informed Lou it also was the fourth time he had hit three or more home runs in a game, another record.

The odds of anything pushing Lou out of the spotlight on this particular day were infinitesimal. But sure enough, that afternoon in New York John McGraw announced to the press that, after thirty seasons as manager of the Giants, he was retiring. First baseman Bill Terry, Gehrig's counterpart at the Polo Grounds, would henceforth be player-manager.

At 59, McGraw was sour, sickly, and just two years away from the grave. He had complained long and hard about the kind of game Ruth's and Gehrig's fence-busting had wrought. "Nowadays," he moaned, "the game has become a case of burlesque slugging, with most of the players trying to hit home runs." It's tempting to suggest that his announcement was intended to overshadow Lou's moment in the sun, but he had actually made up his mind the day before. All the same, had Mugsy been looking to deliver one last back of the hand to demonstrate his distaste for the modern game, he couldn't have timed his announcement better. For the next several days, the story of McGraw's retirement and memories of his remarkable career dominated sports pages and radio programs.

New York baseball writers gather in St. Petersburg, Florida, in 1931 to cover spring training. Dan Daniel of the *World Telegram* (second from right, top row) and Frank Graham of the *Sun* (bottom row, second from right) were particularly fond of Gehrig. In 1933 Daniel informed Lou that he was closing in on the record for consecutive games played. Until then, neither Lou or anybody else had bothered to count.

Lou's salvo helped signal that the Yankees were back. By now the lineup had changed substantially from the Murderers Row days of just a few short years ago, though the runs still came in big chunks: 1,002 in 1932, the third straight season a thousand or more Yankees had crossed the plate. Ruth (.341, 41 home runs, 137 RBI), Gehrig (.349, 34, 151), Lazzeri (.300, 15, 113), and Combs (.321) were still raising havoc, but the left side of the infield had new faces in shortstop Frankie Crosetti and third baseman Joe Sewell. Speedy Ben Chapman (he would win three straight stolen base crowns between 1931 and 1933) was in left field, and

Another writer who grew close to Lou was Fred Lieb of the *New York Post*. After the 1931 season, Lieb (sitting fourth from left in the front row) organized an All Star team that traveled to Japan for a series of exhibition games. Lou, standing at right behind Mickey Cochrane and Frankie Frisch, had his hand broken by a pitch in the sixth game, forcing him to sit out the final eleven contests.

a rocklike receiver from Louisiana, Bill Dickey, was behind the plate. Although Herb Pennock and George Pipgras remained old reliables on the mound, the young arms of Lefty Gomez (24-7), Red Ruffing (18-7), and Johnny Allen (17-4) were most instrumental in the Yankees leading the league in ERA for the first time since 1927. With this blend of established and hungry young players, the Yankees won 107 games in 1932. The dethroned Athletics finished a distant second, 13 games back.

That year's World Series against the Chicago Cubs fairly bubbled with subplots. Yankees manager Joe McCarthy, who had taken over the team in 1931, was still bitter over his treatment by the Cubs. After leading Chicago to a pennant in 1929, he had been dismissed for finishing second in 1930. A win over his old team would make for sweet revenge.

And then there was the perceived ill-treatment of the Babe's old buddy, Mark Koenig. The ex-Yankees shortstop, who had spent the last two seasons in Detroit, was acquired in mid-August by the Cubs. Although he batted .353 and displayed a steady glove down the stretch, his new teammates voted him only a half share of the pennant and World Series money. This outraged Ruth, who called the Cubs a bunch of cheapskates. The Cubs responded in kind, the newspapers picked up the cudgel, and suddenly the war of words was on.

New York won the first two contests at Yankee Stadium easily, 12-6 and 5-2. Lou contributed five hits, including the games' only home run, while Ruth was held to a pair of singles. The lopsided results failed to quiet either side as the Series shifted to Wrigley Field for game three.

The air was blue with taunts and insults hours before game time. "I'd play for half my salary if I could hit in this dump all my life," Ruth yelled at the Cubs' bench after depositing nine balls into the stands during batting practice. Even Lou joined in the jockeying, which grew more vicious and profane once the game started.

In the top of the first inning, with Combs on second and Sewell on first, Ruth got around on one of Charlie Root's offerings and sent it soaring into the right-center-field bleachers. Two frames later, Lou lined a Root pitch into the same general area. The home runs only momentarily muzzled the Cubs, who battled back to a 4-4 tie by the time Ruth came to the plate in the fifth with one out and nobody on.

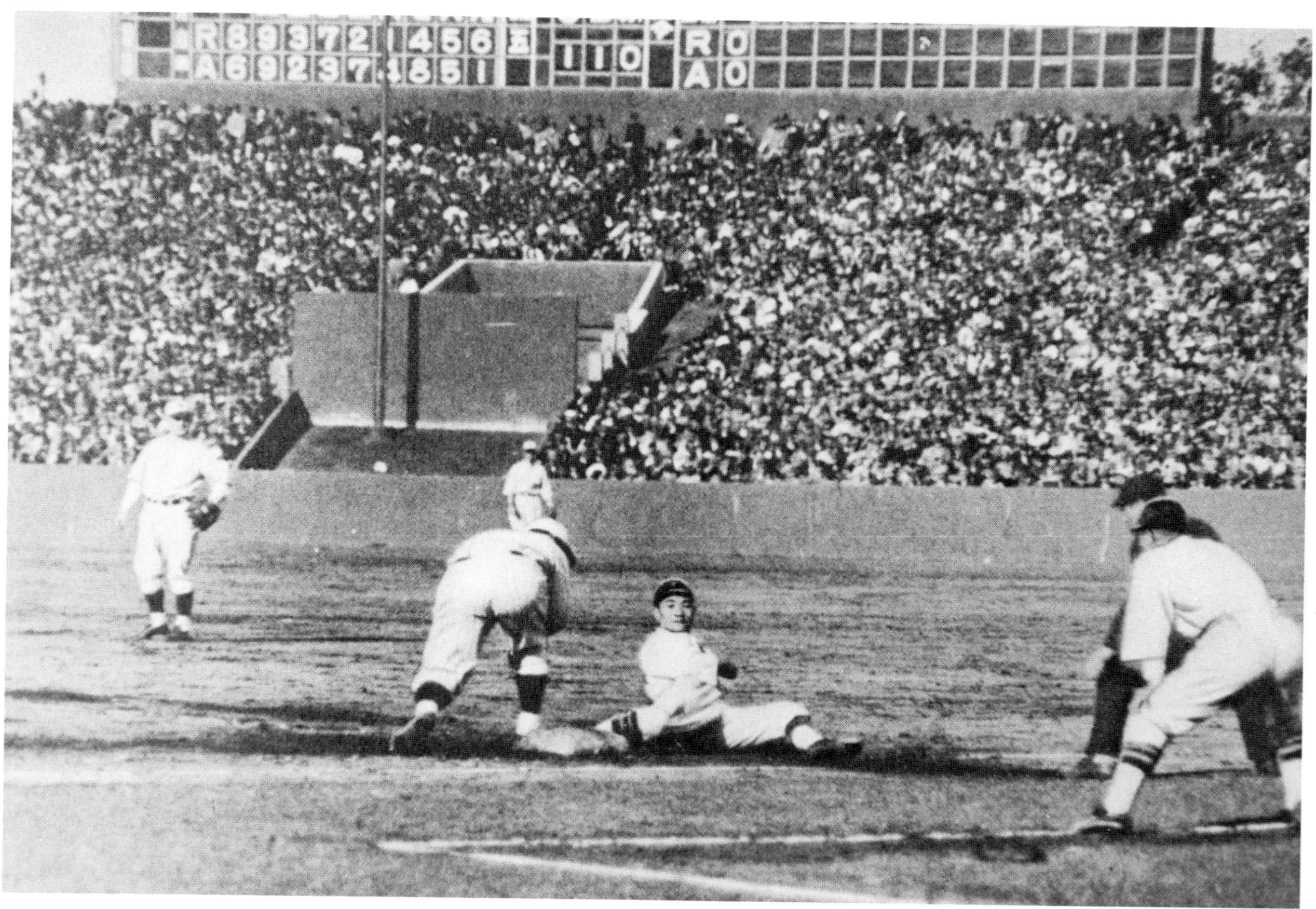

Lou takes a pickoff throw during the Japanese series as second baseman Frankie Frisch looks on.

Lemons and other debris littered the grass as Ruth and the Cubs jawed at each other between pitches. He took two strikes from Root, gesturing after each one. On Root's third delivery, a change-up, Babe uncoiled in that familiar corkscrew fashion and launched the ball far over the head of center fielder Johnny Moore—farther, in fact, that anybody had ever hit the ball at Wrigley Field. "Babe Ruth connects and here it goes!" Tom Manning of NBC Radio screamed into his mike. "And it's a home run! It's gone! Whoopee! Listen to that crowd!"

Clasping his hands like a victorious prizefighter and wearing a big grin, Ruth merrily circled the bases on his pipe stem legs. Lou greeted him at the plate.

The heart of the Athletics' lineup. From left: Jimmie Foxx, Mickey Cochrane, Al Simmons.

"You do the same thing," Babe said with a wink.

Predictably, Root's first pitch to Lou knocked him down. He got up, brushed himself off, stepped back into the box, and then blasted Root's next delivery into the temporary bleachers in right. It was his second homer of the game and the fourth that he and Ruth had hit off Root in the last hour of play. Pat Malone replaced the shell-shocked Cubs starter, but it made little difference. The Yankees won the game, 7-5, then closed out the Series with an 11-6 pounding the following afternoon.

Did Ruth call his shot? The answer will be debated until the sun grows cold. Some maintain that if Ruth had tried to show Root up by pointing to the seats, Root—an ornery ol' cuss—would have sailed the next pitch down Babe's ear canal. Others remain convinced that the game's ultimate showman actually produced what he advertised. Their position is backed by photographs and recently uncovered home movie footage that indeed show Ruth pointing at…well, something. But at what? The fence? The Cubs' bench? A hot dog vendor?

Babe Ruth crosses the plate at Shibe Park while Mickey Cochrane glares out at the mound. Runs were cheap in the Philadelphia-New York battles of the late twenties and early thirties.

Gehrig, who was on deck and thus had a ringside seat to what transpired, maintained it was Root's windpipe: "Babe was jawing with Root and what he said was, 'I'm going to knock the next pitch right down your god-damned throat.'" Gabby Hartnett, squatting behind the plate, said Babe had held up two fingers, indicating the number of strikes on him, and announced, "It only takes one to hit it."

Whatever the truth, by the following day stories about the incident began appearing in newspapers that—significantly—had originally ignored any mention of it.

Lefty Grove (left) and George Earnshaw combined for 146 victories during the Athletics' three pennant-winning seasons. In 1931 Grove went 31-4 and was not knocked out of the box until late August when Gehrig hit a grand slam off of him.

Frankie Crosetti, the only surviving Yankee regular from the '32 team, was there when the called shot happened. Or, more correctly, didn't happen, he says. Now retired in California, the old shortstop remembers that day and its aftermath as clearly as yesterday's dinner.

"Christ, I've been saying this for years, but nobody wants to believe me," he said. "They still say he pointed. They want to make a big story out of it. I guess they want to sell books. As far as I'm concerned, he did not point. When he had two strikes on him, he kind of stepped out of the box and he just raised one finger towards the Cubs' side, right in

Gehrig Ties All-Time Record With Four Straight Home Runs

EQUALS TWO MARKS IN 20 TO 13 VICTORY

Lou Ties Record of Four Circuit Drives in One Game as the Athletics Are Beaten.

DUPLICATES LOWE'S FEAT

He Connects in First Four Times at Bat and Nearly Makes Fifth in Ninth.

RUTH PRODUCES HIS 15TH

Total Base Marks Fall, With 50 for Yanks, 77 for Both Clubs—Victors Tie Team Homer Record.

By WILLIAM E. BRANDT.

Special to The New York Times.

PHILADELPHIA, June 3.—Henry Louis Gehrig's name today took rank in baseball's archives along with Bobby Lowe and Ed Delehanty, the only other sluggers who, in more than half a century of recorded diamond battles, ever hit four home runs in one major league game.

Largely because of Gehrig's quartet of tremendous smashes the Yankees outstripped the Athletics in a run-making marathon, winning, 20 to 13, after twice losing the lead because of determined rallies by the American League champions.

Homers by Combs, Lazzeri and Ruth, the latter the Babe's fifteenth of the season, enabled the Yankees to tie the all-time record of seven homers by one club in one game, performed three times before 1900, by Detroit, New York and Pittsburgh, of the old National League and once in modern times, by the Athletics on June 3, 1921.

Yankees Set Team Mark.

The Yanks, with their twenty-three hits, also set a new modern club-batting record for total bases, with fifty, which eclipsed the previous modern major league mark of forty-six and the American League's best total of forty-four. This achievement fell short by only five bases of the all-time record, set by Cincinnati in 1923. Both clubs' total of seventy-seven bases also set an American League mark.

Gehrig in his first four times at bat hammered the ball outside the playing area. In the first and fifth innings he sailed balls into the stands in left centre. In the fourth and seventh he fired over the right-field wall.

Saltzgaver was on base when Lou connected in the first inning, but the other three came with the bases empty. His fifth-inning homer, which made him the first man in baseball history ever to hit three homers in one game for the fourth time, came after Combs and Ruth had reached Earnshaw for drives over the right-field wall.

Lazzeri Clears Bases.

Lazzeri's drive into the left-field stands in the ninth, the last Yankee homer, came with the bases filled. In Philadelphia's half of the ninth Jimmy Foxx, the major league leader, sent his nineteenth homer of the year shooting into the left-field stands.

Cochrane had driven the ball over the right-field wall in the first inning, but the collective homer total, nine, fell one short of the major league record for both teams in a game.

The outcome of the game evened the series, two to two, but the crowd of 5,000 seemed to concentrate on encouraging Gehrig to hit a fifth homer and thus surpass a brilliant record in baseball's books.

Lou had two chances. He grounded out in the eighth, but in the ninth he pointed a terrific drive which Simmons captured only a few steps from the furthest corner of the park. A little variance in either side of its actual line of flight would have sent the ball over the fence or into the stands.

As it was, Lou's four homers tied the all-time record of Lowe in hitting for the circuit in four successive times at bat in 1894. Only three of Delehanty's were in successive times at bat. Both Lowe and Delehanty had a single in the same game with their four homers, so that Gehrig fell one short of tying their record for total bases.

Gehrig's four made his season's total eleven, six of which have been hit against Philadelphia, four off Earnshaw and two off Mahaffey.

The defeat of the Mackmen, coupled with the Indians' double victory, dropped the Athletics to fifth place, Cleveland supplanting them in fourth.

Lazzeri's homer with the bases filled was his fifth hit of the game. He and Gehrig each drove in six runs.

The box score:

Lou Gehrig

New York Times

Shibe Park, site of Lou's greatest day in the majors—four home runs in a single game. Not even Ruth had ever done that before.

John McGraw and Connie Mack play bottle caps. Gehrig's hard luck continued when McGraw picked the same day Lou hit four home runs in Philadelphia to announce his retirement as manager of the Giants.

front of his face. And of course, the Cubs' players were razzing him. So when he raised his finger he said something like, 'I've got one more strike left.' That's what he meant: he's got one more strike left."

According to Crosetti, Ruth almost immediately realized that there was no advantage to denying a story that gilded his legend.

"The next day the papers were writing that he had pointed and all that stuff. [Before game four] the players were talking about it in the dugout, what the newspapers had said about him. Well, I'm right there when I heard Babe say, 'If they want to think that I pointed, let them. I don't care.' I distinctly remember him saying that in the dugout with the players around."

Lost in all the hullabaloo was Lou's performance, perhaps the most sensational ever in a four-game Series. He'd hit .529 with three home runs and a double and scored or driven in 17 runs. "I didn't think anybody could be that good," marveled one Cub. In the wake of Babe's final and most memorable World Series home run, he may have been the only one to notice.

Gehrig, genuinely happy for his bash brother, never openly bemoaned his second-fiddle fate.

"I'm not a headline guy, and we might as well face it," he responded

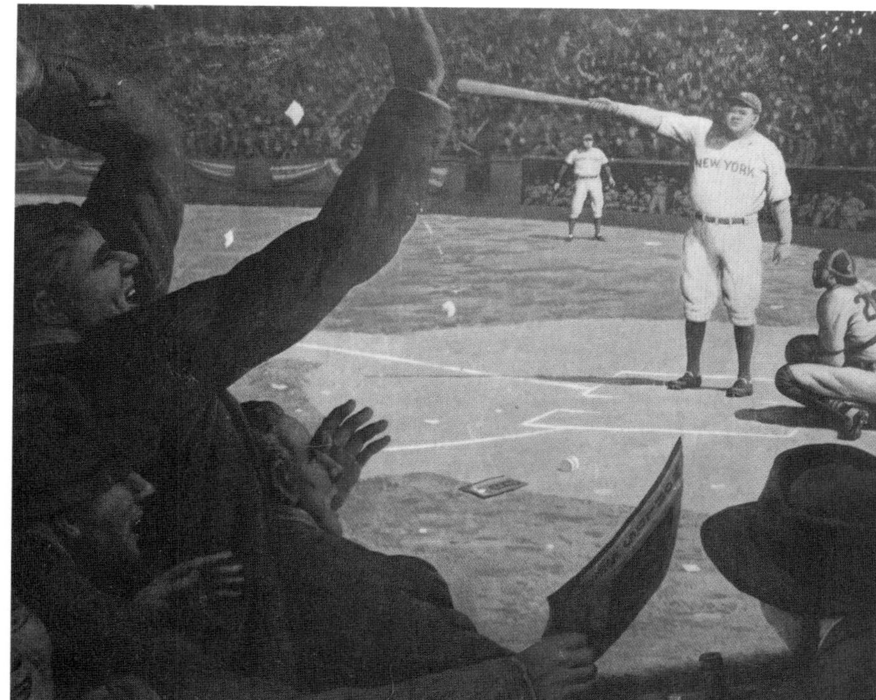

Did he or didn't he? This artist's rendition would have you believe that Babe Ruth actually did call his shot in the 1932 World Series. Whatever the truth, it's a fact that the Bambino banged Charlie Root's pitch into the center-field bleachers at Wrigley Field. Gehrig, greeting Ruth at the plate, followed with his own home run. But no one remembers that.

once when the topic came up. "I'm just a guy who's in there every day. The fellow who follows the Babe in the batting order. When Babe's turn at bat is over, whether he strikes out or belts a home run, the fans are still talking about him when I come up. If I stood on my head at the plate, nobody'd pay any attention."

This was actually changing. After the called shot, the trajectories of the home run twins would soon intersect. While Babe's Roman-candle career began its inevitable nosedive, Lou's star would continue to steadily climb ever higher.

CHAPTER Six

A NEW BEST GIRL

ELEANOR: I left some underthings on my chair and I can't seem to find them. Have you seen them?
MOM GEHRIG: I already washed them.
ELEANOR: Oh, thank you Mrs. Gehrig, but that really wasn't necessary. I can wash myself.
MOM GEHRIG: I wash every day. You do not.
ELEANOR: [Long pause] Boy, that roast beef was good. Sure wish I could cook as well as you do.
MOM GEHRIG: You live here when you get married and you do not have to cook.
ELEANOR: Thank you. But, uh, Lou and I really want our own apartment.
MOM GEHRIG: You do not wash. You do not cook. I know how to take good care of Lou and you do not. Better you should live here.
ELEANOR: You can't let go of him, can you? You just cannot let go of him!
MOM GEHRIG: Not . . . let go?
LOU: What's going on?
ELEANOR: I'm getting out of here!
MOM GEHRIG: Let her go! She's no good for you!
LOU: Quiet, Mom!

—A Love Affair: The Eleanor and Lou Gehrig Story

THE YANKEES' high spirits after their World Series sweep of the Cubs contrasted sharply with the suffocating despair wrought by the Great Depression. Hard times had fallen like an anvil on New York City, which in 1932 was home to one million jobless and a record number of business failures. This situation accounted for the elevators no longer running between the 42nd and 67th floors of the Empire State Building (there were no tenants) and the 20,000 empty seats for the opening game of the Series at Yankeee Stadium. Some desperate New Yorkers took to selling apples and shining shoes; in June the police counted nineteen shoeshine stands on one block alone. Others simply gave up; that year the city recorded its highest suicide rate in a quarter-century.

Pullman slashed the price of an upper berth by twenty percent, but road trips brought ballplayers no relief from the sea of blank and hungry faces. Half of Cleveland's work force was unemployed; in Detroit, the once-booming auto industry was down to just a quarter of its 1929 production. At the time of Babe Ruth's called shot at Wrigley Field, some 660,000 Chicagoans were out of work. The following spring, as Franklin D. Roosevelt took office in the White House and the Yankees trained in Florida for the 1933 season, nearly 13 million Americans—a quarter of the labor force—were desperately looking for any kind of job. "Steel, factories, railroads, newspapers, agriculture, baseball—we rode down together and we'll ride back together," Baseball Commissioner Judge Kenesaw Mountain Landis, said optimistically. His prediction ultimately proved correct, although the recovery wouldn't truly become complete until the Second World War cured the country's lingering economic woes.

Having suffered a forty-percent drop in attendance in just four sea-

Eleanor and Lou.

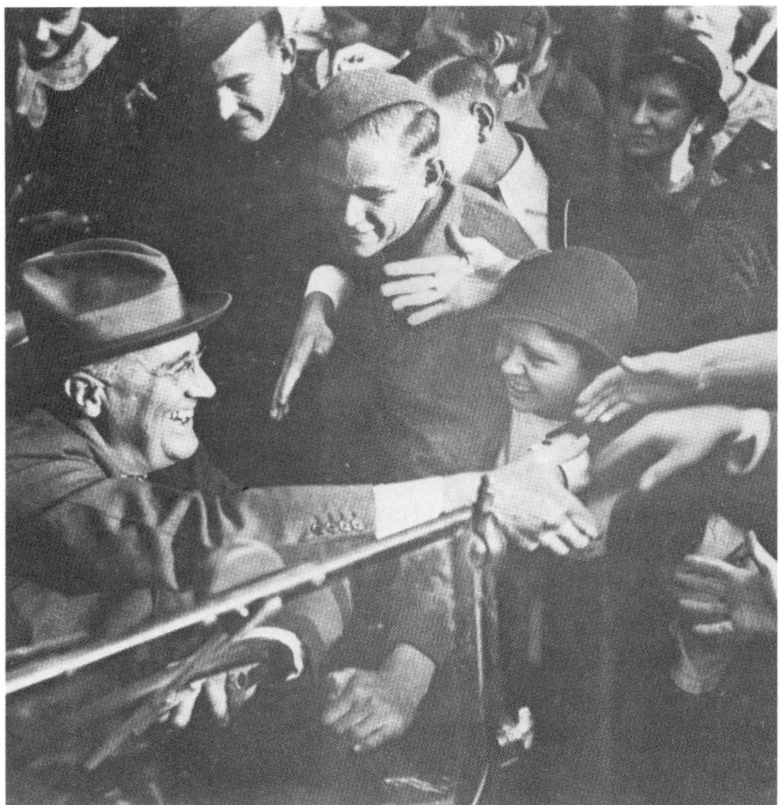

Signs of the times. In Detroit, an unemployed auto worker posted his predicament for the world to see, while in New York an enterprising victim of the Depression optimistically advertised three-cent "prosperity sandwiches." President Franklin D. Roosevelt, seen here shortly after taking office in 1933, often forgot his troubles inside the ballpark. " I am the kind of man who wants to get plenty of action for his money," said FDR, whose ideal game was "one that guarantees the fans a combined score of not less than 15 runs, divided about 8 to 7."

sons, baseball had no choice but to tighten its belt. Rosters were reduced from 25 to 23 men, playing managers were encouraged (thus eliminating one more paycheck), and pay cuts became a fact of life. The average salary of a big leaguer dropped from $7,500 in 1929 to $6,000 in 1933.

Ruth, his body slowing down just as the turnstiles stopped spinning, saw his salary reduced from $70,000 in 1932 to $52,000 in 1933. Babe's new wife (he had married Claire Hodgson in 1929 after his first wife

Giants first baseman Bill Terry (second from left) took over managerial duties from John McGraw in 1932 and led the team to a World Series win over Washington the following season. In an era of outstanding first basemen, Terry was the best fielder of the lot. He also hit a lot: .341 lifetime and a .401 mark in 1930, the last time any National Leaguer topped .400. Terry managed the Giants to two more pennants in 1936 and 1937, but each October they were routed by the Yankees.

Helen, from whom he had been estranged for years, died in a fire) had helped curtail his profligate ways through trust funds, investments, and a daily allowance. So, a subsequent pay cut to $35,000 for 1934 had negligible effect on his toned-down lifestyle. The pride of the man who had once left a hundred-dollar tip for a ham sandwich, however, was stung. Jacob Ruppert reminded his fading star that he remained the best-paid player in the game.

Gehrig, just a few years removed from his impoverished youth, had never gotten into the habit of spending money, even when times were fat. As a long trail of waitresses and parking lot attendants could attest, Lou could squeeze a nickel until the buffalo on it turned blue. His pay, which had been $25,000 since 1928, was cut to $23,000 for the 1933 and 1934 seasons. Unlike Ruth, he didn't squawk. With the average American worker earning a little less than $17 a week (when he worked), Lou considered himself a very fortunate fellow to be pulling down twenty-five times that amount for just playing a kids' game each afternoon. Every down-on-his-luck street-corner vendor he encountered made him that much more determined to keep a death grip on his job and the comfortable lifestyle he had created for himself and his parents.

In 1933, when Lou turned thirty, that lifestyle continued to revolve around the Gehrigs' white corner house in New Rochelle in Westchester County. He seemed contented there. "You know, guys," he had told reporters more than once over the years, "I don't really need much else. I get everything I want at home."

During the off-season and home stands, there often was a small riot inside: ballplayers, writers, a parrot, canaries, a couple of dogs and, of course, Mom and Pop, who typically conversed with visitors in English

Bam! Another Slam

Lou Gehrig's bases-loaded home run in a high school tournament game in Chicago foreshadowed a big-league specialty. During his career in pinstripes, the Iron Horse cracked 23 grand slams, easily the most in baseball history. Far behind are Willie McCovey (18), Jimmie Foxx and Ted Williams (17 each), Babe Ruth and Hank Aaron (16 each), and Gil Hodges (14). Lou also ranks high in bases-loaded triples, with six. Ahead of him are John Shano Collins (8) and Stan Musial (7). Collins, however, had but one grand-slam homer during his career, Musial nine.

Why so many slams and near-slams for Gehrig? An easy answer is that he simply concentrated harder when the sacks were full. But Gehrig, one of the most insecure sluggers ever to be enshrined at Cooperstown, *always* bore down. The heavy-hitting Yankees did give Lou more opportunities to bat with the bases loaded, but on the flip side, because Ruth batted ahead of Gehrig in the lineup, it may be that Babe's base-clearing blasts actually cost his slugging mate several chances.

The most likely explanation is luck, which has been defined as preparation meeting opportunity. In Lou's case, not only did serendipity present him with many chances to produce four runs with one swing of the bat, he had the superior ability to capitalize on those chances. The 23 times he came through in "grand" style are listed below.

Date	Opposing Team (Pitcher)	Inning	Final Score
	1925		
July 23	Washington (Fred Marberry)	1	NY, 11-7
	1927		
May 7	at Chicago (Ted Lyons)	9	NY, 8-0
July 4	Washington (Bobby Burke)	6	NY, 21-1
	1928		
May 11	Cleveland (Joe Schaute)	6	NY, 7-6
	1929		
September 10	Detroit (Phil Page)	1	NY, 10-9
September 18	Cleveland (Milt Shoffner)	7	NY, 12-2
	1930		
May 22	at Philadelphia (Bill Shores)	1	NY, 20-13
July 31	at Boston (Ed Durham)	7	NY, 14-13
	1931		
August 29	at Philadelphia (Lefty Grove)	6	PHI, 7-4
August 31	Washington (Lloyd Brown)	5	WAS, 6-5
September 1	Boston (Ed Morris)	3	NY, 5-1

	1932		
May 26	at Washington (Alvin Crowder)	6	NY, 5-0
September 9	at Detroit (Earl Whitehill)	3	DET, 14-13
	1934		
May 10	Chicago (Lee Stine)	5	NY, 13-3
May 13	Cleveland (Lloyd Brown)	1	NY, 8-0
June 10	Philadelphia (Bill Dietrich)	1	NY, 7-3
July 5	Washington (Wally Stewart)	3	NY, 8-3
	1935		
July 7	at Washington (Bobo Newsom)	5	NY, 11-1
August 21	at St. Louis (Jim Walkup)	3	NY, 14-2
	1936		
August 15	at Philadelphia (Randy Gumpert)	8	NY, 16-2
September 9	at Cleveland (Oral Hildebrand)	2	NY, 12-9
	1937		
August 31	at Cleveland (Mel Harder)	5	NY, 7-3
	1938		
August 20	at Philadelphia (Buck Ross)	1	NY, 11-3

while yelling at the pets in German. The commotion often carried over to the dinner table.

"Lots of times," said Lou, "I would have all my dinner finished before Mom and Pop started. They would argue about baseball instead of eating. Pop would say I should have done this, and Mom would come back by telling him I should have made the play some other way. I just listened to 'em argue about it."

Best of friends. From left: Bill Dickey, Lefty Gomez, and Lou.

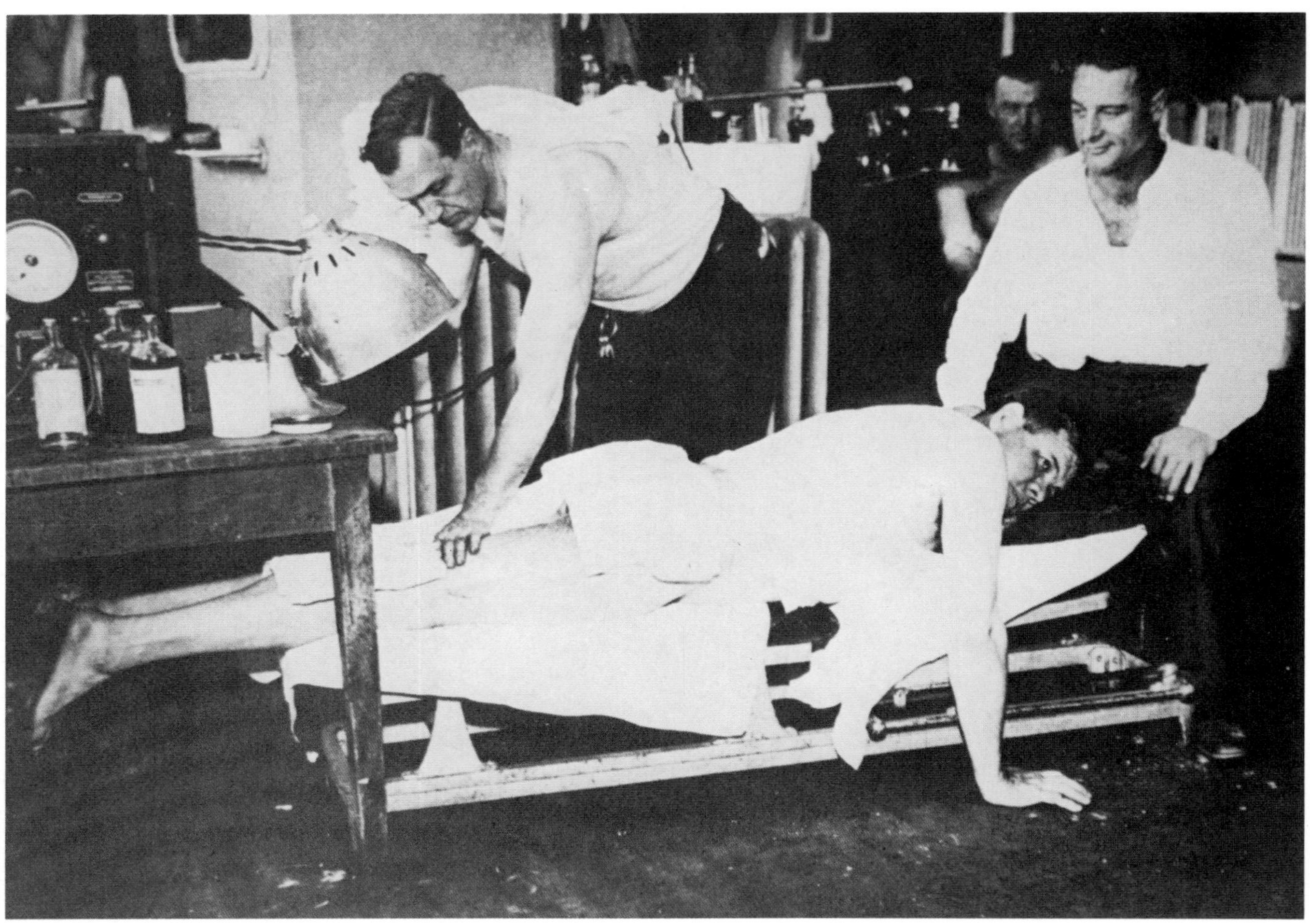

By 1932 Ruth was slowing down, his drop in production matched by a corresponding drop in salary. He desperately wanted to manage the Yankees. Jacob Ruppert fended off his overtures, saying, "How can you manage the Yankees when you can't even manage yourself?"

Now that Lou was entering his prime as a ballplayer and a breadwinner, he began to assert himself a bit more at home and inside the locker room, albeit in his same understated, natural way.

"Lou didn't want people fussing over him," recalled Frankie Crosetti, who joined the Yankees as a rookie shortstop in 1932. "He didn't like people who popped off or bragged. I think that's why he took a liking to me when I came up as a twenty-one-year-old kid. I was very quiet, you know. I never opened my mouth. Lou made me feel like I belonged. On game days he'd pick me up, take me down to the ballpark, and after the game he'd drop me off back at the hotel."

Lou literally made Crosetti feel at home. One day, when the rookie came down with a bad cold, Lou received Joe McCarthy's permission for both to leave an exhibition game early. Lou drove Crosetti to New Rochelle where Mom Gehrig fixed the boys a hearty meal and concocted her special cold remedy.

"After dinner she made me drink the tallest glass of hot red wine," Crosetti said. "The biggest goddamn glass you ever saw. I'd never heard of that before. But I drank it."

Mom tucked Crosetti into Lou's bed while Lou crashed on the couch. "I slept like a baby," remembered Crosetti. "And the next morning I was fit as a fiddle. That's the way he was. He was great. His folks were great."

Lou often called his mother his "best girl," a whimsical expression of endearment that he came to regret as he began contemplating settling down. Mom took a dim view of the girls Lou brought home to meet her and regularly voiced her objections about anyone her son was particularly sweet on. Frustrated, Lou nonetheless heeded his mother. In fact, when he joined Fred Lieb's exhibition tour of Japan in the fall of 1931, he returned home with a staggering amount of gifts for Mom—$7,200 worth of ivory, silk and Oriental jewelry. The tour had only paid him $5,000.

Joe McCarthy, hired to manage the Yankees in 1931, was a no-nonsense disciplinarian. "He was a tough guy but he really knew the game," said Lefty Gomez. "We went through a lot of schooling with him. He was always trying to be perfect in everything, on and off the field."

As a ballplayer, particularly one as handsome and well-known as Lou, "You always had your opportunities," reflected infielder Bill Werber, a Duke University graduate who played with and against the Yankees throughout the 1930s. "Lou was monogamous even as a single fellow. He didn't mess around. He and Bill Dickey roomed together, and Dickey was a pretty solid fellow."

Dickey, a strapping country boy born in Louisiana and raised in Arkansas, had solved the Yankees' catching problems practically from the moment he reported to the team at the end of the 1928 season. His seven World Series rings, eleven All Star game selections, .313 average over 16 seasons (including a high of .362 in 1936) and Hall of Fame plaque suggest those who called him history's best all-around catcher knew what they were talking about.

In Werber's opinion, "Bill Dickey really had more to do with the success of the Yankees of the thirties than anybody. He was the brains of the club. He was not a college-educated man, but he had a great deal of common sense. A very level headed fellow. The pitchers recognized this and they respected him. When Dickey called for a pitch, he expected the pitcher to throw it. If he didn't give his best effort, Bill would walk out halfway to the mound and throw the ball at him from 25 or 30 feet away. Knock his ass off right off the mound."

Dickey, already respected for his field leadership and his insistence on playing hurt, grew in his teammates' estimation in 1932 after he married Violet Arnold, a gorgeous blond chorus girl. Lou thought highly of the laconic backstop's blend of professional intensity and personal

Babe and family in 1929. From left: daughter Dorothy, wife Claire, and stepdaughter Julia.

integrity. Coupled with their common affection for bridge and fishing, it was almost inevitable that he and Dickey would quickly become best friends and roommates. Listening to Dickey talk of the joys of matrimony undoubtedly got Lou thinking in the same direction.

Another future Hall-of-Famer appeared on the scene about this time. Vernon "Lefty" Gomez, whose alternate nickname of "Goofy" neatly summed up his personality and philosophy of life, seemed on the surface to be an odd addition to Joe McCarthy's squad of no-nonsense warriors. The gangly, wisecracking, rubber-faced pitcher from Rodeo, California, never stopped putting the needle to his more serious-minded teammates. They, in turn, rarely missed a chance to rib him over the extraordinary size of his "slugger," which had almost cost him a job in the major leagues. Cy Slapnicka, the Cleveland scout who later signed Bob Feller, actually forfeited the Indians' option to buy Gomez from the San Francisco Seals after seeing him undressed in the clubhouse. "Anybody who's got as big a prick as he's got can't pitch winning ball in the major leagues," Slapnicka told several chagrined reporters.

Slapnicka's illogic cost Cleveland the services of the game's top left-hander of the thirties. Between 1930 and 1942, Gomez won 189 games for the Yankees, leading the American League in victories and ERA twice and strikeouts three times. He was a perfect 6-0 in World Series play and won three of the first five All Star games. Lou apparently saw something in Goofy's musings over the world's need for a revolving fishbowl ("for tired goldfish," he explained), because the two men became great friends.

"Best thing to happen to Gehrig was running around with Gomez," commented one Yankee. "Gomez could loosen anybody up. An odd couple? Absolutely. But Lou felt at ease with him. Who wouldn't? Gomez took the burden off everybody." Despite his zany reputation, Gomez's formula for success was anything but goofy: "clean living, a fast outfield—and that big fellow Gehrig at first base."

In 1933 that big fellow finally began to step out of Ruth's shadow. Although the Yankees finished second to Washington, Gehrig's numbers that season were once again of championship caliber. He finished third

Lou Gehrig and Eleanor Twitchell on their engagement day, August 16, 1933.

Lou and Eleanor, just moments after being married.

in home runs and batting, led in runs scored, and trailed only Philadelphia's Triple Crown winner, Jimmie Foxx, in slugging, total bases and RBI. And for the eighth consecutive season, he started every game of the schedule.

Opponents marveled over Gehrig's durability. "We used to try to step on his feet at first base and everything," said Elon "Chief" Hogsett, a submarining southpaw for the Tigers and Browns. "But he'd play with a broken thumb, broken fingers."

Lou's dedication was as much a product of his insecurity as anything else. Sit out a game and who knew what might happen? Lou couldn't help but be aware of the social turmoil swirling about him. In an era of universal labor unrest and massive unemployment, where the tricks of keeping a job ranged from dyeing one's hair to painting the foreman's garage, workers in all fields understood that life—and bosses—offered few guarantees.

The interesting thing about Lou's eventual 2,130-game playing streak is that the first two-thirds of it unfolded in absolute anonymity. No one in 1933 was calling him the Iron Horse. Midway through the season, Lou had played in nearly 1,300 straight games, an accomplishment that no one in that less record-fixated age was aware of until sportswriter Dan Daniel brought it to Lou's attention one morning at breakfast. Game number 1,000—a significant milestone and the kind of nice, round number that the press loves—had come and gone early in the 1931 season without a mention. Now, however, Lou stood on the threshold of breaking his one-time teammate Everett Scott's record of 1,307 consecutive games played.

The record fell with precious little fanfare at Sportsman's Park in St. Louis on August 17, 1933. After the first inning, time was called and American League president William Harridge presented Lou with a silver statuette at home plate. A couple of minutes later, the Yanks and Browns were back at it, St. Louis winning the game despite Lou's two hits.

At about this time, observers detected a frost forming over Ruth and Gehrig's friendship. The chill was evident even to a youngster named

Gehrig's Reported Annual Salary

Season	Salary	World Series Share
1923	$ 3,500*	
1924	3,000	
1925	3,750	
1926	6,500	$ 3,418
1927	7,500	5,592
1928	25,000	5,532
1929	25,000	
1930	25,000	
1931	25,000	
1932	25,000	5,232
1933	23,000	
1934	23,000	
1935	31,000	
1936	31,000	6,431
1937	36,750	6,471
1938	39,000	5,783
1939	36,000	5,542
Totals	$369,000	$44,001

* Includes $1,500 signing bonus

Lou and the man who controlled the purse strings, Jacob Ruppert.

The first All Star game was played July 6, 1933, at Chicago's Comiskey Park. Lineups were determined by a vote of the fans. Lou, who easily outpolled Jimmie Foxx, would be the starting first baseman six straight times through 1938, hitting home runs in the 1936 and 1937 contests.

Nobody could ever say that Babe Ruth didn't rise to the occasion. Who else but the aging Bambino would hit the first home run in All Star competition? And who else would be waiting to shake his hand at the plate but that other fellow in the lineup, Lou Gehrig?

Edwin Diamond. His father, Chicago sportswriter Louis Diamond, had taken him to the first All Star game a few weeks earlier at Comiskey Park. Wandering around the field collecting autographs prior to the game, Edwin was lucky enough to have his photograph taken with Gehrig (who had been overwhelmingly voted to the first of six consecutive All Star starts), Ruth, and Al Simmons. While it's possible to read too much into one photograph, Diamond believes that the two Yankees' body language speaks to their strained relationship at the time.

"Gehrig exuded absolute warmth and friendliness," said Diamond, today a New York-based journalist. "As you can see by the picture, he has his arm around me as I'm holding a ball. Ruth was kind of morose and standoffish. I can't remember if Lou or someone asked him to be in the photograph, but it's clear he doesn't want to be there. Of course, a nine-year-old boy doesn't know the meaning of the word 'morose.' But what I remember through the years, and what the picture shows, is Gehrig's warmth and charm, especially in relation to Ruth."

A culmination of factors was behind the breakup. In 1933 Ruth, eight years older than Lou, outhomered Gehrig, 34 to 32, but the overall quality of his game had slipped. Now thirty-eight years old, he found it hard to keep his weight down and his enthusiasm up. He frequently sat out the second game of doubleheaders and left other games early because of a variety of aches and pains. With Lou coming into his prime, Ruth couldn't help but envy his youth and his favored-son relationship with McCarthy.

Ruth barely spoke to McCarthy, whom he considered ill-equipped to manage a major-league ball club. After all, Babe argued time and again, McCarthy had never even played big-league ball. For several years Babe's contention had been that, because of his star quality, seniority, and knowledge of the game, he deserved a shot at managing the Yankees, especially after Bob Shawkey had proved a one-season bust after replacing Miller Huggins. But never for a single second did Jacob Ruppert and Ed Barrow consider Ruth. How could he manage the Yankees, they reasoned, when for years he had demonstrated to the world that he couldn't even manage himself?

Even Babe's teammates recognized this. "When I become manager," Ruth told Ben Chapman, a fast, young outfielder from Tennessee, "you won't be stealing bases at your discretion."

"When you become manager," replied Chapman, "send me to St. Louis."

Joseph Vincent McCarthy, a product of Philadelphia's sandlots, had spent almost twenty years playing and managing in the minors before finally getting his break as skipper of the 1926 Chicago Cubs. McCarthy

Eight-year-old Edwin Diamond at the 1933 All Star game with three of baseball's biggest stars: Ruth, Gehrig, and Al Simmons.

It seems only right that Detroit's Hall of Fame second baseman Charlie Gehringer (seen here with his mother) should immediately follow Lou Gehrig in the *Baseball Encyclopedia*. In addition to sharing the right side of the infield in six consecutive All Star game starts, the two were remarkably similar in tastes, temperament, and ability. Born just three weeks apart in 1903, each was celebrated for his quiet competitiveness, aboveboard morality, and popularity among opposing players and fans. Both abhorred hunting, loved ice skating, and were considered "frugal Germans" and momma's boys. They played against each other for sixteen years and, true to their character, hardly ever spoke a word to each other.

was a managerial success from the start, taking the Cubs from the basement to a pennant in just four seasons. He was an absolute nut about fundamentals, drilling ten-year veterans over and over again in the proper methods of bunting, turning the double play, and hitting the cutoff man. McCarthy valued tact, discipline, honest labor, and quiet professionalism above all else. For this reason he was drawn instantaneously to players like Gehrig, Dickey, and Crosetti.

McCarthy "couldn't stand shirts unbuttoned and hairy chests showing," said Lefty Gomez, whose 20-win seasons allowed him to remain one of the few wild cards in the Yankees' deck. "He could really get on you for an open shirt. 'You don't go in a bank and see people with shirts unbuttoned and hairy chests,' he would say. He thought playing for the Yankees called for being the same kind of gentleman who would work in a bank."

By the time McCarthy wrapped up his Hall of Fame career with the Red Sox in 1950, he would be responsible for eight more pennants and seven world championships, all with the Yankees. His career winning percentages in the regular season (.614) and postseason (.698) remain the highest of any manager. In 24 big-league seasons none of his teams ever finished out of the first division—a tribute to his philosophy of fielding ballplayers who were also good citizens.

Good citizens like Lou. "What a wonderful fellow that Gehrig was!" McCarthy reminisced in retirement. "Always hustled. Never gave a moment's trouble. Just went out every day and played his game and hit the ball." McCarthy's generous praise inspired Lou to strive ever harder to live up to expectations.

"Lou was a hell of a hustler," agreed Bill Werber, now retired and living in Florida. "I saw him make one play that remains with me to this day. I use it sometimes in talks to church groups and at athletic banquets as an example of a person giving more of himself than might be expected."

On this particular afternoon at Yankee Stadium, the batter lined the ball between Gehrig and the bag into the right-field corner. The runner on first tore around second and headed for third. "Ruth fielded the ball and threw it to Lazzeri, who relayed it to third," remembered Werber. "The ball scooted off to one side and I fully expected the runner to come on in. But Lou was there, backing up third!

"You know, when the ball was hit past him, he was out of the play. But he cut across the middle of the diamond and damned if he wasn't backing up the throw. That saved a run and was one of the greatest plays I ever saw. It's one of those instinctive but telling things. The great ballplayers have it."

Lou had always lapped up praise, but he was careful not to display a swelled head. Although he was by now an acknowledged superstar and one of the senior players on the team, he generally kept a low profile and kept his mouth shut.

"He probably figured there's no use trying to outmaneuver Ruth as far as publicity goes," said Detroit's own quiet wonder, Charlie

Lou slides into third base at Navin Field in 1934 while Marv Owen awaits the throw. The Tigers won the pennant that season and their first world championship the next, while the Yankees finished second each year.

Gehringer. "Whatever town the Yankees were in, all of their writers would flock to Ruth." By the early 1930s, "Gehrig was probably a better all-around player by far, but he'd get no special attention even though he'd hit just about as many home runs."

Lou, like McCarthy, was a stickler about presenting the proper public image, even on the long train trips between cities. This seemed a waste of effort since the traveling sportswriters were intimately aware of most players' peccadillos but rarely wrote about them.

Werber regularly played bridge with Gehrig, Ruth, and Dickey on the train during his two partial seasons (1930 and 1933) with New York.

"Babe would get out the cards," said Werber. "He was a good bridge player. Gehrig was too. Ruth carried a big glass with him and a fifth of Seagram's. He'd fill that glass right up to the top with whiskey. About eight inches, I'd judge. On top of that he'd pour a little water. He'd sip

The 1934 home run derby turned out to be no contest, as Lou slugged 49, en route to capturing batting's Triple Crown.

that for about two hours. Eventually it would make him merry and jocular, and he'd begin to give Gehrig bad bids to irritate him."

Lou, who limited himself to an occasional beer or glass of his mother's homemade elderberry wine, remained sober and unflappable, concentrating on his cards while Dickey kept score. Finally, said Werber, Ruth would "stick up his big middle finger and give Lou the raspberries. 'Well,' Lou'd say, 'figure up what we owe you. The bridge game's over.'"

On other occasions Ruth, corroded by jealousy and emboldened by alcohol, openly denounced McCarthy. On a train trip to St. Louis, Babe slammed down a poorly played hand. "Hey!" he bellowed in his bullhorn voice. "I butchered that one just like McCarthy handles the goddamn pitchers!"

Lou was furious at this breach of etiquette. Sitting in on the game were a pair of sportswriters, who were more shocked by Lou's response than by Ruth's outburst. His face growing dark, Lou folded his cards and told his one-time idol that he had a big mouth. A day later he was still brooding. Ruth, said Lou, "pops off too damn much about a lot of things."

One of those things was Mom Gehrig's alleged insult of Ruth's young daughter, Dorothy, who visited the Gehrigs' house one day dressed in some rather nondescript clothes. Mom, who didn't care for Babe's second wife, Claire, thought the former show girl favored her own daughter Julia over her stepdaughter.

"Why doesn't Claire dress Dorothy as properly as she dresses Julia?" she asked. The remark got back to Claire, who in turn told Babe. He, in turn, informed Lou in the clubhouse that Mom should "mind her own goddamned business!"

Ruth, of all people, should have known that his sensitive and protective teammate would never tolerate such an attack on his mother. Babe's moral outrages typically lasted all of ten seconds, but those ten seconds were enough to earn Lou's eternal emnity. Ruth should have considered himself lucky that he didn't get a punch in the nose as well.

But even as one of Lou's longest lasting personal relationships was deteriorating, a new one was rapidly blossoming into the most meaningful of his life. In 1928 he had been introduced before a game at Comiskey Park to a slightly untamed young woman named Eleanor Twitchell. Lou took notice of her brown hair and eyes, upturned nose, and oval face, but seemed disinterested. He tugged on the bill of his cap, mumbled "Nice to meet you, ma'am," then disappeared into the dugout.

Three years later, however, they met again at a party. This time, Eleanor recalled, "I was alone, but not for long. The 'shy one' suddenly became the bold one, singled me out, and spent the whole time giving me a shy man's version of the rush."

Eleanor, two years younger than Lou, had grown up during the heyday of Al Capone's Chicago. In fact, she had once been poker partners with the wife of underworld boss Johnny Torrio, who was driven from power (and back to Italy) at the point of a

Lou's number at the Polo Grounds was held by Mel Ott, who broke into John McGraw's outfield when he was only seventeen. Between 1926 and 1942 the Giants' number 4 was number one in homers six times; on another occasion Philadelphia pitchers intentionally walked him five times—once with the bases loaded—to prevent him from tying Chuck Klein on the final day of the season. Weighing only 165 pounds, Ott utilized a distinctive leg kick to loft two-thirds of his career 511 homers over the Polo Grounds' 256-foot fence.

Mickey Cochrane was sold to Detroit in the winter of 1933 and drove a perennial second-division club to pennants his first two seasons behind the wheel. His 1934 stats weren't much—.320 with two home runs—but his field leadership earned the fiery backstop the Most Valuable Player Award the same year Gehrig won the Triple Crown.

tommy gun. In an era where young women delighted in offending their mothers' Victorian sensibilities, Eleanor smoked cigarettes, wore short dresses, painted her face, drank bootleg gin, danced the Charleston and Black Bottom, and dabbled in Mah-Jongg, crossword puzzles, and the other escapist fads of the day. However, she was far from the empty-headed flapper she sometimes appeared to be. She loved books and the opera, shot a mean round of golf, and was a very capable horsewoman. By the time of her second meeting with Lou, a mild heart condition had convinced her to slow down her pace. Like many young single ladies trying to ride out the depression, she was actively looking around for the ideal husband, all the while keeping several less desirable candidates on a string.

That night Lou mustered enough courage to ask if he could walk her home. She said yes, but was disappointed when he abruptly left her at her apartment door with a simple "good night."

A week later a package arrived for Eleanor, who had spent the interval idly wondering if she had "lost the zip on my fastball." She hadn't. Inside was a diamond cut-crystal necklace that Lou had just brought home from his exhibition trip to Japan. Lou, Eleanor marveled, "was breaking more records for restrained behavior: taking the girl home, not even working up a good-night kiss, and a week later sending her jewels."

The relationship percolated over the next couple of years. They exchanged notes, met for dinner when the Yankees were in town, and talked long-distance on the phone. Exactly who proposed to who was never sorted out. But by the time Lou was gathering acclaim for overhauling Everett Scott as baseball's new iron man, he and Eleanor were making wedding plans.

Mom was far from happy. An undomesticated society girl for her beloved Louie? Eleanor might as well have been a piano player in a brothel. She couldn't cook, couldn't wash, couldn't take care of her son like he needed to be taken care of. A trip to the Windy City to meet her prospective daughter-in-law was a complete disaster. Mom returned to the family fortress in New Rochelle and, like some matronly senator passing judgement in the Roman Coliseum, turned her thumb down. This time, however, Lou wiggled out from under it.

"Mom is the most wonderful woman in the world," he told Fred Lieb. "She broke up some of my earlier romances, and she isn't going to break up this one."

It wasn't for lack of trying. Eleanor, who had been working as a secretary for Chicago's "Century of Progress" centennial exposition, gave notice in September 1933 and moved in with the Gehrigs while she and Lou shopped for an apartment. Mom Gehrig "betrayed an awkward,

As noted in this Stookie Allen cartoon, by the end of the 1934 season, the Iron Horse had played in 1,504 consecutive games.

Gehrig, Jimmie Foxx, and Earl Averill watch Babe take his cuts at Meiji Shrine Stadium in Tokyo during their 1934 exhibition tour of Japan. The Americans played—and won—17 games in 12 cities.

even blundering resentment at every step," Eleanor revealed forty years later in her colorful memoir, *My Luke and I:*

> We are talking about a formidable person when we're talking about Lou's mother, not just a mild irritant to a spoiled girl who had led a carefree life until running into the Gehrigs' iron fence. Formidable, built something like a lady wrestler, with yellowish gray hair snatched back in a bun. No hairdresser for her, certainly no makeup. Not that it would have mattered anyway, since she was in a state of steaming perpetual motion, no idle hands, chores around the clock. A huge breakfast to be prepared for her husband and son, then an attack on the sinkful of dishes, then an almost compulsive session with the vegetables and meat for the night's dinner.
>
> Finally, she would jam a hat on her head and leave for Yankee Stadium *with* Lou, in time for batting practice. Afterwards, back in the kitchen while Pop walked the dogs again and the parrot kept shouting baseball lingo until he was covered for the night. And at last the evening meal, starting with caviar on toast, thick soup, a Caesar salad, meat, potatoes, the vegetables, oversized dessert, the whole works....
>
> After dinner and the dishes, we would settle in the living room. Mom would grab either the crochet or knitting bag and get her fingers flying, uttering sage little philosophies like "what goes up must come down," and Pop would invariably nod in agreement. Sometimes a glint would creep into her steel-blue eyes, and I'd swear she was figuring out how to "acquire" me as a part-time maid and full-time playmate for her son.

Eighteen-year-old Eiji Sawamura became a national hero when he struck out Gehrig, Foxx, Ruth, and Gehringer in a 1-0 loss to the American All Stars. Ten years later the college pitcher was lost on a troopship torpedoed by a U.S. submarine.

The old-fashioned triangle between Eleanor, Lou and Mom reached its apex of acrimony after a wedding date was set. "I'm not going to be there!" Mom insisted. Lou, who had no doubt that she meant it, asked Fred Lieb to intercede.

The ceremony was to take place on Long Island on September 29, 1933, after Lou had played the first couple of innings of that afternoon's scheduled contest with Washington. A few days before the wedding, Mom was in her regular seat at Yankee Stadium when Lieb approached her. "Mom," he said, "Lou would like me to bring you to the wedding on Long Island."

"I have absolutely no intention of going," responded Mom, who then knocked the sportswriter back on his heels with an especially vicious personal attack on Eleanor. Then, two days before the wedding, she and Eleanor had an ugly argument over drapes that left "the other woman" threatening to call off the wedding. Mom seemed to be on the verge of pulling out a last-licks victory.

Lou had had enough. On the morning of September 29, he phoned the mayor of New Rochelle, a chubby middle-aged lawyer named Walter G. C. Otto. Eleanor had found a fourth-floor apartment at 5 Circuit Road, which she and Lou were busily preparing to move into. Soon the mayor, accompanied by a posse of motorcycle cops, arrived on the scene. As carpenters, carpet installers, and the plumber respectfully doffed their caps and held their tools silent, Mayor Otto pronounced Lou and Eleanor husband and wife. Then the motorcycle caravan, sirens wailing, whisked Lou to the ballpark. It wouldn't do for the Iron Horse's playing streak to be interrupted by something as relatively innocuous as a wedding.

Unlike many ballplayers, Lou rarely played golf, believing it would mess up his baseball swing. One day, however, while following Babe Ruth and Grantland Rice around a course, he picked up Ruth's midiron. "He took a smooth easy swing and hit a perfect shot some 200 yards," recalled Rice. "I couldn't get him to hit another."

The following day Eleanor's aunt hosted a small reception at her Long Island home. Fred Lieb stopped by, Mom Gehrig in tow. To everyone's surprise and relief, she behaved. "See, I acted like a good girl," she proudly told Lieb on the way back home. "I didn't raise any hell, did I?"

There's something to be said about the matrimonial bed. The following year, as the Yankees battled Detroit for the flag, Lou enjoyed one of his greatest seasons. On June 25 against the White Sox, he became the fourth Yankee to hit for the cycle. (He would repeat the feat three years later against St. Louis.) On July 5, he cracked his fourth grand slam of the season, establishing a new club record. In all, he sent 49 balls flying over the fence, a leading major-league number that represented a personal best. With Ruth hitting but 22 round-trippers in his final season in New York, it also marked the first and only time Buster outhomered Babe in the same season.

Lou also led the circuit in hitting (.363) and runs batted in (165),

One of Lou's favorite pastimes was fishing, a hobby he shared with Eleanor and several close friends including Bill Dickey and Fred Fisher. He was particularly fond of jellied butterfish and often spread newspapers on the living room floor and gobbled up clams as if they were popcorn.

making him the first Yankee to win batting's Triple Crown. Eleanor couldn't help rubbing it in. "You know how managers are afraid of too many brides on the club," she gleefully said. "Young husbands usually have off seasons. Well, I guess Lou's Ellie didn't hurt his ball playing any in our first year of married life."

In 1934, a Triple Crown season was not nearly the rarity it was to become after the Second World War. In fact, Jimmie Foxx and the Phillies' Chuck Klein had both turned the trick the previous year.

A *New York Sun* photographer took a picture of Frank Graham Jr. wearing the cap of his favorite ballplayer. "He gave me the cap," the sportswriter's son recalled, "which I found to my chagrin was too small for me. I suppose he was a bullet head, whereas I was a round head."

Although Lou was the *Sporting News*'s choice as most valuable player, he finished no better than fifth in the baseball writers' voting for their more prestigious MVP award. Catcher-manager Mickey Cochrane earned the laurels instead for leading the Tigers to an unexpected pennant.

After the season Gehrig joined Foxx, Cochrane, and Ruth on Connie Mack's squad of All Stars for an exhibition series in Japan. It was on this trip that Lou's estrangement with Ruth took on a sordid overtone.

On the boat ride over, Babe and Claire Ruth initially avoided Lou and Eleanor as best they could. "The Ruths don't ever speak to the Gehrigs anymore," little Julia Ruth told a friend on the voyage. Finally, one day Eleanor passed by Claire, and they exchanged hellos. Claire then invited Eleanor back to the Ruths' cabin, where Eleanor discovered Babe "sitting like a Buddha figure, cross-legged and surrounded by an empire of caviar and champagne."

There are conflicting stories regarding what happened next. Some say Claire, Babe, and Eleanor got innocently bombed on champagne; others say that at some point Babe and Eleanor not-so-innocently wound up under the sheets. What is certain is that Eleanor was out of Lou's sight for two hours, cause enough to have her worried husband launch a stem-to-stern search that had some crew members postulating that she might have somehow fallen overboard. "I'd been 'overboard' all right," recalled Eleanor, "but the one place Lou had never thought to check out was Babe Ruth's cabin."

Ice skating was Lou's favorite off-season conditioner. One observer noted that his powerful legs rivaled those of any speed skater.

After Eleanor was found to be safe, Lou gave her the silent treatment. As they dressed for dinner, Babe suddenly appeared in the doorway, his arms opened wide in a jovial gesture of friendship. Lou may have had in mind an incident that occurred a few years earlier when Ruth reportedly stole a girl that he had been smitten with. While Lou, in his usual aw-shucks fashion, had probably still been working up the nerve to ask her out, Ruth had used his fame and charm to casually bed her. At any rate, Lou would have nothing to do with Ruth's overture. He turned his back on him and continued to dress in silence until Babe finally left the cabin—and, in effect, Lou's life.

Did the lusty Babe and adventurous Eleanor, their judgment addled by alcohol, sleep together? It seems highly unlikely, although gossip hinting that they had circulated for many years afterwards. Lou evidently didn't believe it—he wouldn't have stayed married if he had—but its salacious nature embarrassed him and destroyed any faint hope of reconciliation between him and Ruth.

"They were never friends again," said Bill Dickey. "You know that famous picture of Babe hugging Lou when Lou had that retirement ceremony at the stadium in 1939? Well, Babe put his arms around Lou and hugged him but, if you look close, Lou never put his arm around the Babe. Lou just never forgave him."

CHAPTER Seven

UTTERLY DEPENDABLE

G is for Gehrig,
The Pride of the Stadium;
His record pure gold,
His courage, pure radium.

—Ogden Nash, *Line-up for Yesterday*

IN 1927, even after clouting 47 home runs and driving in 175 runs, the American League's most valuable player found it impossible to shuck his perpetual supporting role to Babe Ruth. Franklin P. Adams, the newspaperman whose verse saved Joe Tinker, Johnny Evers, and Frank Chance from obscurity, had fun with Lou's relative anonymity. "Gehrig," he said, "was the guy who hit all those home runs the year that Ruth broke the record."

Seven years later, however, Gehrig could finally be described as the guy who hit all those home runs...period. For when he and Eleanor returned from their trip to the Orient (which they had extended to include a tour of Egypt and Europe), they discovered that the Yankees had given Babe his unconditional release. Lou's porcine, sullen, forty-year-old teammate was free to strike his own deal, which he promptly did with the Boston Braves. The Braves were as pathetic as Ruth proved to be. After hitting .181 in 28 games, Ruth quit. Despite all he had done for the game, he would never realize his dream of managing a major-league team. And after 1935, he would rarely attend a game at Yankee Stadium.

From strictly an entertainment standpoint, this was a shame, for the last half of the decade belonged to Lou and the Yankees. After three straight second-place finishes from 1933 to 1935, the Yankees would become the first team ever to win four straight world championships. Along the way, the newly christened "Bronx Bombers" would introduce a slew of new heroes including a tall, quiet, handsome twenty-one-year-old Italian from San Francisco who had torn up the Pacific Coast League.

Joseph Paul DiMaggio, said Lefty Gomez, "became a big star almost as soon as he joined the Yankees. The man I felt sorry for was Lou

Lou's homer helped Monte Pearson to a World Series win over the Giants in 1936.

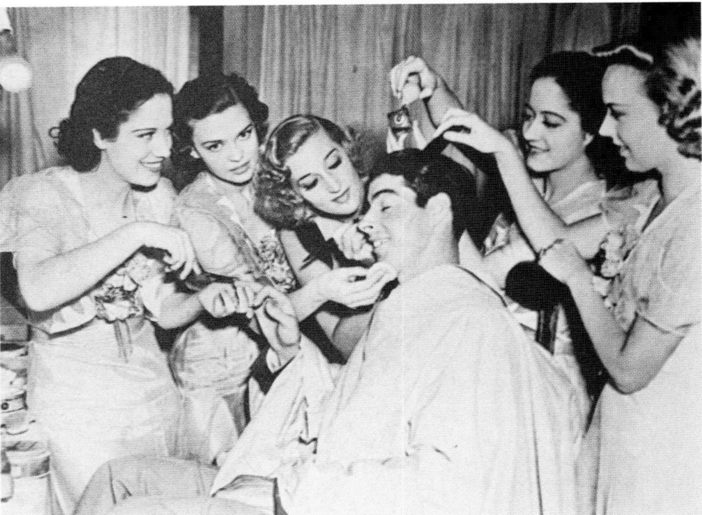

After only one season out of Ruth's shadow, Lou was gently pushed aside by the more graceful, but equally taciturn, Joe DiMaggio. The rookie center fielder, despite attempts to glamorize his image in the 1937 movie ***Manhattan Merry-Go-Round***, valued his privacy even more than Gehrig.

Gehrig. He had always played behind Ruth, and finally Ruth quit, and he had it all to himself in 1935. Now in '36 Joe comes along. Lou had another big year, but Joe was the rookie sensation so he got all the attention."

With his gleaming black hair and dark pinstriped suits, DiMaggio (who pronounced his name *DiMah-zhee-o*) was a study in elegance. Long before he married the world's most glamorous woman, Marilyn Monroe, this quiet son of a fisherman was recognized as being someone whose class, ability, and style set him apart. "Joe never could have played in Brooklyn," a writer once noted. "He's too perfect."

During his career, the Yankee Clipper would win three Most Valuable Player Awards and be named to thirteen All Star squads in 13 years. In the clubhouse he was taciturn and withdrawn. Having been teased as a child for his imperfect English, he had long ago dispensed with the notion of small talk being necessary to a full and happy life. Instead he filled his time drinking cup after cup of black coffee and chain-smoking cigarettes, which made his effortless grace on the diamond all the more remarkable. He didn't run as much as glide across center field, chasing down fly balls with an impossibly small glove. And his batting stance—feet planted wide apart and his bat held straight up and motionless—was classic in its composition. His flowing swing produced a .325 lifetime batting average (including two batting titles), 361 home runs, and a record 56-game hitting streak. He quickly supplanted Gehrig as New York's favorite immigrant son.

"The relationship between Joe and Lou was very good," said Gomez. "They never had a cross word that I know of. They were both quiet fellows, and they got along. But it just seemed a shame that Lou never got the attention he deserved. He didn't seem to care, but maybe he did."

A lesser man might have resented DiMaggio. Early in the 1936 campaign, veteran umpire George Moriarty, unimpressed by Joe's advance billing, called two questionable pitches strikes. When DiMaggio glanced back, Moriarty snarled, "Turn around."

"Leave the kid alone, George," Lou yelled from the on-deck circle. "If you call 'em right, he won't have to turn around."

"When you're a rookie, you never forget that," remembered DiMaggio, who went on to bat .323 with 29 homers and 125 RBI for the season. He followed that up with a big-league best of 46 home runs and 167 RBI in 1937.

Lou lights up—a habit he tried to hide from members of Lou Gehrig's Knot Hole League of America.

Lou also enjoyed solid back-to-back seasons. In 1936, the *Sporting News* named him most valuable player (his fourth and final MVP award) on the strength of his .354 batting average, 49 home runs (tops in the majors), and 152 RBI. He easily outdistanced everybody in both leagues in slugging (.696) and runs (167). The following year he was third in the American League in batting (.351), home runs (37), runs (138), RBI (159), slugging, and total bases. He also received the ultimate sign of respect from pitchers, leading the majors in walks both seasons.

With DiMaggio batting third and Gehrig fourth, the Yankees rolled over the New York Giants in a pair of Subway Series.

It didn't appear to be easy at first, however. Carl Hubbell, the Giants' 26-game winner and National League MVP, pitched a seven-hit gem in the 1936 Series opener at the Polo Grounds, which the Giants won, 6-1. With Hubbell masterfully blending his storied screwballs with curves and change-ups, the Giants did not record a single fly ball out.

"Our philosophy in those days was to try to hold the opponent's big guy to singles," explained catcher Harry Danning, the Giants' signal caller for ten seasons. "We figured, you can't get him out, he's gonna hit .350 no matter where you pitch him. And if he comes up at a time where he can beat you, then you walk him.

"When we played in the Polo Grounds, we always tried to make the batter hit the ball on the ground or in the big part of the outfield. Sometimes you could do that by throwing sinkers, and sometimes you could do that by letting off a fastball a little bit. You know, make the batter hold up his swing a little bit. Then he'd hit it to center field."

Danning, who has a photograph of himself watching Lou Gehrig cross home plate after hitting a home run off the Giants, can only laugh at the strategy. "That was our philosophy. But it didn't work too well with that Yankee team. They creamed us."

The Yankees had too many big guys, a point they drove home with an 18-4 pasting in the second game. They won the third game, too, but had to face Hubbell again in the fourth.

Not everybody was enchanted with the image of the Yankees captain. "He was too cheap, that's what it was," Roger "Doc" Cramer recalled in his old age. "And he was self-centered. He'd have a beer and drink with you, if you bought it. Otherwise, he wasn't buying you one." The crusty Cramer, who broke his collarbone diving for a Gehrig line drive in 1932, was not universally loved in his day.

The Ultimate Road Warrior

Most ballplayers perform better in front of the home folks than they do on the road. A variety of factors are involved, but the most obvious is the benefit of eating, sleeping, and playing in familiar surroundings. Lou Gehrig, who was devoted to his parents, was a "home boy" sixty years before the term became popular. The combination of home cooking and Yankee Stadium's inviting right-field fence would naturally lead one to assume that Lou performed much better in New York than on the road.

Not so. Historians can't speak about the effect of Mom Gehrig's pickled eels on her son's batting performance. But statistical analysis reveals that Yankee Stadium, long considered friendly to left-handed hitters, actually hurt Lou more than it helped him. Lou didn't pull the ball as much as his partner, Babe Ruth; consequently, a fair share of his line drives died in the Death Valley expanses of center and left field. On the road, however, where Lou generally encountered parks with shorter power alleys, these same drives often wound up against or over the fence.

Pete Palmer, the guru of home/away baseball statistics, argues that Lou would have been better off playing half the season at any other American League park except Washington's. Lou's comparatively low lifetime batting and slugging averages at Yankee Stadium (.329 and .620, respectively), while obviously still respectable, bear this out. By comparison, Gehrig hit an aggregate .351 inside foreign parks and slugged the ball at a .644 pace. He hit .381 at Detroit's Navin Field and .380 at Chicago's Comiskey Park. He also smashed 52 home runs at Sportsman's Park in St. Louis. These figures only hint at the devastation he wrought away from New York.

No player in baseball history has ever made himself so much at home on the road. In 1930 Gehrig accumulated 26 doubles, 27 home runs, and an amazing 117 RBI in 78 away games—a full season's work for mere mortals. The ribbies remain the standard for road performers and are more than any big leaguer has ever compiled in a single home season. Gehrig also owns the next best road marks: 98 RBI in 1927 and again in 1931. The 1927 season saw Lou set several other still-standing road records: most doubles (36), most total bases (247, which he tied in 1930), highest slugging average (.805), and most extra-base hits (69). In 1931 he established another record by getting on base 186 times in 77 away contests.

The following charts list Gehrig's lifetime batting performance at home and away against each of the other seven American League teams, as well as his combined home/road totals against each team. The numbers underscore a great irony: baseball's ultimate home boy was also its greatest road warrior.

At Yankee Stadium

Club	Games	AB	R	H	BA	2B	3B	HR	RBI	SA	BB	SO
Boston	153	547	137	199	.364	32	8	40	155	.671	93	50
Chicago	153	567	133	180	.317	34	11	40	149	.628	87	38
Cleveland	151	553	119	172	.311	19	11	39	113	.597	92	56
Detroit	158	541	127	172	.318	25	12	32	117	.586	121	49
Philadelphia	156	537	127	178	.331	29	11	34	142	.616	112	70
St. Louis	155	568	140	199	.350	37	17	40	149	.687	110	48
Washington	155	551 1	08	177	.321	27	13	26	130	.559	105	65
Totals	1080	3861	882	1269	.329	206	83	251	947	.620	713	376

On the Road

Club	Games	AB	R	H	BA	2B	3B	HR	RBI	SA	BB	SO
Boston	159	601	143	205	.341	50	14	30	161	.621	116	63
Chicago	151	595	149	226	.380	50	11	37	154	.687	111	47
Cleveland	154	603	143	199	.330	50	15	34	152	.632	94	69
Detroit	155	583	143	222	.381	65	13	22	149	.650	119	55
Philadelphia	150	583	137	195	.334	37	11	45	151	.667	101	73
St. Louis	156	576	153	207	.359	37	6	52	157	.715	140	48
Washington	158	596	129	190	.319	42	10	22	116	.534	107	58
Totals	1084	4140	1006	1452	.351	329	79	242	1043	.644	795	413

Combined

Club	Games	AB	R	H	BA	2B	3B	HR	RBI	SA	BB	SO
Boston	312	1148	280	404	.352	82	22	70	316	.645	209	113
Chicago	304	1162	282	406	.349	84	22	77	303	.658	198	85
Cleveland	305	1156	262	371	.321	69	26	73	265	.615	186	125
Detroit	313	1124	270	394	.351	90	25	54	266	.619	240	104
Philadelphia	306	1120	264	373	.333	66	22	79	293	.643	213	240
St. Louis	311	1144	293	406	.355	74	23	92	306	.701	250	96
Washington	313	1147	237	367	.320	69	23	48	246	.546	212	123
Totals	2164	8001	1888	2721	.340	534	163	493	1990	.632	1508	789

A record Series crowd of 66,669 packed Yankee Stadium for the contest, which would either tie the Series or give the Yankees an insurmountable edge of three to one. Going into the game Hubbell had won 17 consecutive times: 16 regular season victories plus the Series opener. He seemed unbeatable.

Under blue skies, the Yankees struck for a run in the bottom of the second, then opened up a two-run cushion the following frame when Red Rolfe singled in Crosetti. DiMaggio fouled out, bringing Lou to the plate.

Unfortunately for the Giants, who celebrated pennants in 1936 and 1937, they fielded only one famous slugger. The Yankees fielded several and thus won the battle of New York both Octobers.

Larrupin' Lou, the Bronx Buckaroo

Lou Gehrig a major motion picture star? On the surface, the idea seems preposterous, although Hollywood studios never gave up trying to make cinematic heroes out of such popular star athletes as Babe Ruth, Red Grange, Tom Harmon, and Joe DiMaggio. Once in a while they struck pay dirt, as in the case of Johnny Mack Brown, who scored the winning touchdown for Alabama in the 1926 Rose Bowl and then went on to a long career in westerns.

The Yankees' first sacker lacked Brown's natural charm and screen presence. But in the late 1930s, the heyday of low-budget B-westerns, Larrupin' Lou's quiet masculinity and instant name recognition were enough for Twentieth Century-Fox to put him in front of the cameras for a starring role in a sagebrush saga called *Rawhide*. While he received a good bit of teasing about it, his performance in the 1938 release was judged by some to be surprisingly good.

In a way, the role was a natural. Lou had been a sucker for horse operas ever since he was a boy. In fact, the archetype for the shoot-'em-up genre was filmed the same year he was born and not far from his birthplace. In 1903 the Edison Company produced *The Great Train Robbery* near Passaic, New Jersey. It was a runaway success. A flood of one- and two-reelers followed, reflecting the country's fascination with a part of its history that had recently ended and had since been romanticized practically beyond recognition. As a kid, Lou was captivated by the escapades of Tom Mix, Bronco Billy Anderson, Ken Maynard, Bob Steele, Buck Jones, Hoot Gibson, and William S. Hart. For the most part, these men of the frontier were the strong, silent type—necessarily so, since talkies were still years off.

With the advent of sound, the singing cowboy soon became the rage of the 1930s. Technically speaking, Gene Autry wasn't the first singing cowboy; Ken Maynard was. But his success at Republic Pictures inspired a small army of yodeling, guitar-toting balladeers, most notably Roy Rogers (actually Leonard Slye from Cincinnati) and Woodrow Maurice "Tex" Ritter. Even John "Duke" Wayne (born Marion Morrison) tried warbling on screen.

Mass-produced westerns, while immensely popular, were considered low-brow entertainment and usually consigned to neighborhood movie houses, not the ornate palaces where the prestigious A-films were booked. That didn't stop Lou from frequenting them when he could. To prevent a scene, he would park his car a block down from the theatre, then enter just as the lights fell and the movie began. Sitting in the dark in the back row, the Iron Horse could avoid recognition by noisy fans and lose himself in such formulaic fare as *Brothers of the West*, a 1937 release starring Tom Tyler. In dialogue typical of most westerns, Tom is alerted to the presence of approaching villains by his most trusted companion.

"Wait a minute!" Tom warns the heroine. "There's someone out there spying on us. That was my horse . . . he always tips me off!"

Westerns were produced in conveyor-like fashion. Bill Kennedy, a former clubhouse boy for the Cleveland Indians in the early 1920s, appeared in more than forty of them.

"In those days, when you tried to get a job in a western, you'd be asked three questions. Number one: 'Can you ride a horse?' You have to be able to do your own fast mounts. They made those movies so fast—six, seven days—they didn't tolerate any mistakes. You've got to make your mount and get the hell out of town, you know, with the posse following. You can't make a mistake because it'll throw them back.

Lou and co-star Smith Ballew.

"Number two: 'Can you do your own fight scenes?' You had to do your own fight scenes because it saved them the cost of a stunt man.

"Then finally: 'Can you act?' That was third."

During his career Kennedy was punched out by Gene Autry, rode with the Cisco Kid, and shot a blind man in *Silver City Bonanza.* In that movie, Kennedy was paid $400 each for a couple of dogfight scenes, but only $350 for his acting. "That should have told me something," he said.

Making the grade wasn't quite as rigorous if you possessed musical talent or a famous name, which is how Smith Ballew and Lou Gehrig came to team up in *Rawhide.* Ballew was hired by Twentieth Century-Fox in 1936 because of his background as a singer and orchestra leader and his resemblance to Paramount's star, Gary Cooper. Thanks to such forgettable works as *Hawaiian Buckaroo,* where between songs Ballew saves a cattle ranch in Hawaii, his western career was short-lived. But director Ray Taylor thought veteran writer Dan Jarrett's screenplay for *Rawhide* was a suitable vehicle to showcase Ballew's vocal talents, especially with the captain of the New York Yankees sharing the screen.

Lou, meanwhile, owed his presence in Hollywood to his tireless agent, Christy Walsh, who had first gained notoriety as Babe Ruth's ghostwriter and agent. Walsh and Lou had been friends for many years, and the agent had a genuine interest in seeing Lou capitalize on his fame. But with Walsh, commerce often clashed with good taste.

Proof of that was Lou's initial foray into the entertainment field in 1936. Walsh floated the rumor that his client might be right for the movie role of Tarzan, which Johnny Weissmuller—winner of three Olympic gold medals in swimming—had been handling since 1931. Walsh had publicity stills of Lou taken in a leopard-skin loincloth, including one where he was menacingly brandishing a giant papier-mâché club like the clean-up hitter on some neanderthal nine. The shots, circulated to newspapers throughout the country, were so out of character for the normally reserved Gehrig that even Joe DiMaggio had to smile. Finally the would-be king of the jungle said, "The hell with this Tarzan stuff!"

Not one to be put off by ridicule, especially when it wasn't directed at him, Walsh helped arrange a one-picture contract with Sol Lesser of Principal Productions in March 1937. Lou underwent a series of screen tests, then traveled to California after that year's World Series to film the sixty-minute production.

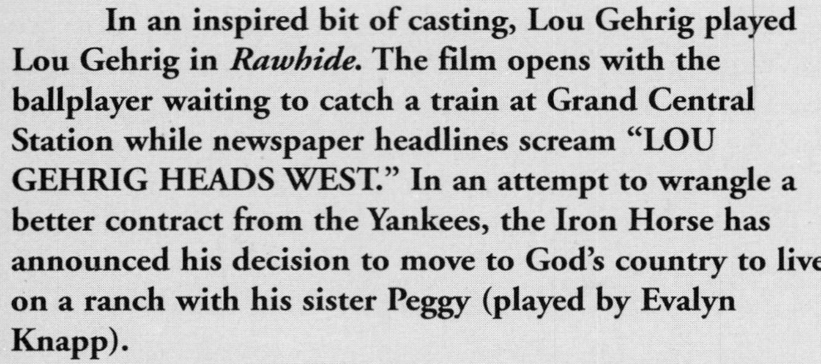

Before he began work on *Rawhide*, Lou had never been on a horse before in his life (although he had worn cowboy duds as part of his and Babe Ruth's "World Series Rodeo" barnstorming tour at the end of the 1928 season). But by the end of three days, Lou had mastered the art of the giddap on Snookie, a mild-mannered pinto the studio had provided him as a mount. To make it appear that Larrupin' Lou was galloping faster than he was, the film was speeded up in the projection room.

In an inspired bit of casting, Lou Gehrig played Lou Gehrig in *Rawhide*. The film opens with the ballplayer waiting to catch a train at Grand Central Station while newspaper headlines scream "LOU GEHRIG HEADS WEST." In an attempt to wrangle a better contract from the Yankees, the Iron Horse has announced his decision to move to God's country to live on a ranch with his sister Peggy (played by Evalyn Knapp).

"I'm gonna wallow in peace and quiet for the rest of my life," he tells reporters, one of whom has handed Lou a cowboy hat as a farewell gift. "I'm gonna hang up my spikes for a swell old pair of carpet slippers."

But varmints quickly appear on the horizon, forcing Lou to team up with a singing lawyer named Larry Kimball (Smith Ballew). As promos for the movie breathlessly described: "Batting against bullets . . . the 'Iron Man' of baseball becomes the West's man of steel and helps your favorite singing cowboy ride the rustlers off the range!" Lou's throwing and batting talents are displayed. During a knockdown, drag-out fight in a pool hall, he skillfully bounces billiard balls off the noggins of several bad guys. He also prevents a rancher from signing over the deed to his property by batting a ball through a window.

And Lou is given a chance to warble a few notes: "I traded [my bats] for riding boots and seven-gallon hats. I played the major leagues for years with versatility. I seldom missed the flies I chased, but now the flies chase me . . . ."

The final scene has Lou receiving a telegram from the ball club. To the relief of Lou (and more than a few reviewers), he doesn't have to quit his day job. "Your terms acceptable," the message reads. "Report at once for spring training."

When Lou did, in March 1938, he was surrounded by reporters and players who wanted to hear of his exploits in Tinseltown. Was it true that he had sent Eleanor, who was waiting back home in New York, a nightshirt with several actresses' autographs scribbled across it? (No, it most certainly wasn't true. Christy Walsh had done it without Lou's knowledge.) And had he kissed his horse? "That's my own affair," Lou joked back. Teammate George Selkirk commandeered a mule and, with two wooden guns and a clothesline for a lasso, galloped around the infield.

The world premiere of *Rawhide* was held in St. Petersburg, allowing the Yankees and their spring-training partners, the St. Louis Cardinals, to join in the fun. Mayor Al Lang and New York owner Jacob Ruppert led a parade down Main Street, which included baseball clown

Al Schacht, Pepper Martin's "Musical Mudcats," and a local high school band. The mayor had Lou imprint his foot in a square of wet cement, after which he stood in the theatre lobby and greeted several "distinguished guests"—the local chamber of commerce.

Reviews varied. Bland Johaneson of the *New York Daily Mirror* concluded that "He was no mushy actor . . . in fact, he's no actor at all." The Cardinals' resident critic, Dizzy Dean, weighed in with his opinion. "Cowboys an' hosses? Well, that Gehrig don't look like no cowboy to me. I guess he must be one of the hosses in this flicker."

Lou brushed aside all speculation that he might trade in his spikes for spurs. "I have been told by my motion-picture connections that I could quit baseball and make a go of it on the screen," he said. "It's fun to make a movie. But it's greater fun to hit a ball out of the stadium."

Lou got smacked around in a barroom scene from *Rawhide*. But as always, the good guys ultimately won.

An early death prevented Larrupin' Lou from climbing back into the saddle again. But could the city kid from New York have become a major western star? At least one authority on the subject, Don Miller, thinks the answer is yes. Lou "took to the open range like the Yankee Stadium infield," he observed. "Had he remained in films . . . Gehrig boded fair to become a threat to John Wayne, whom he resembled."

A straight-arrow kind of guy, Lou certainly appreciated the lack of ambiguity between the good guys and the bad guys. Like the Duke, Gehrig publicly embodied the "cowboy code" that at least two cinematic cowboys, Gene Autry and the Lone Ranger, openly espoused. In fact, when Autry outlined his Cowboy's Ten Commandments (similar to the boy scout's oath), they could have passed for Lou's own personal moral code:

Never take unfair advantage, not even of an enemy. Always tell the truth, and be gentle with children, the elderly, and animals. Be tolerant of other races and creeds. Help people in distress, work hard, and keep yourself pure in thought, speech, action, and personal habits. Respect your parents, all women, and the laws of your country. Do not drink or smoke. (One out of two wasn't bad for Lou, who had a three-pack-a-day habit.) And finally, remember that a cowboy is always a patriot.

Western movies started to fade in popularity after the Second World War. But then they gained new life with the advent of television, whose airings of old B-movie favorites recharged the genre and inspired scores of original weekly shows: *Gunsmoke, Wagon Train, Cheyenne, The Lone Ranger, Wanted: Dead or Alive, Bonanza,* and *Have Gun, Will Travel.* One of the best carried the name of Lou's horse opera. *Rawhide*, featuring squinty-eyed Clint Eastwood as cowhand Rowdy Yates, first galloped into America's living rooms in January 1959 on CBS and lasted seven seasons in prime time. One of the worst appropriated Lou's nickname. *The Iron Horse* debuted one Monday night in September 1966. The hour-long western starred Dale Robertson as a devil-may-care type who wins a railroad in a poker game. Unfortunately for the ABC network, the show didn't have its namesake's endurance. Fifteen months after it first aired, poor ratings derailed *The Iron Horse.*

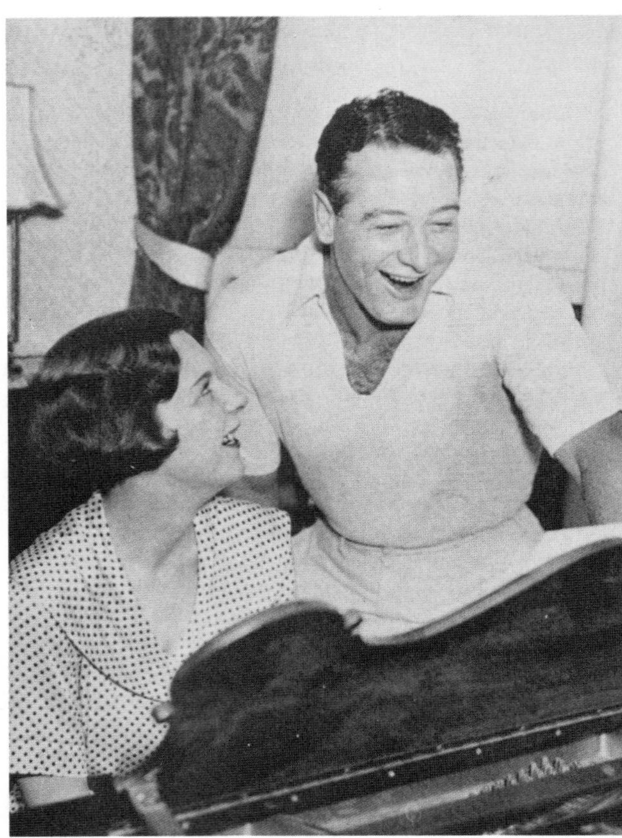

Flippant and adventurous, Eleanor Gehrig was able to coax her husband out of his shell during their eight years of marriage. "He was so totally straight," she said, "and I was the dash of spice in his life."

Prior to the Series, Hubbell and Gehrig had shared the cover of *Time* magazine, which suggested the two rivals were on equal footing. In Lou's mind, they weren't. Hubbell's knee-high screwballs frustrated him, as they did most batters. In the 1934 All Star game, Lou had been one of the five consecutive batters "King Carl" had struck out in succession, a spell of brilliance that has grown in the game's folklore. Lou would do little better in two World Series, touching the left-handed Hubbell for just two hits in a dozen times at bat. He would strike out four times, ground out four times, pop up once, and fly out once.

But even when he was held to a .167 average by a pitcher, Lou could be dangerous. He proved it now, as he awaited a full-count delivery. Hubbell spun a curve ball—high and inside—and Lou smashed it into the right-field bleachers for a two-run homer and an insurmountable 4-0 lead. The Yankees went on to win the game and the Series.

Of all Lou's thrills in baseball, his home run off Hubbell ranked as the best, he claimed. "He was all pitcher. If he had stopped us that day, with that incredible pitch of his, he would have been very tough in a seventh game. I've had thrills galore. But I don't think any of them top that one."

The following October was practically a repeat, the Yankees beating the Giants in five games. Hubbell recorded the Giants' only win, despite a ninth-inning solo home run by Lou—his second and final hit off the master screwballer in two World Series. The RBI was his 34th in post-season competition, allowing him to pass Ruth as the all-time run producer. Although no one knew it at the time, Lou's tenth Series home run would be his last.

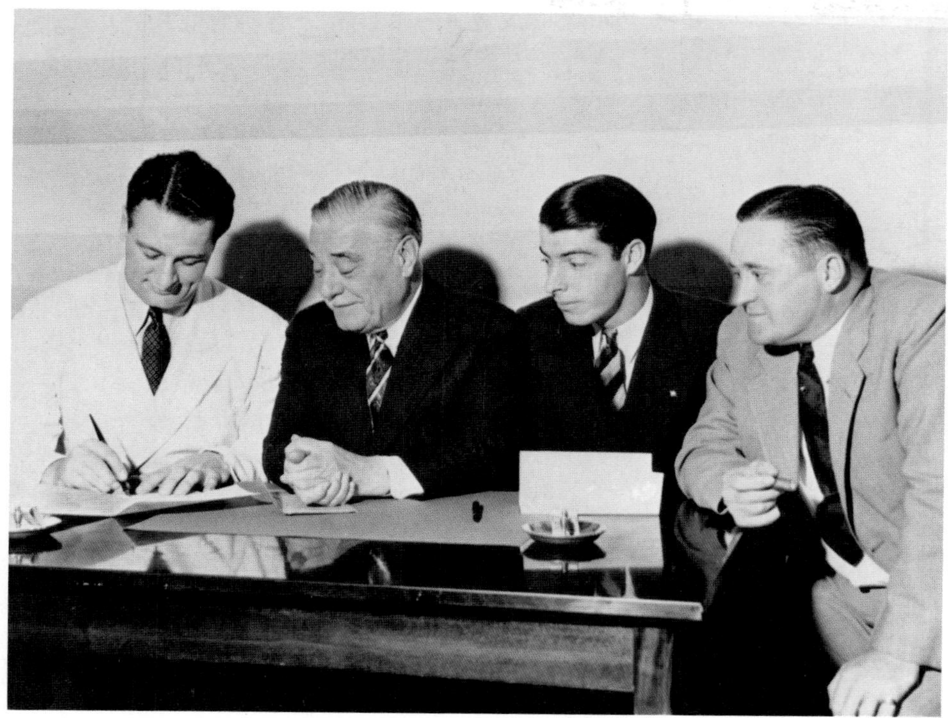

Jacob Ruppert, Joe DiMaggio, and Ed Barrow look on as Lou signs a $39,000 contract for the 1938 season.

Having been the triggerman of two consecutive world championships, Lou signed a $39,000 contract for 1938. Meanwhile, DiMaggio held out for $45,000, which had the public and the Yankees' front office thinking him a swellheaded ingrate. When Ed Barrow pointed out that not even Gehrig had ever made that much money, DiMaggio responded, "It's too bad that Gehrig is so underpaid." Joltin' Joe finally signed a one year deal for $25,000.

While DiMaggio's worth was principally to be found in his lethal bat and fly-paper glove, Lou's added value was in his being there, day in and day out, a tower of strength as familiar and imposing as the green-skinned lady holding a torch aloft in New York Harbor. For all of his slugging, the cornerstone of Lou's fame was his reputation as an iron man—the "Iron Horse," as sportswriters had begun calling him after he shattered Everett Scott's record.

Chugging along through the summers, Lou had downplayed the streak, even as it increasingly defined him as a player and as a person. "I have the will to play," he said. "Baseball is hard work, and the strain is tremendous. Sure, it's pleasurable, but it's tough." If he was circumspect about his motivation, he had already demonstrated that he would go to considerable lengths to keep it going.

One only had to examine his Triple Crown season, during which he overcame a fearful beaning and debilitating attacks of back pain to once again appear in every game.

On June 29, 1934, he was hit square in the head by a fastball during an exhibition game with the Newark Bears in Norfolk, Virginia. (Incidentally, the pitcher, Ray White, was a fellow Columbia University alum.) While Lou toppled over like a felled tree, Joe McCarthy jumped up in the dugout. "My God!" he yelled. "There goes the pennant!"

It took five minutes to revive Lou, who was then rushed to a local hospital. Doctors reported a bad concussion and recommended Lou stay

In 1936, Lou set a record by ripping 14 home runs off Cleveland's pitching staff, which included a teenaged fireballer named Bob Feller. The rookie sensation had first seen Gehrig back in 1928 when the Larrupin' Lous and Bustin' Babes had barnstormed through Iowa. Rapid Robert had since grown to the point that in 1937 he fanned Gehrig three times in one game, all on curves. "Just keep pitching, Bob," Lou said afterwards. "You're going to do all right in this league."

in bed for a couple of days. Instead, Lou accompanied the team to Washington. Suffering from a terrible headache and sporting a knot the size of a grapefruit, but with his streak of 1,414 games on the line, Lou insisted on playing. To everyone's amazement, he banged out three triples in three at-bats until rain washed out the game (and Lou's triples) in the fifth inning.

Two weeks later the Yankees visited Navin Field for an important series with the first-place Tigers. On July 13, Lou slapped a second-inning single and then fell down halfway to first. Straining mightily, he barely made the bag, but then refused to leave the game. The following inning, when he could barely bend over in the field, he signaled to McCarthy that he couldn't continue. Jack Saltzgaver ran out to replace him.

The Yankees' trainer worked on Lou into the night, administering heat treatment and massages to his stiff back. Lou barely slept. The thought was that he was suffering from lumbago, a form of rheumatism. It was a convenient and logical explanation for the occasional pains he had been experiencing in his back and leg muscles for the last couple of years. Come morning, he was soaked in sweat and hardly able to move. But he reported to the park and talked McCarthy into letting him play.

"I don't think I can go nine today," he said, wincing. "But I'd like to keep the streak alive, Joe, because I'm sure I can play tomorrow. Would you do me a favor? Let me lead off. I'll take my first bat, then I'll get out for the day."

McCarthy penciled in Gehrig as shortstop and leadoff man on his lineup card. Wracked with excrutiating pain, Lou hobbled up to the plate and lunged at the first pitch. Incredibly, it popped off his bat and landed in short right field for a single. After dragging himself to first, time was called and Red Rolfe was inserted as a pinch-runner. Rolfe then stayed in the game and played shortstop while Saltzgaver took over first-base duties. The following afternoon, true to his word, Lou was back in the lineup, collecting three doubles off Tiger-ace "Schoolboy" Rowe.

The gimmick kept Lou's streak alive at 1,427 games, but cheapened it in the eyes of some. "Instead of enhancing his reputation for durability, he sullied it," insisted Bud Shaver of the *Detroit Times.* "He also impugned his reputation for sensibility. If a man is too ill to play, the sensible thing for him to do is refrain from playing. His physical handicaps are apt to be disastrous for his teammates.

"Records preserved in the manner in which Gehrig preserved his at Navin Field prove nothing except the absurdity of most records."

Shaver's criticism begs the question: Just how "pure" of a record was Lou's streak?

In retrospect, not very. Raymond Gonzalez of the Society for American Baseball Research has tracked every game of Gehrig's playing streak, which would reach 2,130 games before ending in the spring of 1939. He discovered that in only one season did Lou play every inning of every game. That was in 1931. Ironically, that fall Lou suffered a broken hand during Fred Lieb's exhibition tour of Japan, an injury that would have sidelined him had it occurred in a regular-season game.

Outside of his home run off Carl Hubbell in the 1936 World Series, Lou's biggest thrill in baseball involved St. Louis's trash-talking speedballer, Jay Hanna "Dizzy" Dean. In the first inning of the 1937 All Star game, Dean struck Lou out with a curve. Two innings later, with Joe DiMaggio on first and a full count on Gehrig, Dean shook off his catcher's sign for another curve and instead threw the "Dean Special," a fastball "as hot as bacon grease." Lou knocked it far over the right-field fence at Griffith Stadium, the one park in the league that had given him fits over his long career. Earl Averill, the next batter, provided a footnote (literally) to Gehrig's blast: he lined a pitch back to the mound, breaking Dean's big toe and effectively ending Ol' Diz's career.

In addition to the farcical game in Detroit when he was listed at shortstop and batted leadoff, Lou was substituted for on nearly 70 other occasions. Typically these were in games where the outcome was no longer in doubt, or in late September affairs where the Yankees had already clinched the pennant. More threatening were the six times during the streak when he was ejected by umpires, for even a mild suspension of one game would have ended his streak.

Gehrig never maintained that he had played every minute of every game, and he never felt that he had to offer any apologies for the streak's somewhat controversial nature. This included the time Ed Barrow reportedly called off a home game on account of rain, even though there was scarcely a cloud in the sky. The extra day of rest allowed Lou, who was nursing an attack of lumbago, to crawl out of bed and resume his streak the following afternoon.

In any case, the streak wasn't the core of what he was all about, merely the by-product. Shaped by self-discipline, he played, not only because he was genuinely passionate about the game, but because that was what he was paid to do. If he was suffering from an injury or a cold, he plunged ahead, a good soldier in good cheer, just as he had since he was a small boy lugging loads of wash home for his mother. He played with torn muscles, colds, concussions, headaches, stiff backs, and fractured fingers, just as he had once stumbled feverishly to school after his mother had tucked him in for the day. At one time or another during Lou's baseball career, each of his fingers was broken, some more than once, and yet he continued to grin and bear it. To play was one thing. But to *try,* to give it one's all despite the obstacles at hand—well, that was the true measuring stick of a person's character.

Lou's ability to play over pain was truly remarkable. A pitcher could

On October 9, 1937, Lou hit his tenth, and last, World Series home run off an old nemesis, Carl Hubbell. The blast also produced his 34th Series RBI, allowing him to pass Babe Ruth in that category. Harry Danning is the disconsolate catcher.

hardly get him out even when he was sick. During the three-game series in Detroit in 1934, Lou had been forced out of two games early and yet managed to bat an even 1.000: six hits in six at-bats. A few weeks before that he had played with a terrible cold. McCarthy finally pulled him after the fifth inning. Of course, by then Lou had collected two homers and two doubles and driven in seven runs!

"My success came from one word—hustle," he explained. "There is no excuse for a player not hustling. Every player owes it to himself, his club, and to the public to hustle every minute he is on the ball field. And that goes for the star as much as for the kid who is fighting to get a regular job."

If he had achieved any success in life, Lou concluded, "It has been because I have been willing to give everything the old college try."

Lou's durability had people wondering about such items as his diet and daily regimen. "Nothing to it," he claimed. "Ten hours of sleep a night, a lot of water, a sensible choice of food, and you'll never have a day's worry in your life."

During the playing season, he had a late breakfast, no lunch, and a hearty dinner. He was partial to vegetables and fruits, avoided pastries and sweets, and had his one and only cup of coffee in the morning.

He also had a fairly wicked tobacco habit. "What I remember about Gehrig is how he used to murder cigarettes," recalled an opponent. "He'd come into the visitors' clubhouse and duck down in the tunnel. His image was everything they said about him, but God, he smoked cigarettes. He'd always come in between innings for a smoke if he wasn't due up." Lou also smoked a pipe, but he refrained from enjoying tobacco whenever kids were around. He knew about the examples ballplayers set, both good and bad.

The image of the corporate Yankee, the one that carried through the forties, fifties, and early sixties, was molded by Gehrig, who Joe McCarthy officially recognized as his surrogate when he named Lou captain in 1935. Lou was the team's first captain since Everett Scott ten years earlier, but players had been following Lou's lead for some time.

Being the captain of the Yankees was more ceremonial than anything, and there were some players who suggested Lou never really cared for the role. In any event, the club was self-policing, remembered Tommy Henrich, who entered the Yankees' clubhouse for the first time as a twenty-three-year-old, free-agent outfielder late in the 1936 season.

"I was in awe," he said. "I was introduced to the ball club, and they cordially shook hands with me. Starting with Lou, the captain, and then DiMaggio, Lazzeri, Gomez, Ruffing, Dickey. Isn't that quite a crew I just rattled off? They were polite. They said, 'Good luck, Tom. Nice to meet you.' And then they went back to whatever it was they were doing.

"I'll tell you, this feeling I had was one of the strongest I've ever had in my life. The atmosphere in that clubhouse was absolutely that of nine guys getting ready to go out and play ball. I said to myself, 'Boy, are these guys pros.' It hit me all over. Heck, our third-string catcher, Art Jorgens, if you loafed around the plate during batting practice, he'd say, 'Come on, bear down.' And I'll tell ya, it's a joy to play with that type of team."

Nobody has ever summarized Lou's value to the Yankees and his place in the club's long history better than Stanley Frank, who followed the team for decades:

Even at thirty-four years of age, Lou was a savvy, aggressive base runner. In the third game of the 1937 World Series, he singled to right, then took second when Giants right fielder Jimmy Ripple threw behind him. In a head-first slide, Gehrig beat the first baseman's throw to second.

> Lou was not the best ballplayer the Yankees ever had. Ruth was number one by every yardstick. DiMaggio was a more accomplished performer in every department except hitting. Mickey Mantle was endowed with much more natural ability. Bill Dickey, a catcher without peer, gave the Yankees a big edge over

Lefty Gomez records the final out of the 1937 fall classic, taking a toss from Gehrig and beating the Giants' Joe Moore to the bag. Gomez was a perfect 6-0 in World Series competition.

Upon the advice of his agent, Christy Walsh, the Iron Horse made tracks for Hollywood. He posed for several beefcake photos, including some that portrayed him as the next Tarzan. The prevailing king of the jungle, Johnny Weissmuller, was amused. "I'll need some first baseman lessons," he said. Lou did look the part of a cowpoke, however, hence his starring role in a shoot-'em-up called *Rawhide*.

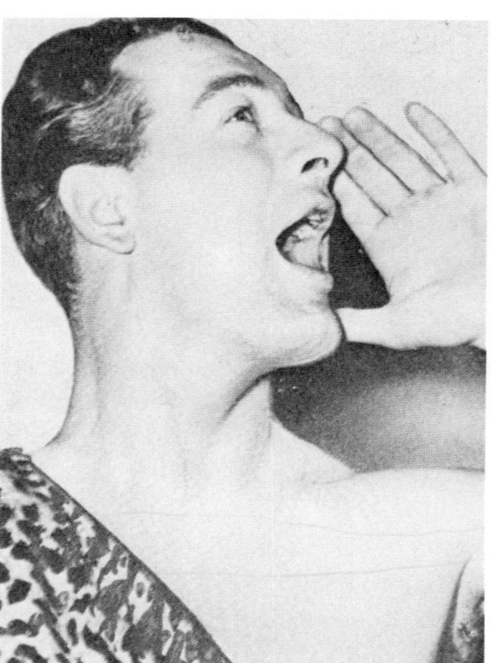

all rivals in the most difficult position to fill and might have been as indispensible to the team as Lou.

Yet Lou was the most valuable player the Yankees ever had because he was the prime source of their greatest asset–an implicit confidence in themselves and every man on the club. Lou's pride as a big-leaguer brushed off on everyone who played with him....

The Yankees had that intangible quality called class. It was a tradition perpetuated by guys such as Dickey, DiMaggio, Gordon, Henrich, Rolfe, Keller, Gomez, and Ruffing, but it stemmed from Lou, and it was the decisive factor in forging their remarkable chain of successes. It is significant that the Yankees never were involved in nightclub brawls or drew adverse publicity from clashes between managers and players until DiMaggio and Henrich, the last men who had been exposed to Lou's influence, had left the club.

Polishing the Yankees' public image was Lou's full-time job. This may seem a trivial point, but he never appeared in a restaurant, hotel lobby, or any other public place without a coat and tie. There was no air conditioning in those days, and Lou, a big man, was as uncomfortable as a polar bear—and sometimes as grouchy—when the temperature hit the 90s. No matter how hot it was, he always was dressed properly in conservative clothes. A Yankee who showed up in a dining room wearing a garish sports shirt without a coat seldom did it more than once.

"You're a big-leaguer," Lou would tell him sharply. "Look like one."

Lou may have lacked flair, and he could often come across as a stuffed shirt, but those close to him knew that suggestions that he was a colorless automaton were unfair. After all, this was a man who had once urinated over the terrace of a friend's Manhattan apartment to break a slump and who playfully referred to his wife as "the old bitch" and "the battle axe." He communicated well with children and animals, neither of which required much from him in terms of sophisticated banter.

Eleanor, who dubbed her husband "Luke" as a way of establishing her claim on him, found he was almost childlike in his pastimes. As a bachelor he had often frequented amusement parks, buying a fistful of tickets for the roller coaster and then spending an hour soaring and dipping through the sky. He faithfully read the Katzenjammer Kids in the comics. He was bonkers for cowboy movies, typically darting into the

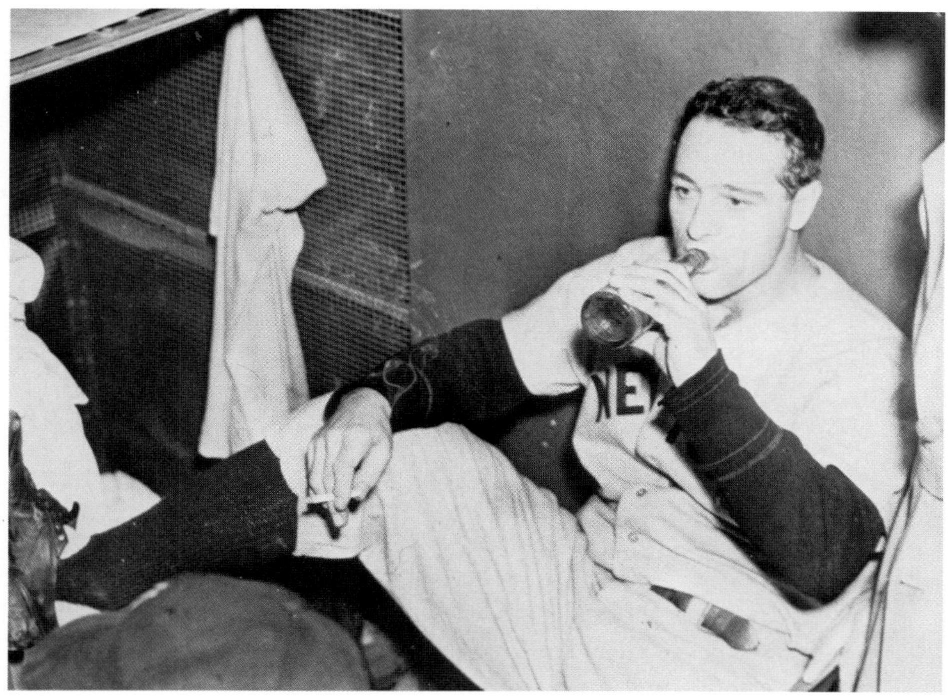

Lou takes a break after a 1937 game. "This Iron Man stuff is just baloney," the recently retired Babe Ruth said. "I think he's making one of the worst mistakes a ballplayer can make. The guy ought to learn to sit on the bench and rest."

Walter "Buck" Leonard, one of only eleven Negro leaguers enshrined at Cooperstown, was often called "the black Lou Gehrig." A durable first sacker with excellent power, Leonard and teammate Josh Gibson were as potent a one-two combination as any that played the game. They led the Homestead Grays to nine straight Negro National League pennants from 1937 to 1945.

back row of the theatre just as the house lights dimmed. Such movies were pure escapism. He didn't have to think, he didn't have to talk, he didn't have to do anything but lose himself in the dark—where he could let down his guard—and be entertained by the likes of Tom Mix and Gene Autry.

From the beginning of their marriage, Eleanor looked to expand Lou's cultural horizons, introducing him to classic literature like *Anna Karenina* and ageless opera like *Tristan und Isolde.* To her surprise, he responded enthusiastically, especially to Wagnerian operas, which because of his fluency in German, he could follow as easily as a Hoot Gibson shoot-'em-up. "So the next thing I knew," said Eleanor, "he was living opera and loving it, and he also was dragging me to the opera house all winter." Lou even bought the librettos to the operas. Then, during the Saturday afternoon radio broadcasts from the Metropolitan Opera House, he would stretch out on the living room floor and follow the action, note by note.

"That's the way he was," Eleanor said, "anything he loved, he embraced to the point of tears, and it was that way in every direction he turned."

Eleanor, a good sport, did everything with Lou, including his favorite activities, fishing and skating. In 1935 she and songwriter Fred Fisher collaborated on a song, "I Can't Get To First Base With You," which was "dedicated to Lou Gehrig." A uniformed Lou appeared on the songsheet cover, cigarette rakishly in hand. While it was no "Peg O' My Heart," one of Fisher's many hit tunes, it did result in Lou's face unexpectedly showing up on top of the thousands of pianos throughout America.

A barometer of Lou's popularity was his growing number of commercial endorsements. While never exactly a celebrity in today's sense of the word, during the 1930s his familiar dimpled face appeared on board games and in advertisements for a wide range of products including cereal, cigarettes, and sporting equipment. Lou's slightly high-pitched voice with New Yawk accent also rang out on the airwaves, resulting in a humorous if embarrassing experience.

Lou was invited onto Robert L. Ripley's popular *Believe It Or Not* radio program, which was sponsored in part by Huskies cereal. All radio was live in those days. Lou, who was being paid for his endorsement, had a simple but important role on the broadcast. When questioned, he was to tell the world that he owed his remarkable success to Huskies.

"Well, Lou," Ripley asked, "what helps you hit all those home runs?"

"A heaping bowlful of Wheaties!" replied Lou.

Millions of Americans listening from coast to coast slapped themselves in the forehead. *Wheaties?* Lou was devastated. He returned the $1,000 he was paid for the ad, even though the cereal manufacturer tried to convince him that they had reaped more publicity from his gaffe than if he had read the line correctly.

Buck Leonard homering at Yankee Stadium in 1939. "I have seen many Negro players who belong in the big leagues," said Gehrig, who barnstormed against blacks many times during his career. "I don't believe there's any room in baseball for discrimination. It's our true national pastime and a game for all." The Yankees, who didn't mind renting its park to Negro leaguers when the team was on the road, would be among the last to desegregate.

No, insisted Lou, who later returned to the show to set the record straight. This time when Ripley asked him his favorite breakfast food, Lou firmly replied: "My favorite is Huskies, and I've tried them all."

As the Wheaties fiasco illustrates, Lou believed in doing the right thing. After he married, he put all of his life savings into a trust fund to provide for his parents' needs. He also gave them the deed to the house in New Rochelle and the keys to a new car. Meanwhile, he and Eleanor continued to sock away most of his regular-season, World Series, and endorsement checks and make plans for his postbaseball career.

Lou gives his mother a kiss at spring training in 1938, the start of his last full season in baseball.

In 1938 retirement still seemed far away. That year he began his 16th season with the Yankees. By now the press portrayed him as a sort of paterfamilias in pinstripes. With the departure of Tony Lazzeri, who was replaced at second base by power-hitting rookie Joe Gordon, Lou remained the sole link between the Bronx Bombers of the thirties and the Murderers Row teams of the twenties. For those whose memories stretched even further, to afternoons at Columbia's South Field or playgrounds in Manhattan Heights, it must have seemed that there had always been a Lou Gehrig at first base and that there probably always would be. As war clouds gathered in Europe and Asia, and America struggled to get back on its feet economically, this sense of continuity was a small but important comfort in a world that seemed to be slowly spinning out of control.

Of course, Lou was more than a symbol. Approaching middle age (he would turn thirty-five during the season), he was still an integral cog in the Yankees machine, which was primed to take another title. From top to bottom, the lineup was filled with stars, including three future Hall-of-Famers—DiMaggio, Gehrig, and Dickey—in the traditional power positions. "They had everything," marveled Harry Danning. "They had good pitching, good hitting, and they had great defense."

Lou on the dugout steps on May 31, 1938. That afternoon at Yankee Stadium, he played his 2,000th consecutive game.

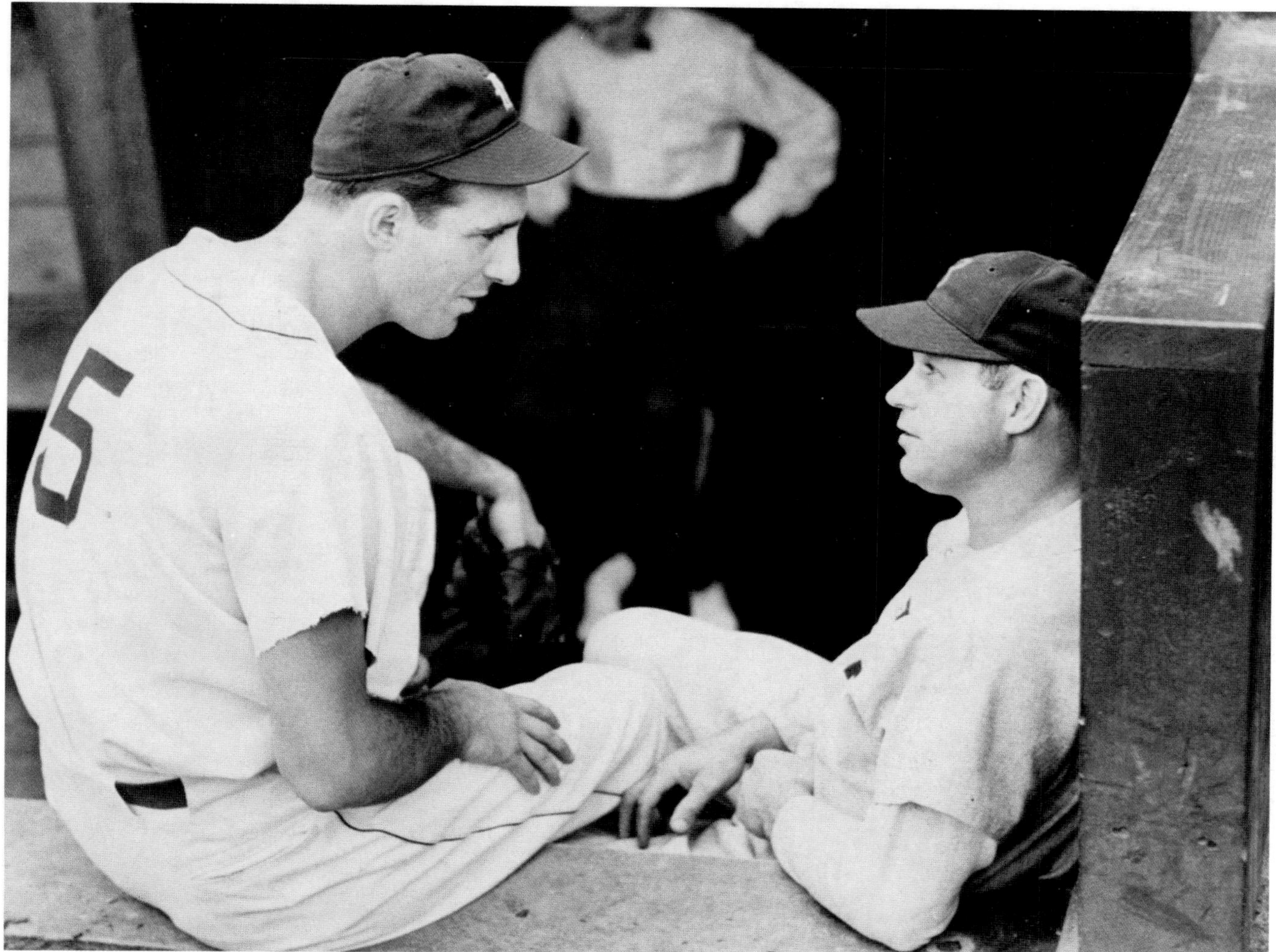

Hank Greenberg talks hitting with Jimmie Foxx late in the 1938 season. That year the Tigers first baseman attracted national attention by ripping 58 home runs, falling just short of breaking Babe Ruth's single-season record. This wasn't his keenest disappointment. That had come the previous summer when he had missed Lou Gehrig's RBI record by one. "Runs batted in are more important than batting average, more important than home runs, more important than anything," he insisted. "That's what wins ball games: driving runs across the plate."

Lou started slowly, which was his style. In spring training observers commented on his tendency to pull away from the plate on good pitches. He also wasn't leaning into the ball as in the past. This time his slump lasted into midseason, taking a little of the bloom off a special occasion. On May 31 Lou played in his 2,000th consecutive game.

Two grand inspired little hoopla. Seven thousand fans watched as Lou cooperated with the press photographers, one of whom posed him with a bushel of baseballs arranged in the magic number. Lou then contributed a single to New York's 12-5 thrashing of Boston.

Before he had left for the park that day, Eleanor had tried to convince him people would remember him better if he voluntarily stopped the streak at 1,999 games. Lou, not quite sure whether his wife was serious or joking, hastily left the house. "All they'll do today is hang a horseshoe of flowers around your neck," she had told him. Sure enough, Lou meekly reappeared in the doorway several hours later, a floral horseshoe hung around his neck and a big grin on his face.

But there was little smiling over his decline. Looking to put some juice back in the offense, as well as to relieve some of the pressure on Lou, McCarthy dropped Gehrig from his familiar cleanup spot to fifth in the order. Tommy Henrich now batted third, followed by DiMaggio.

Lou in 1938 with Mayor Fiorello La Guardia and his wife. Hizzoner was a huge Yankees fan, particularly since, for the first time in history, three of his countrymen—Joe DiMaggio, Frankie Crosetti, and Tony Lazzeri—appeared on the same major-league roster. The Yankees, observed Dan Daniel, "seem to have had a penchant for descendants of the Romans."

Mired in the .250 range, Lou experimented with his swing and sought advice from everyone from batting practice pitchers to park employees. Who knew what was wrong? During a tight game with the White Sox, Lou had even resorted to laying down a bunt! Only Jacob Ruppert dancing nude in the grandstand would have produced a more shocking sight.

Along with his prolonged batting slump, Lou battled recurring bouts of lumbago and an untimely broken thumb. Nobody, least of all Lou, thought he would leave the lineup. "A fractured finger is an injury serious enough to force any ballplayer out of action," observed Edward T. Farrell, "that is, any ballplayer whose name is not Gehrig. It is going to take more than a thumb fracture to produce the unusual sight of the Yankees starting a ball game without Gehrig at first base."

Finally, in early August Lou declared, "What the hell, I'm not hitting with all this change in my batting stance. I've tried everything. I'm going back to my old way. I certainly can't do any worse, and at least I'll feel natural up there."

Lou practically willed his way out of his funk, crashing the ball at a .400 pace in August. The always resourceful slugger even became a base stealing threat again, at least for a game. On September 7 against Boston, he twice walked and stole second, giving him six swipes for the season. Not bad, considering Frankie Crosetti would lead the league with 27. They turned out to be the last stolen bases of Lou's career.

The Bronx Bombers captured a third consecutive pennant, Lou rebounding to post a .295 batting average with 29 homers and 114 RBI. Although he had dipped below .300 for the first time since 1925, he had played every game of the schedule for the 13th consecutive year. It also was the 13th straight season he had reached the century mark in RBI, a record that still stands.

Lou resumed his mild hitting in the World Series against Chicago, gathering just four singles in 14 at-bats. He didn't knock in a single run.

Rookie second baseman Joe "Flash" Gordon (second from left) was an acrobatic fielder and long-ball hitter for the '38 Yankees whose veteran infield included third sacker Robert "Red" Rolfe (second from right) and shortstop Frankie Crosetti. During his last full season in pinstripes, the graying Gehrig hit 29 homers and knocked in 114 runs.

But his sputtering productivity wasn't as glaring as it might otherwise have been because the Yanks manhandled the Cubs in four straight.

Watching from the bench was Wes Ferrell, the veteran hurler Joe McCarthy had picked up from Washington in the late stages of the pennant race. Not long after joining New York, Ferrell won an extra-inning affair over his old employer, as delicious a moment as any that he enjoyed during his long career. Recalling that game many years later, Ferrell's mood turned from jovial to sober.

"You know," he told baseball historian Donald Honig, "something happened in that game. I thought it was curious at the time, though now I can understand it. We should've won the game in nine innings, but Gehrig made a bad play on a ground ball and let the tying run in. Instead of going to the plate and throwing the man out, he went the easy way, to first base."

It was unusual, said Ferrell, "the kind of play you'd never expect him to make." But nobody, reflected the old pitcher, knew at the time that Lou Gehrig was dying.

CHAPTER Eight

—THREE STRIKES—

SAM BLAKE: It's a routine, I'm tellin' you. Why, at a place like this they give you the x-ray, the cardiogram, the metabolism, the flouroscopes, the works. And then they're liable to tell you you've got dandruff . . . I had a talk with the doctor the other day. He said he never ran up against a better physical speciman. Strong as an ox, he said you were. And talk about that x-ray guy, too. Boy, what a send-off he gave you. Heart okay, lungs okay, everything okay. Lou, I'll bet you . . . Here's the doctor.
LOU: Well, how'd I do, doctor?
DOCTOR: I'm afraid you'll have to give up baseball for a while. You see, Mr. Gehrig . . .
LOU: Go ahead, doc. I'm a man who likes to know his batting average.
DOCTOR: I've only made a superficial examination of the tests. I shall need some new x-rays.
LOU: Give it to me straight, doc. Am I through with baseball?
DOCTOR: I'm afraid so.
LOU: Any worse than that?
BLAKE: You heard what the doc said, Lou. He's got to go over the tests again.
LOU: Is it three strikes, doc?
DOCTOR: You want it straight?
LOU: Sure I do. Straight.
DOCTOR: It's three strikes.

—*The Pride of the Yankees*

EARLY IN BASEBALL'S centennial season of 1939, the New York Yankees and Washington Senators visited Arlington National Cemetery for ceremonies honoring Abner Doubleday, the Civil War general and the dubious "inventor" of baseball. To the surprise of those who hadn't seen Lou Gehrig since the previous season, the captain of the Yankees moved around as stiffly as some of the still-surviving members of the Grand Army of the Republic.

Even someone clad in the tools of ignorance could see that something wasn't right. "Say, Bill," Washington catcher Rick Ferrell asked his counterpart on the Yankees, "what the hell's the matter with Lou?"

"Oh, he's slowly getting in shape," replied Bill Dickey, ever protective of his best friend.

It's the opening week of the season and he's still getting in shape? Ferrell asked himself. He let the matter drop.

Ferrell got a closer look at Lou during that afternoon's game. "Gehrig swung at a pitch right down the pipe," he recalled, "and he missed it by six inches." As Ferrell snapped the ball back to the pitcher, he thought: *Something is seriously wrong with this guy.*

People around the game had been saying that for more than a year. The familiar power was missing, some reporters had observed during the 1938 season, and only an extraordinary late-season rally had kept Lou's final numbers remotely close to what people had come to expect from him. Some said Lou was simply getting old. Others speculated that the streak was the culprit. By refusing to take an occasional day off, they said, Lou had played the equivalent of 19 or 20 seasons and was now paying the price.

Gehrig, with his silver temples and weathered face, looked more than ever the part of the elder statesman of the team. But at age thirty-

May 2, 1939: The streak ends.

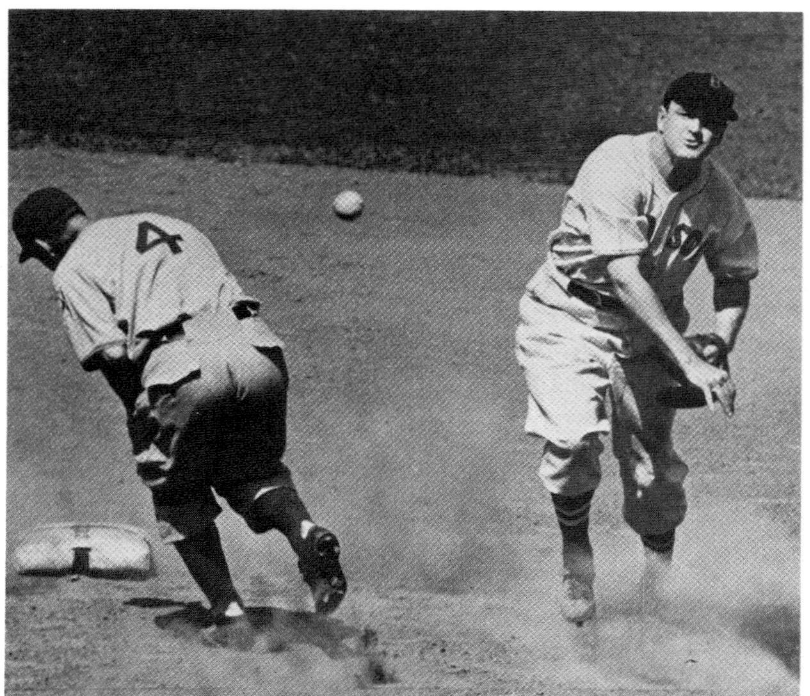

Barely able to lift his feet off the ground, Gehrig is an easy force-out for Boston's Bobby Doerr early in the 1939 season.

five, it was inconceivable that he should be having the problems of an octogenarian tying his shoes or lighting his pipe. During the off-season, he had alarmed Eleanor by falling repeatedly during his favorite winter activity, ice skating. At her request he'd gone to see a doctor, who diagnosed a gallbladder problem. He put Lou on a bland diet. Lou, who'd accepted a pay cut to $36,000 for the 1939 season, arrived at spring training convinced the Florida sun would boil the kinks right out of him.

Lou had always been a notoriously slow starter, but his record in the Yankees' first 27 exhibitions was abysmal. He was batting around .200 and had no extra-base hits in more than 100 at-bats. Ed Barrow later confessed that, in his fifty years in the game, he had never seen a hitter lose his stroke as quickly. Usually that was the last thing to go, he said, pointing to Babe Ruth's ability to hit three home runs in one game even as the forty-year-old slugger faded away with the Boston Braves.

Equally disturbing was Gehrig's decline as a doorkeeper. He made several errors. True, it was only spring camp, but the boo-birds were on him as if it were the World Series.

"His failures have been distressing," wrote Sid Mercer, "and his sensitive nature has been wounded by jibes from the stands. That's something he never had to take before, and it is a bitter pill." Lou's solution was to simply work harder.

It didn't help. His reflexes were so bad teammates openly fretted that he would be unable to get out of the way of a pitch or a line drive. Fresh in their minds was the Bump Hadley fastball that had nearly killed Detroit catcher Mickey Cochrane two years earlier at Yankee Stadium. Cochrane eventually recovered, but he never played again.

Lou's feet hugged the ground like two flat tires. "In Clearwater one day we played the Phillies," said Tommy Henrich. "He tried to go from first to third on a hit. I watched him run to second, and it looked like he was trying to run uphill. He wasn't getting any place."

At one point Joe McCarthy gave Lou the day off to go fishing with Bill Dickey. Henrich filled in at first. Barrow insisted there was no special significance in the move, explaining that the team needed to be ready for any emergency.

"The best of them have got to go some day," said Barrow. "We are all fond of Lou. He's a Yankee institution. Get me right, we've not given up on him yet. There is still some sentiment left in baseball. Gehrig will get every chance...Work is the thing to straighten him out. We will go the limit for him."

During one of the Yankees' last exhibition games as they moved north to begin the regular season, Lou raised hopes that he had finally snapped out of his lethargy by banging out a pair of home runs. They looked good in the box score, but those on hand weren't fooled. The game was played in Norfolk, Virginia, at a park with an extremely short right-field fence. Both balls would have been easy outs in any big-league park.

Nonetheless, Lou was in the lineup when the Yankees opened the season on April 20 against the Red Sox. McCarthy—like Barrow, no sentimentalist—was adamant that his captain would have to decide when to bench himself. On the mound for Boston was Lefty Grove. In his first at-bat, Lou flied to a slender right fielder named Ted Williams, who was making his major-league debut. Later in the game, with a runner on third and one out, Grove made the Yankee Stadium crowd gasp when he walked Joe DiMaggio to pitch to Lou. This would have been unheard of even a year earlier. But the strategy worked. Lou grounded into a double play.

The Yankees managed to beat Grove and win five of their first eight games, but these victories could not camouflage Lou's mounting frustration. In those eight games he had scratched out just four singles in 28 at-bats for an anemic .143 average. He had knocked in only one run. On April 30, in a 3-2 loss to Washington, he came up four times with runners on base and failed to hit. After the game, he shuffled forlornly into the clubhouse, where he overheard some teammates griping about McCarthy keeping him in the lineup.

"Those fellows don't think I can do it anymore," he told Eleanor that night. "Do you think I should quit?"

"All that matters," she answered, "is if you still get satisfaction out of playing."

"How can I get satisfaction," responded Lou, "when I'm hurting the club?"

On May 2, a University of Michigan student named Art Hill and his friend Jim skipped classes and hitchhiked from Ann Arbor to Detroit to catch the Yankees' first visit of the season to Briggs Stadium. As the park announcer ran down the Yankees' starting

After fourteen seasons, Lou finally benched himself at Briggs Stadium in Detroit. This headline news around the country started weeks of speculation: What was wrong with Gehrig?

Gehrig Voluntarily Ends Streak at 2,130 Straight Games

LOU, NOT HITTING, ASKS REST ON BENCH

Gehrig's String, Started June 1, 1925, Snapped as Yanks Start Series in Detroit

RETURN OF ACE INDEFINITE

But Iron Man Who Holds Many Records Hopes to Regain Form in Hot Weather

Record of Gehrig's Streak

	G.	AB.	R.	H.	RBI.	HR.	PC.
1925.....	*126	437	73	129	68	21	.295
1926.....	155	572	135	179	107	16	.313
1927.....	155	584	149	218	175	47	.373
1928.....	154	562	139	210	142	27	.374
1929.....	154	553	127	166	126	35	.300
1930.....	154	581	143	220	174	41	.379
1931.....	155	619	163	211	184	46	.341
1932.....	156	596	138	208	151	34	.349
1933.....	152	583	138	198	139	32	.334
1934.....	154	579	128	210	165	49	.363
1935.....	149	535	125	176	119	30	.329
1936.....	155	579	167	205	152	49	.354
1937.....	157	569	138	200	159	37	.351
1938.....	157	576	115	170	114	29	.295
1939.....	8	28	2	4	1	0	.143
Total..	2,141	7,963	1,880	2,704	1,976	493	.340

*Includes eleven games before consecutive run started.

By JAMES P. DAWSON
Special to THE NEW YORK TIMES.

DETROIT, May 2.—Lou Gehrig's matchless record of uninterrupted play in American League championship games, stretched over fifteen years and through 2,130 straight contests, came to an end today.

The mighty iron man, who at his peak had hit forty-nine home runs in a single season five years ago, took himself out of action before the Yanks marched on Briggs Stadium for their first game against the Tigers this year.

With the consent of Manager Joe McCarthy, Gehrig removed himself because he, better than anybody else, perhaps, recognized his competitive decline and was frankly aware of the fact he was doing the Yankees no good defensively or on the attack. He last played Sunday in New York against the Senators.

When Gehrig will start another game is undetermined. He will not be used as a pinch-hitter.

The present plan is to keep him on the bench. Relaxing and shaking off the mental hazards he admittedly has encountered this season, he may swing into action in the hot weather, which should have a beneficial effect upon his tired muscles.

Dahlgren Gets Chance

Meanwhile Ellsworth (Babe) Dahlgren, until today baseball's greatest figure of frustration, will continue at first base. Manager McCarthy said he had no present intention of transferring Tommy Henrich, the youthful outfielder whom he tried at first base at the Florida training camp. Dahlgren had been awaiting the summons for three years.

It was coincidental that Gehrig's string was broken almost in the presence of the man he succeeded as Yankee first baseman. At that time Wally Pipp, now a business man of Grand Rapids, Mich., was benched by the late Miller Huggins to make room for the strapping youth fresh from the Hartford Eastern League club to which the Yankees had farmed him for two seasons, following his departure from Columbia University. Pipp was in the lobby of the Book Cadillac Hotel at noon when the withdrawal of Gehrig was effected.

"I don't feel equal to getting back in there," Pipp said on June 2, 1925, the day Lou replaced him at first. Lou had started his phenomenal streak the day before as a pinch-hitter for Peewee Wanninger, then the Yankee shortstop.

This latest momentous development in baseball was not unexpected. There had been signs for the past two years that Gehrig was slowing up. Even when a sick man, however, he gamely stuck to his chores, not particularly in pursuit of his all-time record of consecutive play, although that was a big consideration, but out of a driving desire to help the Yankees, always his first consideration.

Treated for Ailment

What Lou had thought was lumbago last year when he suffered pains in the back that more than once forced his early withdrawal from games he had started was diagnosed later as a gall bladder condition for which Gehrig underwent treatment all last Winter, after rejecting a recommendation that he submit to an operation.

Wired Photo—Times Wide World

VETERAN FIRST BASEMAN AND HIS SUCCESSOR
Lou Gehrig and Babe Dahlgren in Detroit yesterday

Gehrig's Streak at a Glance

June 1, 1925
Lou Gehrig's iron-man streak innocently begins when he pinch-hits for shortstop Paul Wanninger in the bottom of the eighth inning in a losing effort against Washington. Walter Johnson induces Lou to fly out to left fielder Goose Goslin.

June 2, 1925
Lou replaces Wally Pipp, who has been injured by a pitched ball in batting practice in the regular lineup. Batting sixth, he collects hits his first three at-bats against the Senators.

June 3, 1925
Aaron Ward pinch-hits for Lou in the bottom of the ninth against Washington left-hander Vean Gregg. It's the first of six times this summer that the Yankees new first baseman will be removed for a pinch-hitter, including twice as early as the fourth inning.

July 5, 1925
Lou barely keeps the streak alive when Fred Merkle, who starts the game at first base, collapses from the heat and is replaced by Lou in the ninth inning.

June 29, 1926
During a contest with Philadelphia, Lou is thrown out of the game after arguing with umpire George Hildebrand—the first of six ejections he would receive during the course of the streak.

September 28, 1930
In the season-closer at Boston, Babe Ruth pitches, Lou plays left field, and Harry Rice takes over first base. The gimmick ends Lou's streak of 885 consecutive games at first base, still a major-league record.

November 1931
In an exhibition game in Japan, Lou's right hand is broken by a pitched ball, forcing him to the bench for the final 11 games of the 17-game tour. Although exhibition games, All Star games, and World Series contests aren't included in his consecutive-games-played record, the injury illustrates how quickly and capriciously the playing streak could have come to an end.

August 16, 1933
Lou ties Everett Scott's big-league record of 1,307 games in a row in the Yankees' loss at St. Louis.

August 17, 1933
In another loss at St. Louis, Lou sets a new record for consecutive games played, garnering two hits and a silver statuette from American League president Will Harridge.

June 29, 1934
Lou is knocked out for five minutes after being hit in the head by a brush-back pitch during an exhibition game in Norfolk, Virginia. Playing with a concussion, he hits three straight triples the following day against Washington until rain washes out the game (and his triples).

July 14, 1934
Gehrig, suffering from lumbago, is entered in the lineup as the leadoff man and shortstop in a game at Detroit. He limps to the plate, singles, then is replaced by pinch-runner Red Rolfe. In the bottom of the first inning, Jack Saltzgaver goes in to play first base. This keeps Gehrig's streak alive at 1,427 games, but the manner in which it is preserved draws criticism from several members of the press.

May 31, 1938
Over his wife's protestations ("Why not stop at 1,999?" she says), Lou plays his 2,000th consecutive game. He collects a single in a 12-5 win over Boston at Yankee Stadium.

September 27, 1938
With the streak now up to 2,121 games, Lou hits the last home run of his career off Washington's Dutch Leonard at Yankee Stadium.

April 29, 1939
Game number 2,129 sees Lou get the final hit of his career—a single off Washington's Ken Chase.

April 30, 1939
In his 2,130th consecutive game, Gehrig goes hitless in a 3-2 loss to Washington at Yankee Stadium.

May 2, 1939
Obviously ailing from some mysterious malady, Lou pulls himself out of the lineup before the opener of a series in Detroit. The Iron Horse's remarkable streak is finally ended after 14 seasons and 2,130 games in a row.

Lou Gehrig at the start of his streak . . . and after.

lineup, Hill turned to his friend in astonishment. "Jesus, they've got Gehrig batting eighth!" At precisely that moment, the announcer said, "Dahlgren, first base."

"And then we knew," remembered Hill. "After 2,130 consecutive games, Lou Gehrig's streak was ending. Having already wasted my profanity on the far less shocking event I had thought I was about to see, I said nothing. Jim and I just looked at each other in wonder."

Unbeknownst to the midweek crowd of 11,379, that morning Lou had gone up to Joe McCarthy's room in the Book-Cadillac Hotel and announced that, for the good of the team, he was benching himself.

"Nobody has to tell me how bad I've been and how much of a drawback I've been to the club," Lou said. "I've been thinking ever since the

A week after his streak ended, Lou appeared tired but in good spirits. "Please omit flowers," he joked to reporters. "And don't write my obituary." Bill Dickey (holding bat) was so upset over his best friend's rapid physical decline that his batting average dropped 55 points.

season opened, when I couldn't start as I hoped I would, that the time has come for me to quit."

"You don't have to quit," responded McCarthy. "Take a rest for a week or so, and maybe you'll feel all right again."

"I just don't know," Lou said disconsolately. "I can't figure what's the matter with me. I just know I can't go on this way." He went on to explain that the final straw had come in the last game against Washington when he had labored mightily to complete a simple fielding play. Like uncles applauding a favorite nephew's wretched performance in the school play, his teammates had profusely congratulated him as they left the field. "I knew then that it was time to get out," he said.

"All right, Lou," McCarthy said. "But any time you want to get back in there, it's your position. I'll put Dahlgren in at first today."

That afternoon, lineup card in hand, Lou walked stiffly out to the umpires gathered at home plate. As if on cue, the entire crowd got on its feet and applauded for a full two minutes.

"There was no shouting, just sustained vigorous applause," said Hill. "But they were on their feet, which meant something in those days. A standing ovation was a ritual act, meant to honor a man's whole career, or some deed of superhuman courage or skill. It was important because it was unplanned; people knew when to do it—and when not to do it, which was most of the time."

Lou acknowledged the crowd with a tip of his cap. Blinking back tears, he ducked into the dugout and took a long drink at the water fountain. Then he found a seat in the middle of the bench, bowed his head, and cried. Teammates looked away, unsure of what to say or do. After several agonizing seconds, Lefty Gomez broke the awkward silence by moseying over from the far end of the dugout.

"Hell, Lou," said Lefty. "It took fifteen years to get you out of the game. Sometimes I'm out in fifteen minutes." Lou laughed, then wiped his eyes.

The tension broken, the Yankees went on to bury the Tigers, 22-2. The twenty-seven-year-old Dahlgren, who as a kid growing up in San

Francisco used to draw Lou's picture on the inside of his binder, hit a home run, doubled off the fence, and had two more drives caught on the warning track. Not that Dahlgren's aging hero was conceding him anything. When photographers asked Lou to pose as if he were cheering Dahlgren on, he refused. He planned on regaining his spot in the lineup, he explained.

For the time being, however, his duties were strictly ceremonial. He took the lineup card to the plate before every game, then watched the action from the bench. Rest was the thing, everyone agreed. On the long train trips between cities, he and his bridge partner, Bill Dickey, continued their games with Red Rolfe and a rotating number of sportswriters. No one commented on the loss of dexterity in Lou's hands when he tried to shuffle and deal the cards. Everybody pretended not to notice when a fork fell out of his hand or when he tripped over a curbstone.

Gehrig never played another major-league game. But on June 12, the day before he was scheduled to enter the Mayo Clinic in Rochester, Minnesota, for a thorough examination, he did suit up one final time in an exhibition game against the Yankees' powerful Triple-A farm team. The Kansas City Blues fielded a lineup that included future big-leaguers Phil Rizzuto at shortstop, Jerry Priddy at second base, Clyde McCullough behind the plate, and Vince DiMaggio (Joe's older brother) in center field. Lou wasn't expected to even be in uniform, but he told Joe McCarthy that he felt an obligation to the 23,864 fans that had packed Kansas City's Ruppert Field hoping to catch a glimpse of the Iron Horse. More likely, he couldn't resist one last go-around before the Mayo Clinic's specialists rendered their judgment.

Lou's final appearance in uniform was a three-inning stint on June 12, 1939, in an exhibition game against the Kansas City Blues. The Yankees farm team featured several future big leaguers, including second baseman Jerry Priddy (left), who that afternoon in Kansas City fielded the last ball Lou ever hit.

Lou, "weak and staggering," as remembered by McCullough, got a standing ovation when he brought out the lineup card. Batting eighth, he grounded to Priddy his only time up. The effort produced another standing ovation.

A revealing exchange took place between Lou and Blues first baseman Johnny Sturm, whose parents also were German immigrants. When the two had played against each other in spring exhibitions, they often practiced their German on each other. This time Sturm asked Gehrig how he felt.

"*Schlect*," replied Lou. Terrible.

New York won, 4-1, the Blues' only run coming in the bottom of the third when pitcher Joe Vance "pushed a hit past the slow-moving Gehrig," reported the *Kansas City Times*. That same inning, everybody in the park held their breath when Lou was knocked on his back by a line drive. After the third out was recorded, Lou left the game for his hotel. All in all, recalled the Yankees' rookie catcher, Buddy Rosar, it "wasn't exactly a pleasant day to play a game of baseball."

Eleanor, suspecting that her husband was suffering from a brain tumor, had scheduled Lou's visit to the Mayo brothers' world-famous clinic. Lou met with Dr. Harold Habein, the chief diagnostician.

"When Lou Gehrig entered my office and I saw the shuffling gait,

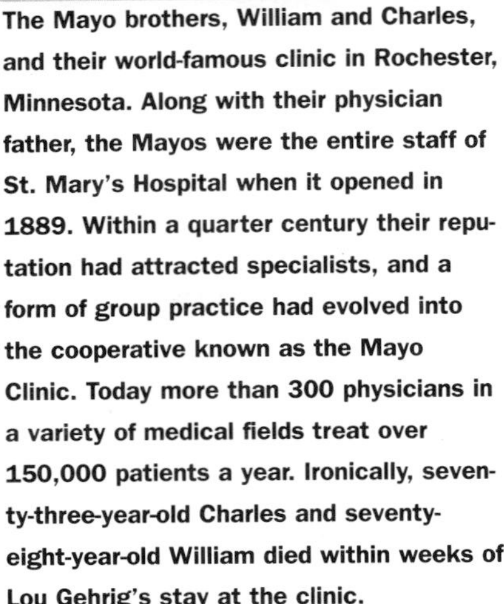

The Mayo brothers, William and Charles, and their world-famous clinic in Rochester, Minnesota. Along with their physician father, the Mayos were the entire staff of St. Mary's Hospital when it opened in 1889. Within a quarter century their reputation had attracted specialists, and a form of group practice had evolved into the cooperative known as the Mayo Clinic. Today more than 300 physicians in a variety of medical fields treat over 150,000 patients a year. Ironically, seventy-three-year-old Charles and seventy-eight-year-old William died within weeks of Lou Gehrig's stay at the clinic.

his overall expression, then shook his hand, I knew," Dr. Harbein said later. "I had watched my mother go through the same exact thing. I excused myself from Lou and went straight to Dr. Mayo's private office. 'Good God,' I told him, 'the boy's got ALS!'"

Five days of tests followed. On June 19, Lou's thirty-sixth birthday, the clinic issued a press release. It read:

> TO WHOM IT MAY CONCERN:
>
> This is to certify that Mr. Lou Gehrig has been under examination at the Mayo Clinic from June 13 to June 19, 1939, inclusive.
>
> After a careful and complete examination, it was found that he is suffering from amyotrophic lateral sclerosis. This type of illness involves the motor pathways and cells of the central nervous system and in lay terms is known as a form of chronic poliomyelitis (infantile paralysis).
>
> The nature of this trouble makes it such that Mr. Gehrig will be unable to continue his active participation as a baseball player, inasmuch as it is advisable that he conserve his muscular energy. He could, however, continue in some executive capacity.
>
> (Signed)
> Harold C. Habein, M. D.

Probably not one in a million Americans had heard of amyotrophic lateral sclerosis before Lou Gehrig was diagnosed with it. Fewer could pronounce it, making it virtually certain that ALS would soon be simply known as "Lou Gehrig's disease"—the first and only time in history that a disease has taken on the name of one of its victims. Such was the power of Lou's fame and the irony of his fate. As Frankie Crosetti said:

"We were all stunned. Just shocked. For a big strapping guy to come down with something like that was…unthinkable."

No one knows what causes ALS, which was discovered in the late nineteenth century by a French physician, Dr. Jean Charcot. The disease gradually destroys the nerve cells in the brain and spinal cord that control a person's voluntary muscles. This causes the muscle tissues to waste away because there are no longer any nerves to stimulate them. The afflicted first notices increasing weakness in a limb, especially a hand. Later other limbs are affected. The muscles twitch and cramp and eventually complete paralysis can result.

About 5,000 new ALS cases are reported in the U. S. each year. Internationally, such well-known figures as British actor David Niven and Chinese leader Mao Tse-tung have contracted and died from the disease. In fact, in a few places around the globe, notably Guam and western New Guinea, the incidence of ALS is extremely high. The reason why baffles the medical community. The only certainty about ALS is that there is no cure. Most often, death occurs between two and ten years after diagnosis.

In Rochester, Lou clutched a pen in his cramped hand and painstakingly wrote a letter to reassure Eleanor:

Dr. Harold Habein, whose mother had died from amyotrophic lateral sclerosis, immediately recognized the symptoms in Lou Gehrig.

> Mornin' Sweet:
>
> Really, I don't know how to start and I'm not much at breaking news gently. But am going to write it as there is no use in keeping you in suspense. I'll tell it all, just as it is.
>
> As for breaking this news to the papers, I thought and the doctors approved, that they write a medical report and then a laymen's [sic] interpretation underneath and I would tell the papermen here that I felt it was my duty to my employers that they have firsthand information and that I felt sure they would give it to the newspapermen. That seemed the most logical way to all of us here and I felt it was such vital news that it wouldn't be fair to have Joe [McCarthy] and Ed [Barrow] read about it in the papers.
>
> However, don't be too alarmed or sympathetic, for the most important thing for me is no fatigue and no strain or major worries. The bad news is "amyotrophic lateral sclerosis." There isn't any cure, the best they can hope is to check it at the point it is now and there is a 50-50 chance for that.

Lou Gehrig Appreciation Day took place July 4, 1939, at Yankee Stadium. Manager Joe McCarthy presented Lou with a trophy inscribed "Your pals of the Yankee team."

There are very few of these cases. It is probably caused by some germ. However, my first question was transmission. No danger whatever. Never heard of transmitting it to mates. If there were (and I made them doubly assure me) you certainly would never have been allowed within 100 feet of me.

I may need a cane in ten or fifteen years. Playing is out of the question and Paul suggests a coaching job or job in the office or writing. I made him honestly assure me that it will not affect me mentally.

They seem to think I'll get along all right if I can reconcile myself to this condition, which I have done but only after they assured me there is no danger of transmission and that I will not become mentally unbalanced and thereby become a burden on your hands for life.

I adore you, sweetheart.

Before the letter arrived, doctors had already called Eleanor. She made them promise not to tell her husband the disease was fatal, but indications are that Lou knew the score even as the Yankees organization hastily prepared a tribute. Rejoining the club in Washington, he was hailed in the train station by a group of Boy Scouts wishing him good luck. Lou waved back, then remarked softly to a companion, "They're wishing me luck, and I'm dying." Later, he made a similar remark to Bill Dickey.

"Lou Gehrig Appreciation Day" was scheduled for an Independence Day doubleheader against the Washington Senators at Yankee Stadium. The perfect baseball weather—warm with blue skies—was in sharp contrast to the somber mood inside the park. Many of the people associated with Lou's life were on hand: members of the '27 Yankees, Wally Pipp,

Everett Scott, even Babe Ruth, with whom he had not spoken for years. Mayor Fiorello La Guardia, Postmaster General Jim Farley, and assorted other dignitaries were there, too. Between games they came out onto the field and stood with the current team of Yankees as Joe McCarthy spoke briefly into the microphone at home plate.

Among other gifts, Lou received a trophy from his teammates. On it was inscribed a poem written by John Kieran of the *New York Times*:

TO LOU GEHRIG

We've been to the wars together;
We took our foes as they came;
And always you were the leader,
And ever you played the game.
Idol of cheering millions;
Records are yours by sheaves,
Iron of frame they hailed you,
Decked you with laurel leaves.
But higher than that we hold you,
We who have known you best;
Knowing the way you came through
Every human test.
Let this be a silent token
Of lasting friendship's gleam
And all that we've left unspoken;
— *Your pals of the Yankee team.*

Lou stands unsteadily as Sid Mercer emcees the ceremony. Several Yankees had been warned by Joe McCarthy to keep their eyes on Lou, who appeared ready to collapse at any moment.

Before Lou stepped to the home-plate mike to deliver his now-famous speech, he took a few moments to compose himself. Murray Becker of the Associated Press, stationed halfway down the first-base line, trained his Graflex on Lou's face. Becker pressed the shutter, then wrote on his caption card: "Lou Gehrig is crying."

Lou, overcome with emotion, sobbed. Sportswriter Sid Mercer, serving as master of ceremonies, had to lean over to hear what Lou, trembling and looking like he was about to fall, said.

"Lou has asked me to thank all of you," Mercer said when he returned to the mike. "He is too moved to speak."

The crowd wasn't having any of that. A chant of "We want Gehrig!" filled the air as Lou blew his nose and wiped his eyes. Finally, after an awkward half minute or so, McCarthy gently led him to the plate. Rows of players stood, solemn as owls, on either side of him. His head bowed, Gehrig began to speak. He strayed slightly from his prepared remarks, which remained on a folded sheet of paper inside his pocket. In the suddenly silent ballpark, his words boomed like artillery.

"Fans," he began, "for the past two weeks you have been reading about the bad break I got. Yet today I consider myself the luckiest man on the face of the earth."

The crowd, hushed to this point, erupted. Lou waited several long seconds for the cheers and applause to subside, then continued.

"I have been in ballparks for seventeen years and have never received anything but kindness and encouragement from you fans. Look at these grand men. Which of you wouldn't consider it the highlight of his career just to associate with them for even one day? Sure, I'm lucky. Who wouldn't consider it an honor to have known

Babe Ruth, tanned and looking fit, impulsively threw his arm around his old teammate after the emotional two-minute speech. The two had not talked for five years.

Exactly one week after Lou Gehrig Day, Yankee Stadium hosted the seventh annual All Star game. Lou, sandwiched between Lefty Gomez and Jimmie Foxx, was the American League's honorary captain.

Jacob Ruppert? Also, the builder of baseball's greatest empire, Ed Barrow? To have spent six years with that wonderful little fellow, Miller Huggins? Then to have spent the next nine years with that outstanding leader, that smart student of psychology, the best manager in baseball today, Joe McCarthy?

"Sure I'm lucky. When the New York Giants, a team you would give your right arm to beat, and vice versa, sends you a gift—that's something. When everybody down to the groundskeepers and those boys in white coats remember you with trophies—that's something. When you have a wonderful mother-in-law who takes sides with you in squabbles with her own daughter—that's something. When you have a father and a mother who work all their lives so you can have an education and build your body—it's a blessing. When you have a wife who has been a tower of strength and shown more courage than you dreamed existed—that's the finest I know.

"So I close in saying that I may have had a tough break, but I have an awful lot to live for."

Lou began to step backward, then quickly leaned towards the microphone and added, "Thank you."

Gehrig's 274-word speech has been called the Gettysburg Address of baseball. There are similarities. Both were short, heartfelt, and partially extemporaneous. But while the exact wording of Lincoln's address can never be known (no tape recorders caught the president's deviations from the original handwritten text), Gehrig's movements and remarks were captured by a swarm of photographers and newsreel cameramen, some of whom looked through viewfinders clouded by moisture.

His speech finished, Lou stood in the warm sunshine and mopped his face with a handkerchief. Babe Ruth came over and impulsively threw his arm around his old teammate. Flashbulbs popped, and 61,808 voices blended into one great, open-throated roar. It was, literally and figuratively, baseball's last hurrah for its beloved Iron Horse.

For all intents and purposes, the transformation of Lou Gehrig began with this simple two-minute speech, although few people at the time imagined that he had delivered his own requiem. Sure, he was ill. But deathly ill? To all those who had watched this johnny lunch bucket in pinstripes dutifully punch the clock every day for fourteen summers, the thought was almost laughable.

But there was no humor in Lou's rapid deterioration. "Before the

Down but not out. That was the message editorial cartoonists across the country attempted to convey as Gehrig battled ALS.

season was over you could see his body go downhill," said Tommy Henrich. "We knew it wasn't an ordinary disease because he was getting weak. His body wasn't coordinated at all."

The Yankees didn't skip a beat with Lou out of the lineup. They won the pennant and the World Series handily, finishing 17 games in front of Boston and then sweeping Cincinnati for its record fourth straight championship. Dahlgren, a flashy fielder, batted just .235 with 15 home runs and 89 RBI during the regular season. He didn't make anyone forget Lou Gehrig. But his two doubles and a home run were instrumental in defeating the Reds.

Lou, who watched the Series from the bench, collected a full post-season share in addition to his regular season salary. But during the summer Ed Barrow, satisfied that the club had gone the limit for its captain, informed Eleanor that the team couldn't be expected to carry

There was a steady stream of visitors to Gehrig's home, and the talk more often than not got around to baseball. Hardly a raconteur, Lou would obligingly point out memorabilia and relate anecdotes associated with them.

Lou accepted a position as a New York City parole commissioner and was sworn in January 2, 1940, by Mayor La Guardia. The official job description didn't include signing baseballs, but it might as well have.

a sick man on its payroll indefinitely. Lou would have to get a job after the Series.

Keeping in character, Lou ignored several lucrative opportunities in the private sector and accepted an offer in public service. On January 2, 1940, Mayor La Guardia swore Lou in as a New York City parole commissioner, a $5,700-a-year job that involved determining release dates for prisoners in city jails.

For the next year, Lou worked six days a week in his Lower Manhattan office interviewing prostitutes, pickpockets, pimps, rapists, con artists, thieves, burglars, addicts, and other petty criminals. Sometimes he visited Rikers Island or the Tombs. Most used the opportunity to practice their "there are no guilty people in prison" speech. If Lou appreciated the irony of listening to society's losers complaining about the "bad breaks" life had handed them, he never let on.

One pugnacious nineteen-year-old from the Lower East Side, an accused rapist named Rocco Barbella, is worth special mention—not for what he was, but for what he later became. A street punk with a penchant for fist fights, Barbella had sometimes gone into Yankee Stadium to steal equipment laying around the field. "Maybe I even got one of Gehrig's gloves," he mused years later.

When Barbella arrived for his hearing, he couldn't believe his eyes. The famous Iron Horse, now gaunt and hoarse, moved on crutches towards his desk as sweat poured off his brow.

"You've caused your mother a

Andover Academy's captain and first baseman in 1940 was future U.S. president George Bush (front row, center). Gehrig "was the player I looked up to most as a kid," recalled Bush, who played in the first two College World Series with Yale. Gehrig "set a standard of quiet excellence, on and off the field. Nothing flashy, no hotdogging, the ideal sportsman." In retirement, Bush said the item he most wished to possess was one of Lou Gehrig's gloves.

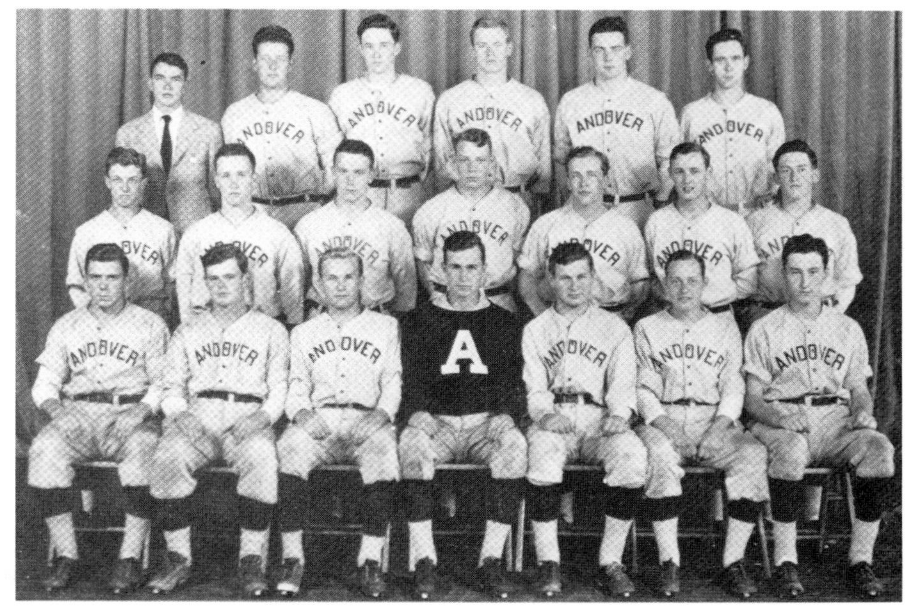

In 1937 Ellsworth "Babe" Dahlgren, newly acquired from the Red Sox, leaps for the ball under the watchful eye of the man he would replace in the lineup two years later. "I never expect to be a Gehrig or anything close to him," Dahlgren, a product of San Francisco's sandlots, said at the start of spring training in 1940. Joe McCarthy agreed and soon traded the good-field, no-hit Dahlgren to the Boston Braves. In his final six seasons, baseball's "Wandering Jew" played for eight different teams, finally retiring in 1947 with Indianapolis of the International League.

lot of grief, haven't you?" asked Lou, reviewing the youth's lengthy probation record. This clearly was a no-no in Lou's book. When he informed Barbella he was recommending that he be sent to a reform school in hopes of straightening him out, Barbella erupted. "Go to hell, you bastard!" he screamed.

Barbella proved less incorrigible than originally thought. He fought his way off the streets to become Rocky Graziano, the middleweight champion of the world. In his autobiography, he admitted that he probably should have shaked Gehrig's hand instead of wanting to kill him.

To fulfill the city's residency requirement, Lou and Eleanor (and a black and white dog named Yankee) had moved from Larchmont into the Riverdale section of the Bronx. They rented a white frame house "where pheasants roamed the lawns and wild roses bloomed along the driveway and walks," said Eleanor. Her mother and two servants helped Eleanor care for Lou, who flatly rejected the idea of having wheelchair ramps installed. Instead, every morning he faithfully received an injection of vitamin E, an experimental treatment suggested by the Mayo Clinic.

The front door was practically a turnstile as players, writers, entertainers, and old friends dropped by daily to keep up his spirits. Mike Bowe, who'd known Lou since semipro days in New Jersey, visited several times. Like all guests, he found Lou cheerful, accommodating, and talking fondly about baseball. He'd point to the walls of photographs and memorabilia and recount anecdotes associated with them. There was never an ounce of self-pity, said Bowe.

As 1940 gave way to a new year, Lou grew too weak to go to work. His hands were so useless Eleanor had to hold his book and read to him. "I wonder what the guys at the ballpark would think of me now," he'd say sheepishly. He continued to dictate correspondence, however, both with parolees and other victims of ALS. It seems improbable that Lou, an intelligent and pragmatic person, didn't realize his fate. But he and his wife bravely kept up fronts, though Eleanor finally had a couple of

Lou's friends and a doctor visit Mom Gehrig and gently tell her the full truth in private.

"For once, she entered our house without a chip on her shoulder," said Eleanor. "She was visiting him for the last time, and I left them alone, no longer worried that she would or could exert the overwhelming influence on his affairs that she had exerted for so long. And she carried it off with something that approached believable grace."

The sick Lou Gehrig stopped by the Stadium only occasionally during the summer of 1940. When he did, there was plenty of good-natured ribbing. Still, sitting stiffly on the bench in his suit, watching his former teammates on the diamond, Lou couldn't help but feel that he was on the outside looking in. "I miss all this," he wistfully told Babe Dahlgren one day.

Meanwhile, the men who tried to replace Lou in the Yankees lineup were found to be lacking by the public and the press. The Yankees finished third in 1940, just two games back of the pennant-winning Tigers. Many thought that the difference between a third-place finish and a fifth consecutive world championship was a healthy Lou Gehrig.

Dahlgren fell into disfavor with Joe McCarthy, who accused him of having "short arms" and then banished him to the Boston Braves. John Sturm took over first-base duties in 1941. "Dan Daniel used to run a column showing what Lou had done that day and what I did," complained Sturm, who batted .239 with three home runs in his sole major-league season. "That was kind of harsh. Here I am, just a rookie, and he's doing that."

Despite Sturm's nonproduction, the Yankees returned to form in 1941. This was the season of Joe DiMaggio's gripping 56-game hitting streak and Brooklyn catcher Mickey Owen's dropped third strike in the World Series. The Yankees won in five games. By then, however, Lou would be gone.

In the spring of 1941 he was, in Eleanor's words, "winding down like a great clock." Tommy Henrich recalled a final visit he made with Bill Dickey, Grantland Rice, and Red Smith.

"He was in bed and you could see from his frame that he was down to about 120 pounds," recalled Henrich. "But his spirits were just the same as always. Just happy. Gee, there was no pity coming out of him at all. Whatever it was that was eating him up, he was taking it as he always did."

"You have to get knocked down to realize how people really feel about you," Lou told a reporter a few months before his death. "I've realized that more than ever lately." Once, when he almost slipped on an icy sidewalk, "four people jumped out of nowhere to help me. When I thanked them, they said they knew about my illness and had been keeping an eye on me."

For the last several weeks of his life, Eleanor was camped by Lou's bedside. "I would not have traded two minutes of the joy and the grief with that man for two decades of anything else," she wrote many years later. "Happy or sad, filled with great expectations or great frustrations, we had attained it for whatever brief instant that fate had decided."

As the group of friends was leaving, someone asked, "Well, Lou, you think you're doing all right?"

"Oh yea," replied Lou. "The doctor told me that I would go downhill and reach a certain point, and then I'd start to come back."

"Did I believe that *he* believed that?" Henrich asks rhetorically today. "No. But that's the kind of guy he was."

Doctors have compared having ALS to being present at your own funeral. At the end the patient is bedridden and as helpless as an infant, unable to move, talk, or swallow. There is no pain. The mind, imprisoned inside a wasted, unresponsive body, remains alert. In such a state, memories become the connective tissue between twilight and dawn.

The crack of wood. The smell of grass. The hum of the infield.

Innings and afternoons.

Lou Gehrig passed away late in the evening of June 2, 1941, sixteen years to the day that he'd replaced Wally Pipp in the Yankees lineup. Eleanor and his parents were by his side. Unlike the cowboy movies and German operas that he had loved so well, there was no dramatic deathbed passage, no surge of orchestral music. He slipped away quietly, nestled contentedly in the shadows.

CHAPTER Nine

ASCENDING TO THE ANGELS

(SETTING: CHRISTMAS DINNER AT A HOUSE IN BALTIMORE)
COUSIN IRENE: When are you getting married, Annie?
DAD: Back in early June, in the garden . . . .
ANNIE: Is this all right with you, Walter?
WALTER: Today I consider myself the luckiest ma-ma-man on the fa-fa-face of the ea-ea-earth [echo effect].
ANNIE: [laughing] The Lou Gehrig line! Remember? Remember, Dad? The Lou Gehrig line from, uh . . . .
WALTER: Pride of the Yankees.
ANNIE: . . . Pride of the Yankees!
DAD: Pride of the Yankees, yea.
[General hubbub at dinner table]
UNCLE MILTON: Baseball. It's baseball. A historical reference.

—*Sleepless in Seattle*

IF NOT FOR the manner of his passing, the only things considered otherworldly about Lou Gehrig would be his playing streak and his numbers in the *Baseball Encyclopedia*. After all, most ballplayers in Gehrig's class are "immortals" in name only, their legacies limited to neat rows of statistics. Although it was obvious by the middle of Lou's career that he too would be remembered by future generations as a great and dedicated ballplayer—nothing more, nothing less—in death he achieved an apotheosis no one back in Yorkville could ever have predicted.

The deification began shortly after Lou Gehrig Day in 1939. The governing members of the Baseball Hall of Fame, which that summer had inducted its charter class at Cooperstown, waived the five-year waiting period and elected Lou by proclamation. The Yankees retired his uniform number (the first time an athlete had ever been so honored), sealed his locker, and erected an honorary monument in the deep recesses of the ballpark. Since then, generations of schoolchildren have left Yankee Stadium convinced that the Iron Horse is buried in center field.

Lou's death naturally inspired a stream of biographies, most of them juvenile titles, for who better to gain from his story than the youth of America? Diamonds around the country became "Lou Gehrig Field." During the war years, his name was carried on a Liberty ship and a fund to provide ambulances for New York City hospitals. Friends sometimes went to extraordinary lengths to keep his name alive. Once, Bill Dickey heard of a war bond rally that was using pledges to determine the city's most popular athlete. Each $25 pledge was worth one vote. It was a horse race between Lou, Babe Ruth, Mel Ott, and football-star Ward Cuff until 320 votes came in for Gehrig. Dickey had settled the issue by wiring a pledge for $8,000.

In 1955 the Phi Delta Theta Fraternity in Oxford, Ohio, created an

The body of Lou Gehrig lay in state at Christ Episcopal Church in Riverdale before being cremated.

GEHRIG

Thousands stood in the rain to view Gehrig. He was buried in Kensico Cemetery in Valhalla, New York, less than an hour's drive from Manhattan. His headstone erroneously says he was born in 1905.

annual Lou Gehrig Award to recognize the major leaguer best exemplifying the qualities of its namesake. Later, the Amyotrophic Lateral Sclerosis Society started handing out a similar honor called the Iron Man Award, with individual chapters in big-league cities also presenting local awards. And in 1989, the U.S. postal service released a first-class stamp bearing Lou's name and likeness.

Then there's "the speech." Its essence, if not the actual words, quickly passed into public domain. The image of a strong man toppled by a mysterious disease, head lowered as he humbly expresses thanks into a microphone, has proved too powerful for publishers, filmmakers, record producers, and advertisers to resist. It's the centerpiece of the most widely played baseball movie of all time, a film that has become as much an American classic as its subject.

The Pride of the Yankees has done more than anything to preserve the popular vision of Lou Gehrig. Before an examination of it, however, it's intriguing to contemplate what Lou's career and life after baseball might have been like had he not died young.

Had Lou remained healthy, it's reasonable to assume that his remarkable physique and extraordinary work ethic would have kept him in the Yankees' starting lineup for several more seasons, at least through the 1941 campaign, after which America's entry into the Second World War probably would have curtailed his playing streak and his career.

Going into the 1939 season, Lou had played 2,122 consecutive games and was on record as saying that he thought 2,500 was an attainable goal. Because a healthy Gehrig was always an asset, no one in the Yankees' organization would have argued against it. Assuming the Yankees had played the full 154-game schedule in 1939, 1940, and 1941, Lou would have already exceeded his goal that Sunday morning when he and the rest of America woke up to discover themselves suddenly at war.

By then Gehrig's career numbers would have been stacked as high as

HENRY LOUIS GEHRIG
NEW YORK YANKEES-1923-1939
HOLDER OF MORE THAN A SCORE OF
MAJOR AND AMERICAN LEAGUE RECORDS,
INCLUDING THAT OF PLAYING 2130
CONSECUTIVE GAMES. WHEN HE RETIRED
IN 1939, HE HAD A LIFE TIME BATTING
AVERAGE OF 340.

Gehrig's Hall of Fame plaque. He was voted into Cooperstown by proclamation in late 1939.

the clouds. Assuming three seasons averaging, say, 180 base hits, 30 doubles, 10 triples, 30 home runs, 120 RBI, and 110 walks—actually a conservative estimate based on past performance—his lifetime totals would be even more impressive than they actually are. He would be in the top ten in hits and doubles; be ranked fifth in home runs, total bases, and walks; and have replaced Hank Aaron as the all-time leader in extra-base hits and runs batted in.

Plus, had Lou managed to cross the plate just 358 more times in these three hypothetical summers (a manageable 119.3 runs per season), he would have slipped past Ty Cobb into first place in runs scored—an achievement that would have amazed those who had once called him Ol' Biscuit Pants.

During the Second World War, Lou's wife and friends kept his name alive by donating ambulances to New York City hospitals.

Finally, his playing streak would have reached a mind-boggling 2,584 games. After seventeen seasons of playing every day with fractured bones, torn muscles, and mild concussions, it would take a world war to get him out of the lineup.

Lou, whose two trips across the Pacific in the 1930s made him one of the few Americans to have heard of Pearl Harbor before the Japanese bombed it on December 7, 1941, would have been thirty-eight years old at the time—past draft age. Being married was worth an additional deferment. But, considering his sense of duty, it's a lead-pipe cinch he would have volunteered, joining fellow American League stars Hank Greenberg and Bob Feller, both of whom immediately enlisted.

Lou loved the water, so he probably would have opted for the Navy. Of course, he may well have spent the duration playing ball for Lieutenant Commander Mickey Cochrane at the Great Lakes Naval Training Station and then later managing service teams at various Pacific bases. Being the kind of guy who would have willingly thrown himself on a grenade to save a foxhole of comrades, he might have disliked the idea of being a noncombatant in a war that eventually claimed more than 400,000 American lives. But it wasn't in his nature to complain.

Naturally, after the war he would return to New York. He would have been forty-two upon his hypothetical discharge in 1945, too old probably to rejoin the lineup, save for a ceremonial send-off that would have included a final, symbolic appearance in the field or at bat. Lou Gehrig Appreciation Day at Yankee Stadium would have been one of those time-honored Sunday affairs where well-wishers and ex-teammates load the honoree at home plate with fishing gear, a loving cup, and a new car. Babe Ruth, just three years away from succumbing to cancer, would have been there. Given the emotion of the afternoon, he might even have thrown an arm around his old slugging mate. Lou, brushing back a tear, would stand at the microphone and undoubtedly pronounce

Movie-pioneer Sam Goldwyn was born Schmuel Gelbfisz in Warsaw in 1879. "When I was a kid," he said, "the only place I wanted to go to was America." Goldwyn arrived New Year's Day, 1899, whereupon he fell on his hands and knees and kissed the ground. After quickly discovering that he had exchanged one Jewish ghetto for another, Goldwyn fled New York's Lower East Side for Gloversville, New York, where he established a successful wholesale glove business. In 1913 he joined forces with his brother-in-law, vaudevillian Jessy Lasky, and an unknown playwright named Cecil B. DeMille to produce *The Squaw Man*, the first feature-length film made in an obscure southern California town called Hollywood. Before he died in 1974, Goldwyn's independently produced films (including *All Quiet on the Western Front, Wuthering Heights,* and *The Best Years of Our Lives*) had joined *The Pride of the Yankees* as examples of artistic but popular movie making.

himself the luckiest man on earth for having known such great teammates and fans. After that, it might have been the coaching box or a front-office position. He might have even become a manager, Joe McCarthy's successor, although Lou and Eleanor's original retirement plans didn't include baseball.

Whatever hats Lou chose to wear, the following decades would have produced its predictable mix of pleasure and sorrow. He would have fished the big waters and battled arthritis. He would have grieved over the loss of his parents and close friends, and he may very well have outlived Eleanor, who passed away in 1984. In fact, given advances in medicine and Lou's constitution, it's not impossible that he would still be alive today, the legendary iron man rusting away in his early nineties but still active, still alert, the elder statesman and guardian of the national pastime. He would be the center of attention at annual Hall of Fame banquets in Cooperstown and monthly card shows in New Jersey, gripping a walker and a fountain pen with the same white-knuckled determination as he did a Louisville Slugger some sixty years earlier. And on Old-Timers Day at Yankee Stadium, when fans need a blast of nostalgia to clear air befouled by the modern game, even Mr. Coffee himself would take a back seat to the indefatigable Iron Horse. For Larrupin' Lou Gehrig, the beloved captain of the Yankees and a last link to some simpler, sepia-soaked past, the cheering would always be the loudest.

But, as we all know, that's not how the script was written.

Sam Goldwyn, like George M. Cohan, was a superpatriot who celebrated his birthday on the Fourth of July. Unlike Cohan, the independent film maker—a Polish Jew who had arrived in New York when he was nineteen years old—didn't know a damn thing about that most American of pastimes, baseball. That didn't stop him from producing the story of Lou Gehrig's life, a film biography that is arguably the best baseball movie ever made. Certainly it is the best known.

Were it not for World War II, *The Pride of the Yankees* might never have been made. But with an entire nation mobilizing for war, the government's cry for patriotic movies struck a nerve with Goldwyn's story editor and executive producer, Niven Busch. Busch, an avid baseball fan well aware of Gehrig's story, suggested a project based on his life.

"I'm not going to make any pictures about ballplayers," said Goldwyn. "If people want to see ball playing, they can go to the ballpark."

"But Sam, he wasn't just any ballplayer," countered Busch. "He was a hero to the young generation of kids today. At the top of his career he got an incurable disease and he died of it, and he died very bravely. His life was sort of an inspiration to people!"

Real to Reel

When Lou Gehrig said goodbye to baseball on July 4, 1939, at Yankee Stadium, he moved all those in attendance and millions more listening to the radio. The moment was later reenacted in the 1942 movie, *The Pride of the Yankees.* Since then, Gary Cooper's words have become widely accepted as Gehrig's own. Here's how the original speech compares with the Hollywood version. You decide which one is better.

Gehrig's Speech:

Fans, for the past two weeks you have been reading about the bad break I got. Yet today I consider myself the luckiest man on the face of the earth.

I have been in ballparks for seventeen years and have never received anything but kindness and encouragement from you fans. Look at these grand men. Which of you wouldn't consider it the highlight of his career just to associate with them for even one day? Sure, I'm lucky. Who wouldn't consider it an honor to have known Jacob Ruppert? Also, the builder of baseball's greatest empire, Ed Barrow? To have spent six years with that wonderful little fellow, Miller Huggins? Then to have spent the next nine years with that outstanding leader, that smart student of psychology, the best manager in baseball today, Joe McCarthy?

Sure I'm lucky. When the New York Giants, a team you would give your right arm to beat, and vice versa, sends you a gift—that's something. When everybody down to the groundskeepers and those boys in white coats remember you with trophies—that's something. When you have a wonderful mother-in-law who takes sides with you in squabbles with her own daughter—that's something. When you have a father and a mother who work all their lives so you can have an education and build your body—it's a blessing. When you have a wife who has been a tower of strength and shown more courage than you dreamed existed—that's the finest I know.

So I close in saying that I may have had a tough break, but I have an awful lot to live for. Thank you.

Cooper's Speech:

I have been walking onto ballfields for sixteen years, and I've never received anything but kindness and encouragement from you fans. I have had the great honor to have played with these great veteran ballplayers on my left—Murderers Row, our championship team of 1927. I have had the further honor of living and playing with these men on my right—the Bronx Bombers, the Yankees of today.

I have been given fame and undeserved praise by the boys up there behind the wire, my friends, the sports writers. I have worked under the two greatest managers of all time, Miller Huggins and Joe McCarthy.

I have a mother and father who fought to give me health and a solid background in my youth. I have a wife, a companion for life, who has shown me more courage than I ever knew.

People all say that I've had a bad break. But today . . . today I consider myself the luckiest man on the face of the earth.

Christy Walsh returned momentarily to his former profession as a cartoonist in order to promote *The Pride of the Yankees*.

Goldwyn remained unconvinced. "Well, he was a ballplayer. I don't make pictures about ballplayers."

But Busch, who saw the project as a perfect vehicle for a young actress he was dating (and would eventually marry), Teresa Wright, persisted. He got the newsreels of Lou Gehrig Day and ran them for Goldwyn. When the lights were flipped back on, Busch found the sentimental Goldwyn crying a river of tears.

"Run 'em again," he said.

After a second viewing, Goldwyn hustled back to his office and called his senior associate in New York, James Mulvey. "Get the rights to the Gehrig story!" he commanded. Mulvey's wife, Marie "Dearie" McKeever, had just inherited her father's quarter-share interest in the Brooklyn Dodgers. She helped smooth the path to an agreement that paid Eleanor Gehrig an estimated $30,000 for the rights to Lou's story. Goldwyn also signed Babe Ruth for the movie.

Ruth's agent, Christy Walsh, served as one of the film's publicists. Walsh tried to create media interest by suggesting a nationwide search was on to find just the right fellow to portray Gehrig. Some actors had offered to play the role for nothing, added Walsh, his nose growing longer with each press release.

Speculation grew. Would the celluloid Lou be Spencer Tracy, Pat O'Brien, John Wayne, Dennis Morgan, or (Ed Barrow's favorite) Eddie Albert? Even "Jarrin' Jack" Kimbrough, star of the collegiate gridiron and a couple of forgettable B-westerns, was mentioned as a candidate.

"But there was only one fella going to play Lou Gehrig," Kimbrough recalls today with a laugh. "And that was Gary Cooper."

Hollywood's original strong, silent type had been born Frank James Cooper in 1901 in Helena, Montana, the son of a state supreme court judge. After a checkered career as a ranch hand, editorial cartoonist, and salesman, he came to Hollywood in 1925 to work as a $10-a-day stunt extra on silent Westerns. Encouraged by cowboy-star Tom Mix, Cooper graduated into meatier roles in such early hits as *Wings*, *The Virginian*, *Lives of a Bengal Lancer*, and *Beau Geste*. At the time Goldwyn committed to the Lou Gehrig project, Cooper had just finished filming *Sergeant York*, a performance that would earn him his first Oscar. Although his most critically acclaimed role wouldn't come until 1953's *High Noon* (for which he would receive his second Oscar), his image as the average joe who triumphs through courage, a good heart, and uncomplicated speech—"Yup" and "They went that-a-way" were his stock utterances—had already been firmly established when Goldwyn signed him for $150,000 to play Gehrig.

As a stable of actresses and studio secretaries could attest, the tall, lanky, blue-eyed actor was all man. He was equally at ease hunting with Ernest Hemingway or dining at a fine restaurant in London. Like Gehrig, he spoke softly and carried a big stick—in Cooper's case, a foot-long member that was the talk of Hollywood. "He's hung like a horse and can go all night," the "It" girl of the twenties, Clara Bow, marveled. Reports of the actor's prowess reached Broadway where Tallulah Bankhead declared, "I'm going to Hollywood to fuck that gorgeous Gary Cooper." She did—once—and never tired of talking about the experience.

Although Lou would have blushed at these kinds of revelations, he undoubtedly would have appreciated the cowboy-like terms often used to describe Cooper's appeal to the movie-going public. According to Frank Capra, "This silent Montana cowpuncher embodied the true-blue virtues that won the West: durability, honesty, and native intelligence." Cooper not only physically resembled Gehrig, his persona, whether innate or acquired, wore well in public—just like Lou's.

"I don't believe his mannerisms were what made him quintessentially American," Teresa Wright, who played Eleanor Gehrig, said of Cooper. "I think the values of the characters he played were generally the values regarded as the American ideal. He played that character so much that it became identified with him.

"This was a paradox of a man. He could easily have gone back and forth in European society…not the typical American. He wasn't just a very sophisticated man with sophisticated values. He was a rather elegant man and liked very nice things. His wife was a very stylish woman. But he played the American ideal. Fundamentally, he cared very deeply about values that we've come to look on as old-fashioned."

Despite his reputation as the all-American male, Cooper, who had been educated in England, had never mastered the art of throwing or hitting a baseball. Before filming began, retired two-time batting champion Lefty O'Doul was hired to help Cooper learn how to throw a ball properly. He spent weeks instructing him.

"You throw a ball like an old woman tossing a hot biscuit," the exasperated O'Doul told the actor. Cooper wintered with his family in Sun Valley where he continued to practice by pitching snowballs.

Meanwhile, Goldwyn's own ignorance about the game became laughably obvious during negotiations to bring ballplaying extras to the set. Walsh, representing Red Rolfe, said the Yankees third baseman wanted $1,500 a week.

Goldwyn pulled Busch aside. "What position did Lou Gehrig play?" he asked.

"First base," he replied.

"*First* base?" said Goldwyn.

"First base," repeated Busch. Goldwyn, under the impression that there were ten bases and a player worked his way up to first, expressed outrage over this perceived inequity.

Teresa Wright and Gary Cooper as Eleanor and Lou Gehrig.

A trio of scenes from *The Pride of the Yankees*. Despite Gary Cooper's inability to throw or hit a baseball, the laconic, unruffled actor was widely applauded as the perfect choice to play Lou Gehrig. "Every line in his face spelled honesty," said Frank Capra. "So innate was his integrity he could be cast in phony parts, but never look phony himself."

"You're robbing me!" Goldwyn screamed at Walsh. "I'm not going to pay through the ass for some lousy... *third* baseman!" Rolfe, unwilling to work for the $500 that Bill Dickey, Mark Koenig, Bob Meusel, and several other of Lou's teammates had accepted, stayed home.

Cooper labored to improve his limp throws, but another problem loomed as production began: He threw and hit right-handed. Gehrig, of course, was a left-handed fielder and batter. But all was not lost. Film editor Danny Mandell approached Goldwyn with the idea of having Cooper bat right-handed and then run to third. The costume department could reverse the numbers and letters on the players' uniforms, he explained. Then, when Mandell flipped the negative in the editing room, the image would be that of a left-hander throwing, batting, and running the bases. Goldwyn readily approved this simple but ingenious solution.

Paul Gallico, who had first written of Gehrig for Columbia's alumni magazine, wrote the story treatment, which was then adapted for the screen by Jo Swerling and Herman Mankiewicz.

The movie has its share of clichés. It opens to the strains of (what else?) "Take Me Out to the Ball Game." The scene where young Lou (played by Douglas Croft) shuts up the bigger kids on the playground by smashing a ball through a window and is then hauled home by a gruff but kindly Irish cop is redolent of scores of baseball films. And what baseball movie is complete without a sick kid in the hospital being promised a home run by the Babe? In *The Pride of the Yankees*, this syrupy scenario is prolonged by having Lou, in a rare display of one-upmanship, promise to hit *two* home runs! Take that, Babe! The kid recovers, of course, and one can almost hear pediatricians sighing off-camera: Thank God, the Yankees are in town.

In 1955, Lou's old fraternity, Phi Delta Theta, presented the first annual Lou Gehrig Memorial Award to Alvin Dark of the New York Giants. Subsequent winners have included Ernie Banks, Al Kaline, George Brett, and Lou Brock.

The supporting cast included veteran actors Elsa Janssen and Ludwig Stossel as Mom and Pop Gehrig, and Walter Brennan (who had just won his third Oscar playing alongside Cooper in *Meet John Doe*) as sportswriter Sam Blake. Brennan's character was loosely based on Fred Lieb, one of Lou's closest friends in the press box. And Ruth, a natural ham who had appeared in several films during his career, did what he always did best: he played himself. Goldwyn didn't know baseball, but he understood that the Bambino still had marquee value. In fact, Babe's name was prominently displayed in advertisements for the movie, while the subject of the biopic appeared in small type and only parenthetically:

GARY COOPER in
THE PRIDE OF THE YANKEES
(The Life of Lou Gehrig)

TERESA WRIGHT • BABE RUTH • WALTER BRENNAN

Once again, Lou was forced to play second banana to Ruth. The pair's rivalry is only hinted at in the movie, and their falling out wholly ignored. The other conflicts in Lou's life—abandoning college for baseball, finding a new "best girl" in Eleanor—are brought to the screen with barrels of sentimentality.

What's missing, maintains Cooper's biographer, Hector Arce, is the John Ford or Frank Capra touch "that makes us feel this is an everyday guy and an American deity at the same time. Cooper has a characteristically wonderful moment when, half-uncomfortable and half-delirious, he's first forced out on the dance floor. In another memorable shot he takes a spectacular fall on a pile of baseball bats. But his 'spontaneous' scenes of horseplay with Teresa Wright are just as forced as the spontaneity that's *supposed* to feel forced after they've learned of his condition."

Wright, two years out of high school and half Cooper's age, remembered that the star prepared quietly between takes. He disliked rehears-

On August 21, 1953, Lou's mother unveiled a memorial plaque at her son's birthplace—a four-story tenement that had become a laundry.

ing and often killed time by whittling planes out of balsa wood or riding his bicycle around the lot. "He didn't make a point of working up an emotion. He did it, and when he was finished, it was finished. Although to the eye it wasn't right, he was instinctively right for film, which was something else again."

The movie covers all the familiar ground of Lou's life except his death, wisely concluding with his farewell speech at Yankee Stadium. The words were doctored for greater effect, although Danny Mandell, seemingly the only person in the entire cast or crew who knew anything about baseball, thought it impossible to improve on the original.

Mandell butted heads with Sam Wood, the film's hard-boiled director, over the climactic scene. Wood, he later complained, "tried to add things that never happened, to make it more dramatic. How could you make a thing like that more dramatic? I got all the newsreels that I could on Gehrig Day, and I cut the whole thing just the way it was in the newsreel, with the exception that they never showed the mother and the father. I had establishing shots of the band marching around, the lineup of the players and all that, which I used. And I inserted closeups of Cooper making the speech, just as it was in the newsreel. There couldn't be anything more dramatic than that."

But Mandell inexplicably ignored the most obvious goof—the scene where Lou decides to finally pull himself out of the lineup in Detroit. In the movie the moment is dramatized by having the public address announcer inform the crowd that Babe Dahlgren was now batting for Lou Gehrig. Realizing the significance of the moment, the people in the stands give Lou a roaring ovation. But as most fans know, being lifted for a pinch-hitter wouldn't have ended his playing streak.

That particular fine point didn't concern Goldwyn. He later explained that the real challenge was preventing the game from overshadowing the personal story.

"As the picture now stands, the baseball is purely a background, and the love story is the dominant factor," he said. To please what was expected to be a predominantly female audience—millions of men were already in the process of being outfitted for dog tags and combat boots—Goldwyn inserted a dance sequence with the gifted duo of Veloz and Yolanda. He also selected as the main theme his and the Gehrigs' favorite song, a sentimental Irving Berlin tune called "Always." It's heard constantly throughout the 126-minute movie, a haunting reprise that hints at tragic but eternal love.

In the end, Sam Goldwyn got the picture he wanted—mawkish but honest, a story that reflected the naiveté and romanticism of the time and survives today as a set piece of the forties.

The Pride of the Yankees premiered in July 1942 in New York City, then moved quickly across the country. Goldwyn, smelling opportunity, jacked up the price of tickets as high as 25 percent. A benefit at the Pantages Theatre in Hollywood, complete with celebrities and floodlights, raised $5,000 for the Naval Aid Auxiliary. Because of blackout regulations, the gala affair was the last nighttime premier for the duration of the war.

Both reviews and receipts were generous. *The Pride of the Yankees* grossed more than $3 million, making it one of the top ten money-makers of the year. The *New York World-Telegram* thought Cooper had "seldom been better than he is as Lou Gehrig. His performance grows, as the character grows, from shy gawky undergraduate to modest, unassuming hero of millions." Eleanor Gehrig proclaimed that she was "completely happy" with the movie, while 1940 presidential candidate Wendell Willkie felt he recognized universal elements of the immigrant experience in the story line.

"Sam, you have done something very important here," Willkie said. "You help democracy everywhere by showing what opportunities there are in America."

"Why shouldn't I?" responded Goldwyn. "Who knows better than I do the opportunities in America?"

The movie earned eight Academy Award nominations and won in three categories. In an interesting twist, Cooper lost the best actor Oscar to a product of Lou's old Yorkville neighborhood, Jimmy Cagney, who was honored for his portrayal of song-and-dance man George M. Cohan in *Yankee Doodle Dandy*.

Cooper, who was too old for the draft, did what he could for the war effort. Although he had little to offer live audiences—he couldn't sing, dance, or juggle—he was a regular at the Hollywood Canteen, where boys in uniform could grab coffee, donuts, and a look at their favorite movie stars.

In October 1943, Cooper joined a troupe entertaining G.I.s in the Pacific. The daily itinerary on the six week, 23,000-mile tour usually

In 1974 Eleanor Gehrig showed off some of Lou's trophies to the press. Two years later she and Joe Durso collaborated on a book that became the basis for a made-for-television movie. *A Love Affair: The Eleanor and Lou Gehrig Story* starred Blythe Danner and Edward Herrmann in the title roles and Patricia Neal as Mom Gehrig. Eleanor died in 1984, having never remarried, and was buried alongside Lou.

The St. Louis Browns hit pregame fungos at Yankee Stadium in the early forties. At the base of the flagpole is the monument to Lou Gehrig, installed just weeks after his death. "The great thing about baseball is the way it never ends; there is always another inning, another game, another season," wrote David Noonan in 1989. "And Gehrig, better than anyone, understood the beauty of that idea, and the power of it. Nothing strange, nothing mysterious, just keep playing and try to win more than you lose. The only real mystery of Lou Gehrig's life was the mystery of his death. Everything else was as clear and simple as a line drive on a sunny day."

included a matinee show, afternoon visits to base hospitals to cheer the wounded, topped by a show in the evening. Performing on an open-air stage, the gang would perform skits, exchange banter with the troops, and sing and dance their hearts out. Even Cooper joined in the riotous rendition of "Pistol Packin' Mama" that closed each show. "Those boys weren't just starved for entertainment," he said, "they were plumb out of their minds."

One night, however, heavy rains moved in. Cooper, figuring the show would be cancelled, napped in his tent. Suddenly an officer rushed in and told him that 15,000 rain-soaked, homesick G. I.s were sitting in the mud. The show must go on.

The troupe did the best it could, considering the conditions. At the end, they couldn't get off the stage.

"Hey, Coop!" shouted someone in the crowd. "How about that Lou Gehrig farewell speech to the Yankees?" Others applauded in encouragement.

"Give me a minute to get it right," he said. Cooper took a short break to recollect the words. Then he approached the microphone and, in a quiet and steady voice, spoke to the suddenly hushed crowd of wet and muddy servicemen.

> I have been walking onto ballfields for sixteen years and I've never received anything but kindness and encouragement from you fans. I have had the great honor to have played with these great veteran ballplayers on my left—Murderers Row, our championship team of 1927. I have had the further honor of living with and playing with these men on my right—the Bronx Bombers, the Yankees of today.
>
> I have been given fame and undeserved praise by the boys up there behind the wire, my friends, the sportswriters. I have worked under the two greatest managers of all time, Miller Huggins and Joe McCarthy.
>
> I have a mother and father who fought to give me health and a solid background in my youth. I have a wife, a companion for life, who has shown me more courage than I ever knew.
>
> People all say that I've had a bad break. But today...today I consider myself the luckiest man on the face of the earth.

Cooper was startled by the reaction. Many of the men were crying. That hundreds of them were destined to never see their wives, children, and homes again—never mind the inside of a ballpark—affected him deeply. By popular demand, for the rest of the tour he ended each show with Lou Gehrig's words, which by now had become his own.

Cooper's own death in 1960 eerily mirrored Lou's. He gave a speech at a Friars Club testimonial, marveling over the good fortune and friends he had enjoyed. At the time he was unaware that the cancer he had been battling was terminal, although his wife and doctors knew. In his final days he lay wasted and shriveled in his darkened bedroom, unable to move, unwilling to complain. Cooper, some said, had faced death just like his most memorable character.

Lou Gehrig's speech has become one of the touchstones of American popular culture. As Cooper discovered, it hardly matters who is delivering the words, or whether they are the real thing or a reasonable facsimile. Most people, great and small, escape a country's collective memory. Not Lou Gehrig. More than fifty years after his death, the mention of his name triggers an immediate and positive response, although we're not always sure why. The ingredients of his legend—the home runs, the streak, the disease, the speech, the movie—are all balled up in the mind.

Gehrig's original claim to fame was as an iron man. But even if some ballplayer succeeds in establishing a new consecutive-game playing streak (as it appears Cal Ripken Jr. might), his legacy is safe. After all, it's not the particulars of the streak, but the story surrounding its ending that has guaranteed his place in folklore.

Lou more than died from amyotrophic lateral sclerosis, he became amyotrophic lateral sclerosis. Part of the reason, naturally, is the tongue-twisting pronunciation, which would make any alternative name welcome. But mostly the legacy is built around his response to encountering an enemy that was new, frightening, and mysterious. Far from expressing fear and despair, Lou exhibited the kind of hope, optimism, and dignity that everyone likes to believe they would display in similar circumstances.

Lou was perhaps not as uncomplicated as he appeared, but his outlook and expectations were simple. Modest, uncomplaining, methodical, and productive, he was the living embodiment of Thoreau's dictum to "live your life, do your work, then take your hat." He certainly was given a bad break, but he never expressed regrets because he truly had none. He had played with and against the greatest names in sports, traveled widely, met famous and important people, accomplished great feats, loved and was loved deeply, and through it all kept true to his own moral code. Cornball stuff, perhaps. But Lou Gehrig continues to thrive as the idealized standard of a less ambiguous age.

Although Lou's life was truncated and tragic, the average American male would gladly trade his own for the one he led. That's the great secret of "the Lou Gehrig line." For when a decent man dying young proclaims himself the luckiest man on the face of the earth, those with lesser gifts can't help feeling that, all things considered, maybe he was at that.

Lou Gehrig's Record with the Yankees

Regular Season

Year	G	AB	R	H	BA	2B	3B	HR	RBI	BB	SO	TB	SA	SB
1923	13	26	6	11	.423	4	1	1	9	2	5	20	.769	0
1924	10	12	2	6	.500	1	0	0	5	1	3	7	.583	0
1925	126	437	73	129	.295	23	10	20	68	46	49	232	.531	6
1926	155	572	135	179	.313	47	**20**	16	107	105	72	314	.549	6
1927	**155**	584	149	218	.373	**52**	18	47	**175**	109	84	**447**	.765	10
1928	154	562	139	210	.374	**47**	13	27	**142**	95	69	364	.648	4
1929	154	553	127	166	.300	32	10	35	126	122	68	323	.584	4
1930	**154**	581	143	220	.379	42	17	41	**174**	101	63	**419**	.721	12
1931	155	619	**163**	**211**	.341	31	15	**46**	**184**	117	56	**410**	.662	17
1932	**156**	596	138	208	.349	42	9	34	151	108	38	370	.621	4
1933	152	593	138	198	.334	41	12	32	139	92	42	359	.605	9
1934	**154**	579	128	210	**.363**	40	6	**49**	**165**	109	31	**409**	**.706**	9
1935	149	535	**125**	176	.329	26	10	30	119	**132**	38	312	.583	8
1936	**155**	579	**167**	205	.354	37	7	**49**	152	**130**	46	403	**.696**	3
1937	**157**	569	138	200	.351	37	9	37	159	**127**	49	366	.643	4
1938	**157**	576	115	170	.295	32	6	29	114	107	75	301	.523	6
1939	8	28	2	4	.143	0	0	0	1	5	1	4	.143	0
Totals	2164	8001	1888	2721	.340	534	163	493	1990	1508	789	5060	.632	102

Bold indicates led league

World Series

Year	Opponent	G	AB	R	H	BA	2B	3B	HR	RBI	BB	SO	TB	SA	SB
1926	St.Louis	7	23	1	8	.348	2	0	0	4	5	4	10	.435	0
1927	Pittsburgh	4	13	2	4	.308	**2**	**2**	0	4	**3**	3	10	.769	0
1928	St.Louis	4	11	5	6	.545	1	0	**4**	**9**	**6**	0	19	**1.727**	0
1932	Chicago	4	17	**9**	**9**	**.529**	1	0	**3**	**8**	**2**	1	19	**1.118**	0
1936	NewYork	6	24	5	7	.292	1	0	**2**	**7**	3	2	14	.583	0
1937	NewYork	5	17	4	5	.294	1	**1**	**1**	3	**5**	**4**	**11**	.647	0
1938	Chicago	4	14	**4**	4	.286	0	0	0	0	**2**	3	4	.286	0
Totals		34	119	30	43	.361	8	3	10	35	26	17	87	.731	0

Bold indicates led Series

BIBLIOGRAPHY

Allen, Frederick Lewis. *Only Yesterday.* New York: Harper & Row, 1931.

Allen, Leslie. Liberty: *The Statue and the American Dream.* New York: Summit Books, 1985.

Allen, Maury. "*Where Have You Gone, Joe DiMaggio?*" *The Story of America's Last Hero.* New York: E. P. Dutton, 1975.

Arce, Hector. *Gary Cooper.* New York: William Morrow & Co., 1979.

Bak, Richard. *Cobb Would Have Caught It: The Golden Age of Baseball in Detroit.* Detroit: Wayne State University Press, 1991.

———. *Ty Cobb: His Tumultuous Life and Times.* Dallas: Taylor Publishing Co., 1994.

Bankes, James. *The Pittsburgh Crawfords: The Lives and Times of Black Baseball's Most Exciting Team.* Dubuque, Iowa: William C. Brown Publishers, 1991.

Barrow, Edward Grant. *My Fifty Years in Baseball.* New York: Coward-McCann, 1951.

Berg, A. Scott. *Goldwyn.* New York: Alfred A. Knopf, 1979.

Berlage, Gai Ingham. *Women in Baseball: The Forgotten History.* Westport, Connecticut: Praeger Publishers, 1994.

Otto L. Bettmann. *The Good Old Days — They Were Terrible!* New York: Random House, 1974.

"Break Up the Yankees." *Colliers,* February 25, 1939.

Broeg, Bob. *Superstars of Baseball.* South Bend: Diamond Communications, 1994.

Bush, George and Victor Gold. *Looking Forward.* New York: Doubleday, 1987.

Chellgren, Norton. "*The Short Career of Lou Lewis.*" Baseball Research Journal, 1975.

Cohen, Richard M. et al. *The World Series.* New York: Dial Press, 1976.

Costello, James and Michael Santa Maria. *In the Shadows of the Diamond: Hard Times in the National Pastime.* Dubuque, Iowa: Elysian Fields Press, 1992.

Cox, James A. *The Lively Ball: Baseball in the Roaring Twenties.* Alexandria: Redefinition, 1989.

Crampton, C. Ward. "Wham! He Hits It!" *Boys' Life,* May 1937.

Creamer, Robert W. *Babe: The Legend Comes to Life.* New York: Simon and Schuster, 1974.

Curran, William. *Big Sticks: The Phenomenal Decade of Ruth, Gehrig, Cobb and Hornsby.* New York: William Morrow & Co., 1990.

Daley, Arthur. "Fabulous Yankees Through Fifty Years." *New York Times Magazine,* March 9, 1952.

Dary, David. *Cowboy Culture.* New York: Alfred A. Knopf, 1981.

Dawidoff, Nicholas. *The Catcher Was a Spy: The Mysterious Life of Moe Berg.* New York: Pantheon, 1994.

Dean, Gordon B. *Iron Horse: A Compilation of Lou Gehrig's Last Years in a Scrapbook.* Privately published.

Dickey, Glenn. *The History of the World Series Since 1903.* New York: Stein & Day, 1984.

Drasen, Richard. *Just Call Me Lou: The Life and Times of Lou Gehrig.* Unpublished manuscript.

Durso, Joseph. *Yankee Stadium: Fifty Years of Drama.* New York: Houghton-Mifflin, 1972.

Easton, Carol. *The Search for Sam Goldwyn.* New York: William Morrow & Co., 1976.

Edelman, Rob. *Great Baseball Films.* New York: Citadel Press, 1994.

Einstein, Charles, ed. *The Baseball Reader.* New York: McGraw-Hill, 1983.

Erickson, Hal. *Baseball in the Movies: A Comprehensive Reference, 1915-1991.* Jefferson, North Carolina: McFarland & Co., 1992.

Evans, Billy. "Baseball's Best Batters." *Baseball Digest,* August 1942.

Feller, Bob and Bill Gilbert. *Now Pitching, Bob Feller.* New York: Birch Lane Press, 1990.

Gallen, David, ed. *The Baseball Chronicles.* New York: Carroll & Graf, 1991.

Gallico, Paul. *Lou Gehrig: Pride of the Yankees.* New York: Grosset & Dunlap, 1942.

———. *The Golden People.* Garden City: Doubleday & Co., 1965.

Gehrig, Eleanor and Joseph Durso. *My Luke and I.* New York: Crowell, 1976.

Gold, Eddie. "Baseball Movies." *Baseball Research Journal,* 1983.

Gonzalez, Raymond J. "Gehrig Streak Reviewed." *Baseball Research Journal,* 1975.

———. "Larrupin' Lou and 23 Skidoo." *Baseball Research Journal,* 1983.

———. "Lou Who? Stole Home 15 Times in His Career." *Baseball Research Journal,* 1978.

———. "Still the Greatest One-Two Punch." *Baseball Research Journal,* 1977.

Graham, Frank. *Lou Gehrig: A Quiet Hero.* New York: G. P. Putnam's Sons, 1942.

———. *The New York Yankees: An Informal History.* New York: G. P. Putnam's Sons, 1948.

Graham, Jr., Frank. *A Farewell to Heroes.* New York: Viking Press, 1981.

Greene, Laurence. *The Era of Wonderful Nonsense: A Casebook of the Twenties.* New York: Bobbs-Merrill Co., 1939.

Greenberg, Hank and Ira Berkow. *Hank Greenberg: The Story of My Life.* New York: Times Books, 1989.

Gregory, Robert. *Diz: Dizzy Dean and Baseball During the Great Depression.* New York: Viking Penguin, 1992.

Hill, Art. *I Don't Care If I Never Come Back.* New York: Simon and Schuster, 1980.

Hirschberg, Al. "The Lingering Shadow of the Iron Man." *Baseball Digest,* October 1963.

Holtzman, Jerome. *No Cheering in the Press Box.* New York: Holt, Rinehart & Winston, 1974.

Holway, John B. *Black Diamonds: Life in the Negro Leagues from the Men Who Lived It.* New York: Stadium Books, 1991.

———. *The Sluggers.* Alexandria: Redefinition, 1989.

Honig, Donald. *Baseball When the Grass Was Real.* New York: Coward, McCann & Geoghegan, 1975.

———. *Baseball Between the Lines.* New York: Coward, McCann & Geoghegan, 1976.

———. *The Man in the Dugout.* Chicago: Follett, 1977.

———. *The October Heroes.* New York: Simon and Schuster, 1979.

Hubler, Richard. *Lou Gehrig: Iron Horse of Baseball.* Boston: Houghton-Mifflin Co., 1941.

Hynd, Noel. *The Giants of the Polo Grounds.* New York: Doubleday, 1988.

James, Bill. *The Bill James Historical Baseball Abstract.* New York: Villard Books, 1986.

Jastrow, Marie. *Looking Back: The American Dream Through Immigrant Eyes, 1907-1918.* New York: W. W. Norton & Co., 1986.

Kirk, Troy. *Collector's Guide to Baseball Cards.* Radnor, Pennsylvania: Wallace-Homestead Book Co., 1990.

Klein, Larry. "Bill Dickey: Baseball's Immortal Catcher." *Sport,* July 1961.

Klingaman, William K. *1929: The Year of the Great Crash.* New York: Harper & Row, 1989.

Kuklick, Bruce. *To Every Thing a Season: Shibe Park and Urban Philadelphia, 1909-1976.* Princeton: Princeton University Press, 1991.

Langford, Walter M. *Legends of Baseball: An Oral History of the Game's Golden Age.* South Bend: Diamond Communications, 1987.

Lieb, Fred. *Baseball As I Have Known It.* New York: Coward, McCann & Geoghagen, 1977.

Lord, Walter. *The Good Years: From 1900 to the First World War.* New York: Harper & Bros., 1960.

Manchester, William. *The Glory and the Dream: A Narrative History of America, 1932-1972.* Boston: Little, Brown, 1974.

McCabe, John. *George Cohan: The Man Who Owned Broadway.* New York: Doubleday & Co., 1973.

McClure II, Arthur S. "The Last Game of the Iron Horse." *Missouri Historical Society Magazine,* Fall 1982.

Mead, William B. *Low and Outside: Baseball in the Depression, 1930-1939.* Alexandria: Redefinition, 1990.

Mosedale, John. *The Greatest of Them All: The 1927 New York Yankees.* New York: Dial Press, 1974.

Nash, Jay Robert. *People To See: An Anecdotal History of Chicago's Makes and Breakers.* Piscataway, New Jersey: New Century Publishers, 1981.

Noonan, David. "Double Legacy of the Iron Horse." *Sports Illustrated,* April 4, 1988.

Palmer, Pete. "Home Park Effects on Performance in the American League." *Baseball Research Journal,* 1978.

Ponsonby, Arthur. *Falsehood in War-Time.* Privately published, Great Britain, 1928.

Reichler, Joseph L., ed. *The Baseball Encyclopedia. 8th ed.* New York: Macmillan, 1990.

Rice, Grantland. *The Tumult and the Shouting.* New York: Dell Publishing Co., 1954.

Reiss, Steven A. *City Games: The Evolution of American Urban Society and the Rise of Sports.* Urbana: University of Illinois Press, 1989.

Ritter, Lawrence. *The Glory of Their Times.* New York: William Morrow & Co., 1984.

———. *Lost Ballparks: A Celebration of Baseball's Legendary Fields.* New York: Viking Penguin, 1992.

Robinson, Ray. I*ron Horse: Lou Gehrig in His Time.* New York: W. W. Norton & Co., 1990.

Russell, Francis. *The American Heritage Book of the Confident Years, 1865-1916.* New York: American Heritage/Bonanza Books, 1987.

Ruth, Babe and Bob Considine. *The Babe Ruth Story.* New York: Signet, 1992.

Seymour, Harold. *Baseball: The Early Years.* New York: Oxford University Press, 1960.

———. *Baseball: The Golden Age.* New York: Oxford University Press, 1971.

Sher, Jack. "Lou Gehrig: The Man and the Legend." *Sport,* October 1948.

Skipper, Jr., James K. "The 1927 Yankees: Great Team, Great Nicknames." *Baseball Research Journal,* 1987.

Smelser, Marshall. *The Life That Ruth Built.* New York: Quadrangle/New York Times Book Co., 1975.

Smith, Curt. *Voices of the Game.* South Bend: Diamond Communications, 1987.

Smith, Packy and Ed Hulse, eds. *Don Miller's Hollywood Corral: A Comprehensive B-Western Roundup.* Burbank, California: Riverwood Press, 1993.

Sobol, Ken. *Babe Ruth and the American Dream.* New York: Ballantine Books, 1974.

Sowell, Thomas. *Ethnic America: A History.* New York: Basic Books, 1981.

Spink, J. Taylor. *Judge Landis and 25 Years of Baseball.* St. Louis: Sporting News Publishing Co., 1974.

Stein, Charles W., ed. *American Vaudeville As Seen By Its Contemporaries.* New York: Alfred A. Knopf, 1984.

Thorn, John and Pete Palmer, eds. *Total Baseball.* New York: Warner Books, 1989.

Voigt, David Quentin. *American Baseball: From the Commissioners to Continental Expansion.* Norman: University of Oklahoma Press, 1970.

———. *American Baseball: From Postwar Expansion to the Electronic Age.* University Park: Pennsylvania State University Press, 1983.

Wells Eddie. "My Four Years with the New York Yankees." Unpublished manuscript.

Whittingham, Richard, ed. *The DiMaggio Albums.* New York: G. P. Putnam's Sons, 1989.

"Why the Yankees Win." *Nation,* September 17, 1938.

Wiley, George T. "New York Yankees vs. Philadelphia Athletics, 1927-1932." *Baseball Research Journal,* 1979.

Williams, Ted and John Underwood. *My Turn at Bat.* New York: Simon and Schuster, 1969.

The day is July 4, 1941, and the event is the unveiling by Bill Dickey and Eleanor Gehrig of the Lou Gehrig monument in centerfield at Yankee Stadium.

INDEX

Bold indicates photo reference

Photo Credits

Andover Academy: 163 bottom
Associated Press: 23, 139
Babe Ruth Museum: 9, 59 top
Bettmann Archives: 41
George Brace: 25, 61 bottom, 70 bottom
Brown Brothers: 1, 2 both bottom, 8, 22 bottom, 24 top, 79, 101
Burton Historical Collection: 34, 35, 46, 52, 57 top, 60 both, 66 bottom, 69 top, 97 top, 99, 137, 138
Chattanooga Regional History Museum: 91
Dick Clark: 142, 143
Columbiana: 29
Culver Pictures: 15, 48
The Detroit News: 114, 115
Detroit Tigers: 145
Edwin Diamond: 113
Filmpix: 175, 176, color 6 middle and bottom
Henry Ford Museum: 118
Hillerich & Bradsby Archives, University of Louisville: 68 both bottom, 87, 116, 129 left
Library of Congress: 5 both, 6, 13, 49, 102 bottom
Mayo Clinic: 156 both, 157
National Archives: 160 bottom
National Baseball Library: 2 top, 7, 10, 14, 16, 17, 22 top, 27, 36, 50, 57 bottom, 58, 73 both, 74, 80 both, 81, 82, 84, 88, 98, 103, 108, 109, 110, 111 bottom, 123, 129 right, 136, 140 top left, 153 both, 158, 159, 177, 180
New York Daily News: 83
New York Yankees: 4, 33, 37, 43, 53, 126
Joe Ritter: 61 top, 96 bottom, 151 top
Reuther Library: 102 top left
Selek Collection: 28, 69 bottom, 122, 127 bottom, color 1 top, color 4 both, color 5 both
The Sporting News: 3, 40, 44, 47 bottom, 67 bottom, 90, 94, 111 top, 117, 120 both, 121, 127 top left, 130, 133, 134, 135, 140 top right, 154, 155, 169, 170 both top, 171, 178
Transcendental Graphics: 42, 56 bottom, 67 top, 86, 89, 119, 125, 140 bottom left, 141, 144 bottom, 146 right, 149, 162 bottom, 164, 179 left, color 1 middle and bottom, color 2 top, color 3 all, color 7 both, color 8 top right
Wide World: 182